101 LETTERS TO A PRIME MINISTER

ALSO BY YANN MARTEL

Beatrice & Virgil

Life of Pi

Self

The Facts Behind the Helsinki Roccamatios

YANN MARTEL

—

101 LETTERS TO A
PRIME MINISTER

—

THE COMPLETE LETTERS
TO STEPHEN HARPER

VINTAGE CANADA

VINTAGE CANADA EDITION, 2012

Published in Canada by Vintage Canada, a division of Random House of
Canada Limited, Toronto, in 2012. Portions of this book originally appeared
in *What Is Stephen Harper Reading?*, published by Vintage Canada in 2009.
Distributed by Random House of Canada Limited.

Vintage Canada with colophon is a registered trademark.

www.randomhouse.ca

Pages 427 to 428 constitute a continuation of the copyright page.

LIBRARY AND ARCHIVES CANADA CATALOGUING IN PUBLICATION

Martel, Yann

101 letters to a prime minister : the complete letters
to Stephen Harper / Yann Martel.

ISBN 978-0-307-40207-3

1. Best books. 2. Martel, Yann—Books and reading.
3. Martel, Yann—Correspondence. 4. Harper, Stephen, 1959–. I. Title.
II. Title: One hundred one letters to a prime minister.

Z1035.9.M36 2012   011'.73   C2012-900998-9

Text design by CS Richardson

Cover image by Emre Ogan

Printed and bound in the United States of America

2 4 6 8 9 7 5 3 1

To Alice, my favourite reader

CONTENTS

INTRODUCTION

This is a book about books. It takes the form of a series of letters. The letters were written by a Canadian writer—me—and sent to a Canadian politician, Prime Minister Stephen Harper. In each letter I discuss a literary work. A novel, a play, a poetry collection, a religious text, a graphic novel, a children's book—the range is wide. I mailed a copy of each work, dated, numbered and inscribed, with the accompanying letter neatly folded inside its front cover, to the Prime Minister's office in Ottawa.

Politely and unfailingly, I did this every two weeks from April 16, 2007 to February 28, 2011; a total of 101 letters accompanying the gift of slightly more than 101 books. Many books, many letters, one essential question hovering throughout: what sort of mind, nourished by what, do we want our leaders to have? My argument is that literature—as opposed to factual non-fiction—is an essential element to a deeply thinking, fully feeling mind in our complex twenty-first-century world. A mind not informed by the thoughtful product that is the novel, the play, the poem, will be capable perhaps of administering the affairs of a people, maintaining the status quo, but not of truly leading that people. To lead effectively requires the capacity both to understand how things are and to dream how things might be, and nothing so displays that kind of understanding and dreaming as literature does. That is my argument, and it is for Canadians, whether regular readers of literature or not, to decide where they stand on the issue.

Does literature make for character, or is it mere entertainment? That is the question.

I received seven replies in total. The first came promptly:

> May 8, 2007
> Dear Mr. Martel:
> On behalf of the Prime Minister, I would like to thank you for your recent letter and the copy of Tolstoy's *The Death of Ivan Ilych*. We appreciated reading your comments and suggestions regarding the novel.
> Once again, thank you for taking the time to write.
> Sincerely,
> Susan I. Ross
> Assistant to the Prime Minister

A long, official silence of nearly two years followed. Then, unexpectedly and in a jumbled order, I received a quick series of four responses, as follows:

For Books 53 and 54, *The Sailor Who Fell from Grace with the Sea*, by Yukio Mishima, and *Louis Riel, A Comic-Strip Biography*, by Chester Brown:

> April 29, 2009
> Dear Mr. Martel,
> On behalf of the Right Honourable Stephen Harper, I would like to acknowledge receipt of your correspondence, with which you enclosed a copy of *The Sailor Who Fell from Grace with the Sea* by Yukio Mishima and a copy of *Louis Riel, A Comic-Strip Biography* by Chester Brown. The Prime Minister wishes me to convey his thanks for sending him these books. You may be assured that your thoughtful gesture is most appreciated.
> Yours truly,

S. Russell
Executive Correspondence Officer

For Book 51, *Julius Caesar*, by William Shakespeare:

May 1, 2009
Dear Mr. Martel,
On behalf of the Right Honourable Stephen Harper, I would like to acknowledge receipt of your correspondence regarding the Social Sciences and Humanities Research Council (SSHRC) and the Canadian Periodical Fund. I would also like to thank you for the enclosure of *Julius Caesar* by William Shakespeare.

Please be assured that your comments have been given careful consideration. I have taken the liberty of forwarding copies of your correspondence to the Honourable Tony Clement, Minister of Industry, and the Honourable James Moore, Minister of Canadian Heritage and Official Languages, so that they may be made aware of your concerns.

Once again, thank you for writing the Prime Minister.
Yours sincerely,
S. Russell
Executive Correspondence Officer

For Book 55, *The Gift*, by Lewis Hyde:

May 22, 2009
Dear Mr. Martel,
On behalf of the Right Honourable Stephen Harper, I would like to acknowledge receipt of your recent correspondence.

Thank you for writing to share your views with the Prime Minister. You may be assured that your comments have been carefully noted. For more information on the Government's initiatives, you may wish to visit the Prime Minister's website, at www.pm.gc.ca.

Yours sincerely,

L. A. Lavell

Executive Correspondence Officer

For Book 52, *Burning Ice: Art & Climate Change*, a collaboration organized by David Buckland and the Cape Farewell Foundation:

June 24, 2009

Dear Mr. Martel:

On behalf of the Right Honourable Stephen Harper, I would like to acknowledge receipt of your correspondence of March 30, which provided a copy of the book *Burning Ice: Art & Climate Change*.

Thank you for providing this material to the Prime Minister. Your courtesy in bringing this information to his attention is appreciated.

Yours sincerely,

P. Monteith

Executive Correspondence Officer

In addition, two of the writers who stepped in to supply the Prime Minister with books when I was not able to do so myself, namely Charles Foran and Alice Kuipers, each received a reply:

For Book 81, *Diary of a Madman*, by Lu Xun:

May 20, 2010

Dear Mr. Foran,

On behalf of the Right Honourable Stephen Harper, I would

like to acknowledge receipt of your recent letters, with which you enclosed a copy of *Century* by Ray Smith, and one of *Diary of a Madman* by Lu Xun.

The Prime Minister wishes me to convey his thanks for sending him these publications. You may be assured that your thoughtful gesture is most appreciated.

Yours sincerely,

S. Russell

Executive Correspondence Officer

For Book 85, *How I Live Now*, by Meg Rosoff:

September 3, 2010

Dear Ms. Kuipers,

On behalf of the Right Honourable Stephen Harper, I would like to acknowledge receipt of your correspondence, with which you enclosed a copy of the book entitled *How I Live Now*.

Thank you for sending this book to the Prime Minister. Your thoughtful gesture is most appreciated.

Yours sincerely,

T. Lewkowicz

Executive Correspondence Officer

I noted in these responses my correspondents' consistent use of initials, with the exception of the very first one, from Susan I. Ross, Assistant to the Prime Minister. Of those that followed from the Executive Correspondence Officers, it was never a Sarah, a Lawrence Andrew or a Penny who replied to me, but always an S., an L. A. or a P. I suppose this gender anonymity accommodated the sensibilities of Canadians to whom it might make a difference whether a reply to their letter to the Prime Minister came from a man or a woman. The effect it had on me was to make clear that the stranger who was writing to me wanted to remain a stranger. And of course each letter is quite formulaic, an acknowledgement rather than a response.

Seven form replies from deputies, ninety-four wilful acts of silence—and not a peep from my intended co-reader. It was a lonely book club. I started it in a moment of frustration. In late March 2007 I was invited to Ottawa to help celebrate the fiftieth anniversary of the Canada Council for the Arts, that towering institution that has done so much to foster the cultural identity of Canadians. The celebrations turned out to be a very pleasant affair, but mostly because of the fellow artists present, fifty in all, of every discipline and tendency, a rainbow of writers, painters, composers, musicians, choreographers and others, each representing one year of the Council's fifty. I was the representative for 1991, the year I received a Canada Council grant that allowed me to write my first novel, *Self.* I was twenty-seven years old and the money was manna from heaven. I made those eighteen thousand dollars last a year and a half (and considering the income tax I have paid in the wake of the success of my second novel, *Life of Pi*, this initial investment by Canadian taxpayers has been well worth it). The eldest artist there, representing 1957, was Jean-Louis Roux, great man of the theatre; the youngest was Tracee Smith, an aboriginal hip-hop dancer and choreographer who had just received her first grant. It was a thrill to be among such a varied gaggle of creators.

The key moment of the celebrations came at 3 p.m. on March 28. We were sitting in the Visitors' Gallery of the House of Commons, waiting. To those Canadians who haven't been, I must mention that the House of Commons, and indeed Parliament Hill as a whole, is an impressive place. It's not just the size of the chamber, its grand design and ornate decoration; it's the symbolism of it. A large part of the history of our nation has been played out within its four walls. While a practical venue, with functional desks, powerful, selective microphones and discreet television cameras, it's also a space of dreams and visions where we Canadians have worked out who and what we want to be. So there I was, in the House of Commons, wowed by the place, and I got to thinking about stillness. I guess the word popped into my head because the unsettling brawl of Question Period was just coming to an end. To read a book, one must be still. To watch a concert, a play, a movie, to look at a painting, one must also be still. Religion, too, makes use of stillness, notably with prayer and meditation. Gazing upon a lake in autumn or a quiet winter scene—that too lulls us into contemplative stillness. Life, it seems, favours moments of still-ness to appear on the edges of our perception and whisper to us, "Here I am. What do you think?" Then we become busy and the stillness vanishes, but we hardly notice because we fall so easily for the delusion of busyness, whereby what keeps us busy must be important and the busier we are with it, the more important it must be. And so we work, work, work, rush, rush, rush. On occasion we say to ourselves, panting, "Gosh, life is racing by." But it's the contrary: life is still. It is we who are racing by.

The moment had come. The Minister for Canadian Heritage, Bev Oda at the time, rose to her feet, acknowledged our presence and began to speak. We artists stood up, not for ourselves but for the Canada Council and what it represents. The Minister did not speak for long. In fact, she had barely started, we thought, when she finished and sat down. There was a flutter of applause and then MPs turned to other matters. We were still standing, incredulous. *That was it?* Fifty years of building Canada's daz-zling and varied culture, done with in less than five minutes?

I remember the poet Nicole Brossard laughed and shook her head as she sat down.

I couldn't quite laugh. What would the equivalent celebration of a major cultural institution have been like in France, say? It would have been a classy, year-long, exhibition-filled extravaganza, with the President of France trying to hog as much of the limelight as possible, that's what. But there's no need to go into further details. We all know how the Europeans do culture. It's sexy and important to them. The world visits Europe because it's so culturally resplendent. We Canadian artists, by contrast, were standing like dolts in a public gallery, getting in the way of more important business. And the thing is, we didn't even ask to be there. We were invited.

From the shadows into which we had been cast, I focused on one man. The Prime Minister did not speak during our brief tribute. He didn't even look up. By all appearances, he didn't even know we were there. Who is this man? What makes him tick? I asked myself. No doubt he's busy. He must be aware every waking minute of every day that he's Prime Minister of Canada. But Stephen Harper must nonetheless have pockets of solitude and idleness during which he contemplates life. There must be occasions when his thinking goes from the instrumental—*how do I do this, how do I get that?*—to the fundamental—*why this, why that?* In other words, he must have moments of stillness. And since I deal in books, reading and writing them, and since books and stillness go well together, I decided, by means of good books, to make suggestions that would inspire stillness in Stephen Harper.

Hence the months and years of reading, thinking, writing and mailing. The books are on a shelf in an office somewhere in Ottawa, I presume. The letters are in your hands.

———

What was I expecting in return? That the Prime Minister would read and reply as fast as I was reading and writing to him? No, I wasn't expecting such diligence. There will always be more books one would like to read than one will have time to read. And thank God for that. It will be a sad day, a sign of a shrunken Earth, when someone will claim to have read every book published. But I did expect that one day I would receive a response more substantial than the mechanical replies I ended up receiving. Isn't that what democracy is about, the accountability of our leaders? As a citizen of the arts, I have a right to know what my Prime Minister thinks about reading, I have a right to know what books shaped him.

Here, for example, are a few imagined replies that would have addressed the core of my inquiry:

The haughty:

Dear Mr. Martel,
Napoleon did not ride into battle with a book in his hands. Politics is action. I will perhaps consider your books when I have won all my political battles.
Yours truly,
Stephen Harper

The principled:

Dear Mr. Martel,
What I do in my moments of leisure is none of your business. Furthermore, I cannot accept your gifts because they possibly place me in a position of conflict of interest in relation to other Canadian writers. I have therefore instructed my staff to donate the books you have sent me to World Literacy of Canada.

Yours truly,
Stephen Harper

The sly:

Dear Mr. Martel,
I cannot thank you enough for the wonderful books you are
sending me. So many hours of reading pleasure. I can't get
enough. Upon reading the Tolstoy, I was deeply struck at how
fragile our grip upon life is. The Orwell had me trembling at
the wickedness of the corrupt, the Agatha Christie panting with
suspense, the Elizabeth Smart weeping with heartbreak, and so
on with each book, a roller coaster of wild emotions. More, more,
please. I've been managing a book every three days.

Your letters are also a source of delight—but if only they
weren't so short! If they were longer, more detailed, then I would
truly be a contented Canadian reader.
Yours truly,
Stephen Harper

P.S. I loved Life of Pi. *But what was that strange island about?*
And what are you working on now?

The practically honest:

Dear Mr. Martel,
I don't have time to read for leisure. I get what I need to know from
briefing papers prepared by my staff. Occasionally I squeeze in a
book on politics or economics. But after my time in office, many
years from now I hope, then I will look at books of my choice.
Yours truly,
Stephen Harper

The brutally honest:

Dear Mr. Martel,
I don't like reading novels or poetry or plays. It feels like a waste
of time. If that bothers you, I don't care.
Yours truly,
Stephen Harper

The openly honest:

Dear Mr. Martel,
I've never been much of a reader of novels and I've done fine
that way. But last week I happened to be standing near the box
where your books are stored and I had a free minute. I looked at
them. Such a variety. It occurred to me that books are like tools.
Some are ploughs, some are hammers, some are spirit levels. I've
picked two books out of the box, the Bhagavad Gita *and* Maus,
which I will try to read in my spare time. That will have to do
for the moment.
Yours truly,
Stephen Harper

Any one of these would have would have answered my main
question about the Prime Minister's reading habits.

What makes me think that Stephen Harper doesn't like reading
literature? Isn't that brazenly presumptuous of me? Has he
actually told me that he hasn't read a novel since high school?
No, he hasn't. Stephen Harper hasn't breathed a word about his
reading habits either to me or to any journalist who has asked
(other than to say, during the 2004 election, that his favourite

book was the *Guinness Book of World Records*). What he reads now, or if he reads at all, or what he's read in the past, remains a mystery. But if I see a man fiercely beating a horse, I feel reasonably confident in concluding that he hasn't read *Black Beauty*. If Stephen Harper were shaped and informed by literary culture, if he read novels, short stories, plays and poetry, he would love them, he would defend them, he would celebrate them. He would not try to scuttle the public means of sustaining our nation's artistic culture, retreating from doing so only when it's politically expedient. If Stephen Harper is informed by literary culture or, indeed, by culture in general, it doesn't show in what he says or what he does. The elimination of the Department of Foreign Affairs' budget for arts promotion abroad, the closing down of the CBC Radio orchestra, the skeletonizing of the CBC as a whole, the exclusion of funding to many of Canada's small literary and arts journals, the imposition of Bill C-32, which aims to loosen copyright protection . . . the list, sadly, goes on. And most of this occurred when Stephen Harper was at the helm of a minority government. What will he do now that he has a majority?

Perhaps the man beating the horse has read *Black Beauty*, but he still wants to beat it. Maybe he thinks the horse will be fine despite being beaten. He may even think it should be beaten for its own good. All the more reason to send him good books, then, in the hope of changing his mind.

But the question still nags and needs to be answered: is it anyone's business what Stephen Harper is reading, has read, or if he reads at all? Is reading not rather like stamp collecting or watching hockey, an activity that resides entirely in the domain of his private life? Shortly after I started my campaign, that's exactly what someone intimated to me. Actually, he barked it in my face. He was furious. This is a gentleman I know in Saskatoon, where I live. He kept repeating that what I was doing was an objectionable "ad hominem attack." And this was no Conservative shouting at me, not at all. He also happens to be a keen reader. An ally, I expected. At home, shaken up, I looked in the dictionary to see what ad hominem meant: Latin for an attack on someone's character rather than on a position or belief he or she might hold. Is asking Stephen Harper to account for his reading habits irrelevant? Worse: is it improper and dishonourable, attacking the private man rather than his public policies?

The answer is simple. As long as someone has no power over me, I don't care what they read, or if they read at all. It's not for me to judge how people should live their lives. But once someone has power over me, then, yes, their reading does matter to me, because in what they choose to read will be found what they think and what they might do. If Stephen Harper hasn't read *The Death of Ivan Ilych* or any other Russian novel, if he hasn't read *Miss Julia* or any other Scandinavian play, if he hasn't read *Metamorphosis* or any other German-language novel, if he hasn't read *Waiting for Godot* or *To the Lighthouse* or any other experimental play or novel, if he hasn't read the *Meditations* of Marcus Aurelius or *The Educated Imagination* or any other philosophical inquiry, if he hasn't read *Under Milk Wood* or any other poetic prose, if he hasn't read *Their Eyes Were Watching God* or *Drown* or any other American novel, if he hasn't read *The Cellist of Sarajevo* or *The Island Means Minago* or *The Dragonfly of Chicoutimi* or any other Canadian novel, poem or play—if Stephen Harper hasn't read any of these or any works like them, then what is his mind made of? How did he get his insights into the human condition? What materials went into the building of his sensibility? What is the colour, the pattern, the rhyme and reason of his imagination? These are not questions one is usually entitled to ask. The imaginative life of our fellow citizens, like their finances, is by and large none of our business. But once these citizens are elected to public office their finances do become our business, and politicians routinely have to account for their financial assets so that we can be assured that they are not acting in self-interest. It's the same with their imaginative assets. Once someone has power over me, as Stephen Harper has, it's in my interest to know the nature and quality of his imagination, because his dreams may become my nightmares. The novel, the play, the poem, these are formidable tools to explore people, the world, life. And a leader must know about people, the world, life. And so to citizens who aspire to be successful leaders, I say: if you want to lead effectively, you must read widely.

I wasn't quite alone in my guerrilla book campaign. For years a complete public record of it was on display on the internet in English and in French. Steve Zdunich set up and maintained these blogs for me for longer than he should have, and then Dennis Duro showed me how I could run them myself. To them I am grateful for their freely given help. I must also thank my parents, Émile and Nicole, who stepped up to translate every letter into French, often with an unacceptably short deadline looming. They are true citizens of the arts, and to them I owe not only love but gratitude. If I love to read and write, it is because they showed me by example. I am also grateful to the University of Saskatchewan's English Department for providing me with the ideal office in which to work. Lastly, I'm thankful to the writers Steven Galloway, Charles Foran, Alice Kuipers, Don McKay, René-Daniel Dubois and Émile Martel who stepped in for me when I went on a book tour and couldn't keep up my correspondence with the Prime Minister.

In the letters that follow are reflected the tastes, choices and limitations of one reader. Some books I had in mind long before I sent them. Others were suggested to me by readers across Canada and even from abroad. Some books I had already read, others were discoveries. In my choices I jumped across the barriers of borders and languages. I make no claim to being a wise or perceptive judge. My hope was simply to show the Prime Minister how the literary word is rich, varied, nourishing, life-changing.

Though my book club with Stephen Harper has come to an end, if there are readers who are dying to jump in with suggestions of their own, I encourage them to do so. Books, like fish, like to move about. Communities are made and then gain by sharing books. Any book club member will testify to the meaty pleasure of talking about a commonly read book with other people. So if you have a book you think Stephen Harper should read, by all means send it to him.

His address is:
THE RIGHT HONOURABLE STEPHEN HARPER
PRIME MINISTER OF CANADA
80 WELLINGTON STREET
OTTAWA ON K1A 0A2

Books make us climb higher, and I always have my hand on a book, as if on a banister. But unlike some readers I know who effortlessly bound up the stairs four steps at a time, floor after floor, never stopping to catch their breath, I creep up slowly. If there's an autobiographical character in my novel *Life of Pi*, it's not Pi, it's the sloth. To me, a good book is a rich lode of leaves and I can read only so many pages before my tummy gets full and I nod off. My banister is more of a branch and from it I hang upside down, nursing the book that is feeding my dreams. I read slowly but continuously. Otherwise I would starve.

Art is water, and just as humans are always close to water, for reasons of necessity (to drink, to wash, to grow) as well as for reasons of pleasure (to play in, to relax in front of, to sail upon), so humans must always be close to art in all its incarnations, from the frivolous to the essential. Otherwise we dry up.

So this is the image I'd like to finish with, the quintessence of stillness and a visual summation of what I tried to convey to Prime Minister Stephen Harper with dozens of polite letters and good books: the image of a sloth hanging from a branch in a green jungle during a downpour of tropical rain. The rain is quite deafening, but the sloth does not mind; it's reviving, this cascade of water, and other plants and animals will appreciate it. The sloth, meanwhile, has a book on his chest, safely protected from the rain. He's just read a paragraph. It's a good paragraph, so he reads it again. The words have painted an image in his mind. The sloth examines it. It's a beautiful image. The sloth looks around. His branch is high up. Such a lovely view he has of the jungle. Through the rain, he can see spots of bright colours on other branches: birds. Down below, an angry jaguar races along a track, seeing nothing. The sloth turns back to his book. As he breathes a sigh of contentment, he feels that the whole jungle has breathed in and out with him. The rain continues to fall. The sloth falls asleep.

THE DEATH OF IVAN ILYCH
BY LEO TOLSTOY
Translated from the Russian by Aylmer Maude
April 16, 2007

To Stephen Harper,
Prime Minister of Canada,
From a Canadian writer,
With best wishes,
Yann Martel

Dear Mr. Harper,

The Death of Ivan Ilych, by Leo Tolstoy, is the first book I am sending you. I thought at first I should send you a Canadian work—an appropriate symbol since we are both Canadians—but I don't want to be directed by political considerations of any sort, and, more important, I can't think of any other work of such brevity, hardly sixty pages, that shows so convincingly the power and depth of great literature. *Ivan Ilych* is an indubitable masterpiece. There is nothing showy here, no vulgarity, no pretence, no falseness, nothing that doesn't work, not a moment of dullness, yet no cheap rush of plot either. It is the story, simple and utterly compelling, of one man and his ordinary end.

Tolstoy's eye for detail, both physical and psychological, is unerring. Take Schwartz. He is in dead Ivan Ilych's very home, has spoken to his widow, but he is mainly concerned with his game of cards that night. Or take Peter Ivanovich and his struggle with the low pouffe and its defective springs while he attempts to navigate an awkward conversation with Ivan Ilych's widow. Or the widow herself, Praskovya Fedorovna, who weeps and laments before our eyes, yet without ever forgetting her self-interest, the details of her magistrate husband's pension and the hope of getting perhaps more money from the government. Or look at Ivan Ilych's dealings with his first doctor, who, Ivan Ilych notices, examines him with the same self-important airs and inner indifference that Ivan Ilych used to put on in court before an accused. Or look at the subtle delineation of the relations between Ivan Ilych and his wife—pure conjugal hell—or with his friends and colleagues, who, all of them, treat him as if they stood on a rock-solid bank while he had foolishly chosen to throw himself into a flowing river. Or look, lastly, at Ivan Ilych himself and his sad, lonely struggle.

How clearly and concisely our vain and callous ways are showed up. Effortlessly, Tolstoy examines life's shallow exteriors as well as its inner workings. And yet this pageant of folly and belated wisdom comes not like a dull moral lesson, but with all the weight, shine and freshness of real life. We see, vividly, Ivan Ilych's errors—oh, they are so clear to us, we certainly aren't making his mistakes—until one day we realize that someone is looking at us as if we were a character in *The Death of Ivan Ilych*.

That is the greatness of literature, and its paradox, that in reading about fictional others we end up reading about ourselves. Sometimes this unwitting self-examination provokes smiles of recognition, while other times, as in the case of this book, it provokes shudders of worry and denial. Either way, we are the wiser, we are existentially thicker.

One quality that you will no doubt notice is how despite the gulf of time between when the story is set—1882—and today, despite the vast cultural distance between provincial tsarist Russia and modern Canada, the story reaches us without the least awkwardness. In fact, I can't think of a story that while completely set in its time, so very, *very* Russian, so leaps from the bounds of the local to achieve universal resonance. A peasant in China, a migrant worker in Kuwait, a shepherd in Africa, an engineer in Florida, a prime minister in Ottawa—I can imagine all of them reading *The Death of Ivan Ilych* and nodding their heads.

Above all else, I recommend the character Gerasim to you. I suspect he is the character in whom we recognize ourselves the least yet whom we yearn the most to be like. We hope one day, when the time comes, to have someone like Gerasim at our side.

I know you're very busy, Mr. Harper. We're all busy. Meditating monks in their cells are busy. That's adult life, filled to the ceiling with things that need doing. (It seems only children and the elderly aren't plagued by lack of time—and notice how they enjoy their books, how their lives fill their eyes.) But every person has a space next to where they sleep, whether a patch of pavement or a fine bedside table. In that space, at night, a book can glow. And in those moments of docile wakefulness, when we begin to let go of the day, then is the perfect time to pick up a book and be someone else, somewhere else, for a few minutes, a few pages, before we fall asleep. And there are other possibilities, too. Sherwood Anderson, the American writer best known for his collection of stories *Winesburg, Ohio*, wrote his first stories while commuting by train to work. Stephen King apparently never goes to his beloved baseball games without a book that he reads during breaks. So it's a question of choice.

And I suggest you choose, just for a few minutes every day, to read *The Death of Ivan Ilych*.

Yours truly,
Yann Martel

REPLY:

May 8, 2007

Dear Mr. Martel:

On behalf of the Prime Minister, I would like to thank you for your recent letter and the copy of Tolstoy's *The Death of Ivan Ilych*. We appreciated reading your comments and suggestions regarding the novel.

Once again, thank you for taking the time to write.

Sincerely,
Susan I. Ross
Assistant to the Prime Minister

LEO TOLSTOY (1828–1910) was a prolific author, essayist, dramatist, philosopher and educational reformist. Born into an aristocratic Russian family, he is best known for writing realist fiction, focusing particularly on life in Russia, and is considered one of the major contributors to nineteenth-century Russian literature. His marriage to Sophia Tolstaya (Tolstoy) produced thirteen children, eight of whom survived into adulthood. Tolstoy wrote fourteen novels (two of his most famous being *Anna Karenina* and *War and Peace*), several essays and works of non-fiction, three plays and over thirty short stories.

ANIMAL FARM
BY GEORGE ORWELL

April 30, 2007

To Stephen Harper,
Prime Minister of Canada,
From a Canadian writer,
With best wishes,
Yann Martel
P.S. Happy birthday

Dear Mr. Harper,

Now that your Flames have been knocked out of the playoffs I guess you'll have more free time on your hands.

I fear that some may criticize me for the second book I am sending you, *Animal Farm*, by George Orwell. It's so well known, and it's another book by a dead white male. But there is time yet to be representative of all those who have harnessed the word to express themselves—believe me, they are varied and legion—unless you lose the next election, which would likely give you even more time to read, but not, alas, according to my suggestions.

Many of us read *Animal Farm* when we were young—perhaps you did too—and we loved it because of the animals and the wit. But it's in our more mature years that its import can better be understood.

Animal Farm has some commonalities with *The Death of Ivan Ilych*: both are short, both show the reality-changing power of great literature, and both deal with folly and illusion. But whereas *Ivan Ilych* deals with individual folly, the failure of one individual to lead an authentic life, *Animal Farm* is about collective folly. It is a political book, which won't be lost on someone in your line of business. It deals with one of the few matters on which we can all agree: the evil of tyranny. Of course a book cannot be reduced to its theme. It's in the reading that a book is great, not in what it seeks to discuss.

But I also have a personal reason for why I've chosen *Animal Farm*: I aspire to write a similar kind of book.

Animal Farm first. You will notice right away the novel's limpid and unaffected style, Orwell's hallmark. You get the impression the words just fell onto the page, as if it were the easiest, the most natural thing in the world to write such sentences and paragraphs and pages. It's not. To think clearly and to express oneself clearly are both hard work. But I'm sure you know that from working on speeches and papers.

The story is simple. The animals of Manor Farm have had enough of Farmer Jones and his exploitative ways so they rebel, throw him out, and set up a commune run according to the highest and most egalitarian principles. But there's a rotten pig named Napoleon and another one named Squealer—a good talker he—and they are the nightmare that will wreck the dream of Animal Farm, as the farm is renamed, despite the best efforts of brave Snowball, another pig, and the meek goodness of most of the farm animals.

I've always found the end of Chapter II very moving. There's the question of five pails of milk from the cows. What to do with them, now that Farmer Jones is gone and the milk won't be sold? Mix it with the mash they all eat, hints a chicken. "Never mind the milk, comrades!" cries Napoleon. "The harvest is more important. Comrade Snowball will lead the way. I shall follow in a few minutes." And so off the animals go, to bring in the harvest. And the milk? Well, " . . . in the evening it was noticed that the milk had disappeared."

With those five pails of white milk the ideal of Animal Farm, still so young, begins to die, because of Napoleon's corrupted heart. Things only get worse, as you will see.

Animal Farm is a perfect exemplar of one of the things that literature can be: portable history. A reader who knows nothing about twentieth-century history? Who has never heard of Joseph Stalin or Leon Trotsky or the October Revolution? Not a problem: *Animal Farm* will convey to that reader the essence of what happened to our neighbours across the Arctic. The perversion of an ideal, the corruption of power, the abuse of language, the wrecking of a nation—it's all there, in a scant 120 pages. And having read those pages, the reader is made wise to the ways of the politically wicked. That too is what literature can be: an inoculation.

And now the personal reason why I've sent you *Animal Farm*: the Jewish people of Europe murdered at the hands of the Nazis also need to have their history made portable. And that is what I'm trying to do with my next book. But to take the rubble of history—so many tears, so much bloodshed—and distil it into some few elegant pages, to turn horror into something light—it's no easy feat.

I offer you, then, a literary ideal of mine, besides a great read.

Yours truly,
Yann Martel

P.S. Happy birthday.

GEORGE ORWELL (1903–1950), born Eric Arthur Blair, was an English novelist, journalist, essayist, poet and literary critic. He was born in India into what he called a "lower-upper-middle class" family. He fought and was wounded in the Spanish Civil War. His two most famous works, *Animal Farm* and *1984*, reflect his signature style as well as his two largest preoccupations: his consciousness of social injustice and his opposition to totalitarianism. He is also well known for his interest in the power of language in politics and in shaping how we view the world. He died from tuberculosis at the age of forty-six.

BOOK 3

THE MURDER OF ROGER ACKROYD
BY AGATHA CHRISTIE

May 14, 2007

To Stephen Harper,
Prime Minister of Canada,
From a Canadian writer,
With best wishes,
Yann Martel

Dear Mr. Harper,

What is there not to like about Agatha Christie? Her books are a guilty pleasure; who would have thought that murder could be so delightful? I've selected *The Murder of Roger Ackroyd* for you. Hercule Poirot, the famous Belgian detective, has rather incongruously chosen to retire to the village of King's Abbot to grow vegetable marrows. But his gardening plans are upset by a shocking murder. Who could have done it? The circumstances are so peculiar. . . .

One of the great qualities of Agatha Christie (funny how she's never referred to simply as "Christie") is that ambition and talent were perfectly matched. In over eighty novels, she delivered exactly what she promised. To do that in literature requires, I think, not only talent and a sound knowledge of one's form but also a good degree of self-knowledge. The result, besides a trail of bodies, is an artistic integrity that has endeared her to generations of readers.

On page 38 I have highlighted a line on George Eliot that I liked: "That pen that George Eliot wrote *The Mill on the Floss* with—that sort of thing—well, it's only just a pen after all. If you're really keen on George Eliot, why not get *The Mill on the Floss* in a cheap edition and read it?"

You might have noticed that I have been sending you used books. I have done this not to save money, but to make a point, which is that a used book, unlike a used car, hasn't lost any of its initial value. A good story rolls off the lot into the hands of its new reader as smoothly as the day it was written.

And there's another reason for these used paperbacks that never cost much even when new: I like the idea of holding a book that someone else has held, of eyes running over lines that have already seen the light of other eyes. That, in one image, is the community of readers, is the communion of literature.

I was in Ottawa recently and while I was there I happened to visit Laurier House, where two of your most illustrious predecessors lived and worked: Wilfrid Laurier and William Lyon Mackenzie King. It's an impressive mansion, with dark panelling, rich carpets, imposing furniture and a hidden elevator. What a perfect setting for an Agatha Christie murder mystery, I thought, which accounts for the book now in your hands.

Did you know that both Laurier and King were voracious readers? I include photographs I took of King's library, which was also where he worked, getting Canada through the Depression and the Second World War and building the foundations of our enviable social welfare system. Remarkable the range and number of books he read, including one that I love, one of the greatest books ever written, Dante's *Divine Comedy*. There was the complete Kipling, too, and all of Shakespeare. A two-volume biography of Louis Pasteur. Books on art. Shelf after shelf of the most varied histories and biographies. There were even what looked like self-help books to do with body and health. Truly a striking library. And let's not forget the piano.

Laurier, who made a country out of an independent colony, was an even more dedicated reader. His library was so extensive that King had it shipped out when he moved in, needing space for his own collection. Laurier's books are now stored at the National Archives.

A part of King's library.

How did they manage to read so much? Perhaps Laurier and King were excellent at time management. Certainly television wasn't there to inform them in part and otherwise fruitlessly devour their hours. Or was it that reading was a natural and essential element of being a respectable, well-rounded gentleman? Was it some ingrained habit of the privileged that gave these two prime ministers permission to spend so much time reading?

Reading was perhaps a privileged activity then. But not now. In a wealthy, egalitarian country like ours, where the literacy rate is high (although some people still struggle and need our help) and public libraries are just that, public, reading is no

And King was a musician, too.

longer an elite pastime. A good book today has no class, so to speak, and it can be had by anyone. One of the marvels of where I live, the beautiful province of Saskatchewan, is that the smallest town—Hazlet, for example, population 126—has a public library. Nor need books be expensive, if you want to own one. You can get a gold mine of a used book for fifty cents. After that, all that is needed to appreciate the investment is a little pocket of time.

I bet you King hurried to bed muttering to himself, "It was Parker the butler, I'm sure of it!"

Yours truly,
Yann Martel

DAME AGATHA CHRISTIE (1890–1977), the award-winning British author referred to by some as "the Queen of Crime," is one of the bestselling authors of all time. She is known the world over for her detective novels and created two of the most iconic detectives in crime-writing history: Hercule Poirot and Miss Jane Marple. She worked as a nurse in World War I, acquiring a knowledge of poisons and illnesses that would later serve her well when writing murder mysteries. In addition to writing more than eighty novels, she wrote several plays, short stories and romances. Many of her stories have been adapted for the screen.

BOOK 4:

BY GRAND CENTRAL STATION I SAT DOWN AND WEPT
BY ELIZABETH SMART

May 28, 2007

To Stephen Harper,
Prime Minister of Canada,
From a Canadian writer,
With best wishes,
Yann Martel

Dear Mr. Harper,

And now a book to be read aloud. I believe that's the best way to read Elizabeth Smart's *By Grand Central Station I Sat Down and Wept*. Because this is a language book, a book where language is the plot, the character and the setting. There is something else, of course, the theme, and the theme here is an old eternal one: love.

So what a perfect book to read in bed at the end of the day and aloud. A book to be shared.

The links between art and life can be reductionist, but this might help you stay afloat in the wash of language: one day Elizabeth Smart read some poems in a bookshop and she fell in love—I'm tempted to say "decided to fall in love"—with the poet, who was George Barker. Good thing for George Barker, because I suspect George Barker will be remembered by posterity more for being "the poet Elizabeth Smart fell in love with" than for his poetry. Smart and George Barker eventually met, in California, and they became lovers and her essential bliss and hell began. Because George Barker was married and would have durable relations with more women than just his wife and Elizabeth Smart. The great number of children he fathered—fifteen in all, including four with Smart—might indicate that he took the consequences of love as seriously as its emotional premise, but I doubt his fathering skills were that good. I am digressing. Elizabeth Smart fell in love with George Barker, it was killing for her heart but it yielded this jewel of a book. In a way, Smart was another Dante and *By Grand Central Station* is another *Divine Comedy*, only the direction of travel is opposite: she started in heaven and made her way to hell.

So, layers of allegorical allusions and metaphorical flights, but at the core of this book is the hard diamond of a passionate love affair.

I'll leave the love affair to your own thoughts and conclusions. What can more easily be talked about is the beauty of the language. Language is the crudest form of metaphor. It is a system of refined grunts in which, by common agreement, a sound we make—say "spinach"—is agreed to represent, to mean, that green leafy thing over there that's good to eat. It makes communicating so much easier and effective, spares one constantly having to point at with bug eyes. I can just see a group of cave people fiercely bobbing their heads up and down and grunting and shouting for joy when they first came upon the idea. It was such a good idea that it spread quickly. What a thrill, involving a fair number of bruising fights, I imagine, it must have been to be the ones who were the first to look upon the world and map it over with words. Different groups of people agreed on different grunts, and that's all right. *Vive la différence.*

And so we have: spinach, épinards, espinacas, spinaci, espinafre, spinat, spenat, pinaatti, szpinak, spenót, ШПИНАТ, السبانخ, and we are the better for it. Because these utilitarian grunts unexpectedly became a world unto themselves, offering their own possibilities. We thought language would be a simple tool directly relaying the world to us. But, lo, we found that the tool has become its own world, still relaying the outer world but in a mediated way. Now there is the word and there is the world and the two are enthralled with each other, like two lovers.

The lovers in the novel were arrested for trying to cross a state border—illicit love being a customs offence at the time—and the first pages of Part Four beautifully capture the coarseness with which the world sometimes greets love.

I thought I'd quote some passages to show you what powerful stuff you have between your hands, but there are too many—I might as well quote the whole book—and to take them out of context somehow seems offensive.

You remember how I recommended Gerasim to you, from *The Death of Ivan Ilych.* Well, in this book, we have Gerasim's equally domestic but petty antithesis: Mr. Wurtle.

Beware of Mr. Wurtle, Mr. Harper.

I can't resist quoting. On page 30:

> But the surety of my love is not dismayed by any eventuality which prudence or pity can conjure up, and in the end all that we can do is to sit at the table over which our hands cross, listening to tunes from the wurlitzer, with love huge and simple between us, and nothing more to be said.

On page 44:

> When the Ford rattles up to the door, five minutes (five years) late, and he walks across the lawn under the pepper-trees, I stand behind the gauze curtains, unable to move to meet him, or to

speak, as I turn to liquid to invade his every orifice when he opens the door.

Grandly romantic? Yes. Highly impractical? Absolutely. But as she asks one of the police officers who arrests her, on page 55:

What do you live for then?
I don't go for that sort of thing, the officer said, I'm a family man, I belong to the Rotary Club.

She might as well have been Jesus, and the officer surely wished later that he had been more like the humble Roman centurion of Capernaum.

There is this paragraph, on page 65, after she has returned to her native Ottawa, banished there for her extraconjugal illegality:

And over the fading wooden houses I sense the reminiscences of the pioneers' passion, and the determination of early statesmen who were mild but individual and able to allude to Shakespeare while discussing politics under the elms.

I wonder if she visited Laurier House.

By Grand Central Station is a masterly—or, better, mistressly—evocation of love. A life untouched by Elizabeth Smart's kind of passion is a life not fully lived. About that, we can take her word.

Who would have thought that language could do so much? Who would have thought that grunts would so recall the miracle of the world?

Yours truly,
Yann Martel

P.S. Please thank Susan Ross, from your office, for replying to me on your behalf about the first book I sent you. Perhaps you could lend Ms. Ross your copy of Ivan Ilych *once you've finished with it?*

ELIZABETH SMART (1913–1986) was a Canadian novelist and poet. She was born into an influential family in Ottawa, and travelled extensively, working in the United States and the United Kingdom. While in London, she read a book of George Barker's poetry and fell in love, first with the writing and then with the man. Their relationship is the basis of her best-known work, *By Grand Central Station I Sat Down and Wept*, which she wrote in British Columbia. She settled in England and continued a long-term affair with the married Barker, with whom she had four children. She worked as a copywriter for thirteen years, then as an editor for *Queen* magazine, and retired to a cottage in Suffolk.

BOOK 5:

THE BHAGAVAD GITA

Translated from the Sanskrit by Juan Mascaró

June 11, 2007

To Stephen Harper,
Prime Minister of Canada,
This book of Hindu wisdom,
From a Canadian writer,
With best wishes,
Yann Martel

Dear Mr. Harper,

With this fifth book, I am taking you in a direction you might find surprising: Hindu scripture. There is much Hindu scripture about, into the thousands of pages. You might have heard of the Vedas, especially the Rigveda, or of the Upanishads, or of the two great Sanskrit epics, the Mahabharata and the Ramayana, among many others. In their lengthy and varied entirety, they are the sum total of the thinking about life of an ancient and still thriving civilization, that which started in the Indus Valley, the place that today we call India. It's all quite dizzying. If you feel that you know nothing, that you are paralyzed with fear and ignorance, don't worry: we all feel that way. I'm sure even devout Hindus feel that way at times.

That feeling of fear and ignorance is in fact a good starting place, because it's exactly how Arjuna feels at the beginning of the *Bhagavad Gita*, the book you now have in your hands. The *Gita* is one short part of the Mahabharata, a much longer text, and it is the best known of Hindu scriptures, certainly the most widely read, and because of that arguably the most important. What Arjuna needs, what I need, what you need, what we all need, is a lesson in dharma, in proper conduct. And that is the lesson that Arjuna receives from Krishna, who is Arjuna's charioteer and friend but who also happens to be the Lord Supreme God of All Things.

Arjuna is on the eve of a great battle. He has asked Krishna to drive their chariot between the two facing armies and he surveys the assembled mass of soldiers. He sees that he has friends and enemies on both sides and he knows that many will die. That is when he loses heart.

Arjuna's battle may have its origins in a real, historical event, but in the *Bhagavad Gita* we are to read it as a metaphor. The true battle here is the battle of life and each one of us is an Arjuna facing his or her life, with all its daunting challenges.

I suggest you read neither the introduction by the scholar nor that by the translator, though Juan Mascaró's translation is excellent; that's why I chose it for you. It's clear and poetic, uncluttered by jargon or pedantry. Read it aloud and you will feel the cosmic wind blowing through the words. But the introductions, leave aside, I suggest, because it is the same thing with Hinduism as with every religion: there are matters of history and there are matters of faith. The Jesus of history is one thing, the Jesus of faith another. Search too far into the Jesus of history and you will lose yourself in anthropology and miss the point. The *Gita* of faith—much like the Jesus of faith—will have its greatest influence on you if you take it entirely on its own terms, making your own way through its grand injunctions and baffling mysteries. The *Gita* is a dialogue between one man and God, and the best reading of it, at least initially, is as a dialogue between one reader and the text. After that first encounter, if you want, scholars can be of help.

There may be ideas here that will irk you. By Western standards, there is a streak of fatalism running through Hinduism that will bother some. We live in a highly individualistic culture and we make much of the exertions of our egos. Perhaps if we took to heart one of the fundamental lessons of the *Gita*—to take action with detachment—we might exert ourselves in a calmer way and see that the ego, in the scheme of things, really is a puny, transitory thing.

Read the *Bhagavad Gita* in a moment of stillness and with an open heart, and it will change you. It is a majestic text, elevated and elevating. Like Arjuna, you will emerge from this dialogue with Krishna wiser and more serene, ready for action but filled with inner peace and loving-kindness.

Om shanti (peace be with you), as they say in India.

Yours truly,
Yann Martel

BOOK 6

BONJOUR TRISTESSE
BY FRANÇOISE SAGAN
Translated from the French by Irene Ash
June 25, 2007

To Stephen Harper,
Prime Minister of Canada,
From a Canadian writer,
With best wishes,
Yann Martel

Dear Mr. Harper,

From London, England, I'm sending you an English translation of a French novel. In this novel people smoke, people get slapped in the face, people drink heavily and then drive home, people have nothing but the blackest coffee for breakfast, and always people are concerned with love. Very French *d'une certaine époque*.

Bonjour Tristesse came out in France in 1954. Its author, Françoise Sagan, was nineteen years old. Immediately she became a celebrity and her book a bestseller.

More than that: they both became symbols.

Bonjour Tristesse is narrated in the first person by seventeen-year-old Cécile. She describes her father, Raymond, as "a frivolous man, clever at business, always curious, quickly bored, and attractive to women." The business cleverness is never mentioned again, but clearly it has allowed Raymond to enjoy freely his other attributes, his frivolity, curiosity, boredom and attraction, all of which revolve around dalliances of the heart and loins. He and his beloved daughter share the same temperament and they are in the south of France for the summer holidays with Elsa, his latest young mistress. This triangle suits Cécile perfectly and she is assiduous at pursuing her idle seaside pleasures, which come to include Cyril, a handsome young man who is keen on her.

But all is ruined when her father invites Anne to stay with them. She's an old friend of the family, a handsome woman her father's age, made of sterner, more sober stuff. She starts to meddle in Cécile's life. Worse, a few weeks after arriving, fun Elsa is dumped when Raymond starts a relationship with Anne. And finally, not long after, Anne announces that she and her father are planning to get married. Cécile is aghast. Her serial frolicker of a father and Anne, husband and wife? She, Cécile, a stepdaughter to Anne, who will work hard to transform her into a serious and studious young person? *Quel cauchemar!* Cécile sets to work to thwart things, using Elsa and Cyril as her pawns. The results are tragic.

After the grim work of the Second World War and the hard work of the post-war reconstruction, *Bonjour Tristesse* burst onto the French literary scene like a carnival. It announced what seemed like a new species, youth, *la jeunesse*, who had but one message: have fun with us or be gone; stay up all night at a jazz club or never come out with us again; don't talk to us about marriage and other boring conventions; let's smoke and be idle instead; forget the future—who's the new lover? As for the *tristesse* of the title, it was an excuse for a really good pout.

Such a brash, proudly indolent attitude, coming with an open contempt for conventional values, landed like a bomb among the bourgeoisie. Françoise Sagan earned herself a papal denunciation, which she must have relished.

A book can do that, capture a time and a spirit, be the expression of a broad yearning running through society. Read the book and you will understand not only the characters but the zeitgeist. Sometimes the book will be one a group strongly identifies with—for example, *On the Road*, by Jack Kerouac, among American youth—or, conversely, strongly identifies against—Salman Rushdie's *The Satanic Verses* among some Muslims.

So that too is what a book can be, a thermometer revealing a fever.

Yours truly,
Yann Martel

FRANÇOISE SAGAN (1935–2004), born Françoise Quoirez, was a novelist, playwright and screenwriter. Sagan's novels centre around disillusioned bourgeois characters (often teenagers) and primarily romantic themes; her work has been compared to that of J. D. Salinger. The writer François Mauriac described her as "a charming little monster." Her oeuvre includes dozens of works for print and performance. She suffered a car accident in 1957, an experience that left her addicted to painkillers and other drugs for much of her life.

BOOK 7:

CANDIDE
BY VOLTAIRE
Translated from the French by John Butt
July 9, 2007

To Stephen Harper,
Prime Minister of Canada,
This witty book on evil,
From a Canadian writer,
With best wishes,
Yann Martel

Dear Mr. Harper,

You've no doubt heard the theory of six degrees of separation, how each one of us on this planet is connected to everyone else through a chain of five people. Well, in a way, you and I are linked through the seventh book I am sending you, *Candide*, by Voltaire. Let me explain. On pages 110 and 111 of Chapter XXIII there is a brief scene in which Candide, having just arrived in Portsmouth, England, witnesses the execution of a British admiral. "Why execute this admiral?" asks Candide.

"Because he had not enough dead men to his credit," comes the reply.

This incident was no invention of Voltaire's. There was indeed a British admiral who was executed for failing to "do his utmost" during a naval battle with the French off the island of Minorca. He was the first and only British admiral so treated by Britannia, and his name was John Byng.

Do you recognize that last name? That's right: Lord Byng of Vimy, of the "King-Byng Affair," Governor General of Canada from 1921 to 1926, and a direct descendant of the ill-fated Admiral Byng. I'm sure you have regular meetings with Lord Byng's current successor, Her Excellency Michaëlle Jean. And the last degree of separation: a direct descendant of both Byngs, Jamie Byng, is a good friend of mine and my British publisher. So there you have it, six degrees of separation: me-Voltaire-Byng-Byng-Byng-Jean-you.

It's in this same Chapter XXIII of *Candide*, in the paragraph just before Admiral Byng's execution in fact, that Voltaire famously dismissed Canada as "a few acres of snow," "quelques arpents de neige." Isn't that amazing? Voltaire speaks of Canada and then right after tells a story about a mutual acquaintance of ours. Mr. Harper, the link between us couldn't be more preordained than that!

One last anecdote. I can also say this of *Candide*: not once but twice I have come upon people reading a book, thought I recognized the title, exclaimed what a great novel it was, anticipating some good talk about the terrible, funny calamities that poor Candide must endure, only to be told by the readers, in both cases women, that the "e" was an "a" and that the book they were reading was not Voltaire's brilliant satire but rather a book on candida, which is a bothersome, often recurring and terribly itchy yeast infection of the vagina. After that, as you can imagine, the conversation became a bit stilted.

Let's get to the point. *Candide*, published in 1759, is a short, funny and engaging tale about a serious problem: evil and the suffering it engenders. Voltaire lived between 1694 and 1778 and was one of the great gadflies of his time. In *Candide* he lampooned what he felt was the facile optimism of the day, an optimism best expressed by the philosopher Gottfried Leibniz's formulation that our world is "the best of all possible worlds" (you might remember that line from an ironic Kris Kristofferson song). The reasoning behind this conclusion was that since God is good and all-powerful, the world cannot be anything but the best conceivable world, with the optimum combination of elements. Evil was thus posited as serving the purpose of maximizing good, since it is in having a choice between good and evil that we fallible human beings can improve ourselves and become good.

Now, we can perhaps agree that adversity can bring the best out of us, and it is still Christian doctrine that we are "perfected by suffering." But such a blithe justification of evil has fairly obvious limits. It might do for the sort of evil that comes as a kick-in-the-behind, as a retrospective blessing in disguise. But will it serve for heinous evil and egregious misfortune?

Voltaire wrote *Candide* in part as a reaction to just such an instance of misfortune. On the morning of November 1, 1755, a cataclysmic earthquake struck Lisbon. Immediately, most churches in the city collapsed, killing thousands of people who were inside. Other public buildings also came down, as did over 12,000 dwellings. Once the tremors had stopped, a tsunami struck the city, and after that, fires wreaked further havoc. Over sixty thousand people were killed and the material damage, in an age still innocent of the destructive power of modern bombs, was unprecedented. The Lisbon earthquake had the same troubling effect on people at the time as the Holocaust had in our time. But whereas the Nazi barbarity had us mostly wondering about human nature, the Lisbon earthquake had people wondering about the nature of God. How could God allow such cruelty to take place in a city as piously Catholic and evangelical as Lisbon, and of all days on All Saints' Day? In what conceivable way could killing so many people in one stroke maximize the good of this world?

Answering such troubling questions—the Holy Grail of theodicy—remains as troubling then as now. Perhaps the answer still is that we lack perspective, that in a way that we mortals just can't understand, great evil is part of a divine plan and makes ultimate sense.

In the meantime, until God comes down and fully explains that plan, evil galls. Voltaire was religiously outraged by the Lisbon earthquake. For him it was clear: there was no Providence, there was no God. To be eternally optimistic in the face of great evil and suffering was not only insensitive to its victims, but morally and intellectually untenable. He set to prove it in the story of Candide, the naive young man from Thunder-ten-tronckh, in Westphalia, who could have had as his motto "All is for the best," such an optimist was he at the start of the novel. Wait till you see all the catastrophes that befall him. The novel ends, when all has been said and done and suffered, with a simple call to quiet, peaceable and collective work: "we must go and work in the garden," "il faut cultiver notre jardin."

That call still stands as perhaps the only practical solution to what we can do in the face of evil: spend our time simply, fruitfully and with others.

Yours truly,
Yann Martel

VOLTAIRE (1694–1778), born François-Marie Arouet, was a French Enlightenment writer and philosopher. He was immensely prolific, writing novels, poetry, plays, essays, scientific papers and historical works. Voltaire was politically active, supporting social reform, free trade, civil liberties and freedom of religion. He was a fierce critic of the Catholic Church. His satire got him into trouble: in 1717, he was imprisoned for eleven months in the Bastille for criticizing the French government; and in 1726 he was exiled from France for three years for insulting a member of the aristocracy. He is buried in the Pantheon in Paris.

BOOK 8

SHORT AND SWEET:
101 VERY SHORT POEMS
EDITED BY SIMON ARMITAGE

July 23, 2007

> To Stephen Harper,
> Prime Minister of Canada,
> A book of concise loveliness,
> From a Canadian writer,
> With best wishes,
> Yann Martel

Dear Mr. Harper,

You said a few years ago that your favourite book was the *Guinness Book of World Records*. Well, as a dedicated reader of those yearly volumes that means that at least on one occasion you read a poem. Simon Armitage, the editor of *Short and Sweet: 101 Very Short Poems*, the latest book I am sending you, says in his introduction that he became interested in very short poetry as a teenager when he read in the aforementioned *Guinness* book what was claimed to be the world's shortest poem:

> Fleas

> Adam
> 'ad 'em

A masterpiece, isn't it? In a single rhyming couplet of four syllables something is suggested about the ancient and intimate relations between humans and animals, about the great antiquity of small, neglected beings, about the shabby reality of our existence, divine origins notwithstanding, and the corruption of this world, inherent even in the Garden of Eden. And there's more: in that rhyme that sounds like "Adam, Adam," is there not a lament? Or is it an accusation? Either way, it could be that the fleas in question are us.

You can't beat poetry for saying so much with so little.

Busy? Tired? Feeling nothing? You're missing on the depth of life that you know is out there but you don't have time to read a big fat novel? Then try this poem, by George Mackay Brown:

Taxman

Seven scythes leaned at the wall.
Beard upon golden beard
The last barley load
Swayed through the yard.
The girls uncorked the ale.
Fiddle and feet moved together.
Then between stubble and heather
A horseman rode.

Notice the extraordinary concision with which a narrative structure is set up, with the emotional questions and possibilities left to ripple through the reader's mind. The marvel of poetry is that it can be as short as a question yet as powerful as an answer. For example, the following poem, by Stephen Crane:

In the Desert

In the desert
I saw a creature, naked, bestial
Who, squatting upon de ground
Held his heart in his hands
And ate of it. I said, "Is it good, friend?"
"It is bitter–bitter," he answered:
"But I like it
Because it is bitter,
And because it is my heart."

I envy that of poets, that ability to create something so small that nevertheless feels so complete, the vastness of existence made to fit into something no bigger than a coin purse. Look at this poem, by Hugo Williams:

Lights Out

We're allowed to talk for ten minutes
about what has happened during the day,
then we have to go to sleep.
It doesn't matter what we dream about.

Repetition suits poetry. Read one of these poems several times and you'll see for yourself: it keeps getting better. In this case, familiarity breeds respect.

A last one, lovely, by Wendy Cope:

Flowers

Some men never think of it.
You did. You'd come along
And say you'd nearly brought me flowers
But something had gone wrong. The shop was
    closed. Or you had doubts—
The sort that minds like ours
Dream up instantly. You thought
I might not want your flowers.
It made me smile and hug you then.
Now I can only smile.
But, look, the flowers you nearly brought
Have lasted all this while.

Short though they are, I wouldn't rush through any of these poems. Rush tends to disturb their echoing stillness. Best to read them aloud, getting the rhythm right, smoothing out the stumbles, slowly getting a sense of their sense.

It's a marvellous exercise in—in what?—in being human, I suppose.

Yours truly,
Yann Martel

SIMON ARMITAGE (b. 1963) is a British poet, novelist and playwright known for his dry wit and accessible style. He is the author of nine books of poetry, and has written and presented works for radio and television. He has earned multiple awards for his poetry, including the *Sunday Times* Author of the Year Award, a Forward Poetry Prize, a Lannan Award, an Ivor Novello Award and the title of the UK's Millennium Poet for his poem "Killing Time." Armitage has been a judge for the Griffin Poetry Prize and the Man Booker Prize for Fiction.

BOOK 9:

CHRONICLE OF A DEATH FORETOLD
BY GABRIEL GARCÍA MÁRQUEZ

Translated from the Spanish by Gregory Rabassa

August 6, 2007

To Stephen Harper,
Prime Minister of Canada,
From a Canadian writer,
With best wishes,
Yann Martel

Dear Mr. Harper,

When I found a used copy of the latest book that I'm sending you, I was pleased that it was a hard cover—a first after eight paperbacks—but I was disappointed with the cover artwork.* Surely, *Chronicle of a Death Foretold*, the short novel by the great Gabriel García Márquez, deserves better than this awkward job. Who chose the purple? It's all so hideous. But you can't judge a book by its cover, isn't that right?

Which is a nice way of broaching the topic of clichés.

A cliché, to remind you, is a worn, hackneyed phrase or opinion. At one time, perhaps in the Middle Ages among monks slowly copying books by hand in a monastery, the notion that nothing of substance can be judged by its surface, expressed in terms of a bound stack of paper and its protective shell, must

---

* The cover features an unappealing drawing of a bride. She looks like a stiff porcelain doll.

have seemed like a dazzling revelation that had the monks looking at each other in amazement and rushing out to sing in full-throated worship to *urbi et orbi*: "Praise be to God! A book can't be judged by its cover! Hallelujah, hallelujah!"

But now, even among people who don't read a book a year, it's a cliché, it's a lazy, thoughtless way of expressing oneself.

Sometimes clichés are unavoidable. "I love you"—a sentence that is foundational to the well-being of every human being, the "you" being another person, a group of people, a grand notion or cause, a god, or simply a reflection in the mirror—is a cliché. Every actor who has to say the line struggles to deliver it in a way that makes it sound fresh, like Adam saying it for the first time to Eve. But there's no good way of saying it otherwise—and no one really tries to. We live very well with "I love you" because the syntactical simplicity of it—one each of subject, verb, object, nothing else—nicely matches its intended truthfulness. So we happily blurt out the cliché, some of us repeating it several times, for emphasis, or some of us saying it all the time, for example at the end of every phone call with a family member. Lovers at a balcony, sons and daughters at war, dervishes whirling—they're all living "I love you" in a way that is not clichéd but essential.

But otherwise clichés should be avoided like the West Nile virus. Why? Because they are stale and flat, and because they are contagious. Convenient writerly shortcuts, hurried means of signifying "you know what I mean," clichés at first are just a froth of tiny white eggs in the ink of your pen, incubated slowly by the warmth of your lazy fingers. The harm to your prose is slight, and people are forgiving. But convenience, shortcuts and hurry are no way to write true words, and if you are not careful—and it is hard work to be careful—the eggs multiply, bloom and enter your blood.

The damage can be serious. The infection can spread to your eyes, to your nose, to your tongue, to your ears, to your skin, and worse: to your brain and to your heart. It's no longer just your words, written and spoken, that are conventional, conformist, unoriginal, dull. Now it's your very thoughts and feelings that have lost their heartbeat. In the most serious cases, the person can no longer even see or feel the world directly, but can only perceive it through the reductive, muffling filter of cliché.

At this stage, the cliché attains its political dimension: dogmatism. Dogmatism in politics has exactly the same effect as the cliché in writing: it prevents the soul from interacting openly and honestly with the world, with that pragmatism that lets in fresh all the beautiful, bountiful messiness of life.

The cliché and dogmatism—two related banes that all writers and politicians should avoid if we are to serve well our respective constituencies.

As for the García Márquez book, I got it for you because of your recent trip to—and renewed interest in—Latin America. The man's a genius.

Yours truly,
Yann Martel

GABRIEL GARCÍA MÁRQUEZ (b. 1927) is an internationally acclaimed novelist, short story writer, screenplay writer, memoirist and journalist. During his long literary career, he has been credited with popularizing the "magical realism" writing style. Márquez, nicknamed "Gabo," sets his stories in Latin America and often addresses the themes of isolation, love and memory. His best-known works are *One Hundred Years of Solitude* and *Love in the Time of Cholera*. He is also well known for his political activism. He received the Nobel Prize in Literature in 1982. Raised in Colombia, he now lives in Mexico City.

BOOK 10

MISS JULIA
BY AUGUST STRINDBERG

Translated from the Swedish by Peter Watts

August 20, 2007

To Stephen Harper,
Prime Minister of Canada,
From a Canadian writer,
With best wishes,
Yann Martel

Dear Mr. Harper,

One day when August Strindberg was still a student at the University of Uppsala, he received a surprising summons: King Karl XV wanted to see him. Strindberg put on his best suit and made the short trip to the Royal Palace in Stockholm. The twenty-two-year-old was from an undistinguished family, he was very poor, and his academic achievements were perfectly average, but the King of Sweden had his reasons for wanting to meet him: he was keen on the arts and he had seen a performance of a historical play that Strindberg had written, *The Outlaw*, and he had liked it. In fact, he had liked it so much that he promised the young man a quarterly stipend so that he could finish his university studies. Strindberg was delighted. Alas, after only two payments and without any explanation, the royal bounty dried up. So it goes. Strindberg dropped out of university.

By all accounts, Strindberg was a miserable sod. He had a boundless capacity to be unhappy, especially in his relations with women. But he also had a mind of immense energy, intelligence and originality, and he wrote brilliant plays.

A brilliant play is something very peculiar. Drama is the most oral of literary forms, far less of an artifice than the short story, the novel or the poem, and far less reliant on publication to fully come into its own; what really counts for a play is not that it be read, but that it be seen, in the flesh. In many ways, life has all the trappings of a play: when you, Mr. Harper, enter the House of Commons, for example, you are walking onto a stage. And you are there because you are playing a role, the lead role. And it is because you are playing that role that you rise and speak. And then in Hansard the next day it reads like a play. It is the same for all of us in life: we move about on various stages, we take on various roles, and we speak. But there is a crucial difference, of course, one that goes to the core of what art is: in a play there is structure and meaning, put there by the playwright, while in life, even after many acts, the structure and meaning is hard to find. Some claim to know of a great playwright who has authored our existence, but even for them structure and meaning remains an ongoing challenge.

So while a play approximates life to a great degree, it is in other ways nothing like life. No one speaks with the concise completeness of the dramatis personae of a play, neither in ways that so quickly yet subtly reveal their character, nor with a tempo that so rises and falls until a climax, nor, usually, in a space so confined as a stage's. In a phrase: life is a play that doesn't make sense, while a play is life that does.

(Admittedly, there are people for whom life makes perfect sense, their vision of things forever untouched by doubt, the entropy of time seeming to have no more effect on them than a gentle breeze on the face. They are the type who will not go for the questioning of life that is a play, indeed, that is all great art. But that is a separate matter.)

The knack for writing plays is a knack I don't have. I have tried to move plot entirely through dialogue, I have tried to express my thoughts on life within the strictures of speech, I have tried to develop an ear for the way people speak—to laughable, unpublishable result. Notice how the word is play-*wright*; it may sound like *write*, but originally the act of writing a play struck the English as more akin to the work of a carpenter than of a writer. The world of letters is indeed easily divided between those who *write* and those who *wright*. There are exceptions—Samuel Beckett, for example—but those who can do both successfully are not many.

There are three plays in the volume of Strindberg that I have sent you. It is the middle play, known either as *Miss Julia* or *Miss Julie*, that I recommend to you. In it you will read dialogue that is so brilliant, so crackling with tension, so straightforward on the surface yet hinting at such turmoil and complexity, that it will, paradoxically, all seem perfectly natural to you. That is the sign of a great play in the naturalist tradition: how easily it flows. One gets the sense that the playwright just sat down with a good, simple idea and it all came out in an easy afternoon's work. I assure you that that is like thinking that all Michelangelo had to do was chip away from the block of marble everything that didn't look like David.

Miss Julia, which was first performed in 1889, is about confinement, principally the confinement of sexual roles and the confinement of class. Miss Julia and Jean, her servant, meet, match and clash, with tragic consequences. I would love to see the play actually performed on a stage. The alchemy of great play, great director and great actors is rare, but when it happens—I am remembering now a performance long ago at Stratford of

Eugene O'Neill's *Long Day's Journey into Night*, with Hume Cronyn and Jessica Tandy—it makes for an experience of an intensity that is, in my estimation, unmatched in the literary arts.

You will notice that the previous owner of your copy of Strindberg wrote copiously in the margins. This annoyed me at first, this defacing of *Miss Julia*. But finally I was charmed by the intruder's thoughts and opinions. The handwriting is large, clear and loopy; I think it is a young person writing, likely a young woman. Above Jean's comment that "on the way back by the barn I looked in and joined the dancing," our hypothetical young woman writes "*joie de vivre*." When Jean impudently tells Miss Julia that he knows that Kristin, the cook, talks in her sleep because "I've heard her," our young woman observes "Kristin's his mistress." She variously thinks Jean to be "practical" or "realistic," while Miss Julia is "totally impractical." Other short notations of hers are "dramatic moment," "flirting," "bourgeoisie," "gives her warning," "seduction" and "trag. everyth falling apart" [sic].

One last thing, to elucidate a point easily missed: the "Turkish pavilion" on page 90 that Jean mentions sneaking into as a child, the "finest building I'd ever seen," the walls "covered with pictures of kings and emperors," his first time "inside a castle," is just a fancy outhouse—and the way out he is forced to take when he hears someone approaching is the exit you'd least like to take if you were in an outhouse.

Yours truly,
Yann Martel

AUGUST STRINDBERG (1849–1912) is best known for his plays, but he also wrote short stories, novels, poems and volumes of autobiography.

In addition to his writing, he was a painter and photographer, and experimented with alchemy. In life and in his art, he was pessimistic and his works were marked by his overt satirizing of Swedish society. Strindberg's plays fall into two categories—naturalistic and expressionistic—and he is considered one of the pioneers of Expressionism. He wrote dozens of plays, the most famous of which are the naturalistic *Miss Julia* and *The Father*.

BOOK II

THE WATSONS
BY JANE AUSTEN
September 3, 2007

To Stephen Harper,
Prime Minister of Canada,
From a Canadian writer,
With best wishes,
Yann Martel

Dear Mr. Harper,

The great Jane Austen. She is a shining example of how art—like politics—can take the least promising ore and transform it into the finest metal. Austen had three things going against her: she lived in *rural* England, she was middle class in the age before that class exploded with possibilities, and she was a woman. That is to say, her life was hemmed in by limitations.

England during Austen's lifetime—1775 to 1817—was in the full throes of the Industrial Revolution, and revolutions are occasions of great upheaval and renewal, both for the arts and for politics. But Austen mostly missed out on this revolution because she lived outside of the urban centres that were at its heart. And in the genteel hinterland where she lived, she was a member of a most precarious class: the landless *middle* class, with a class she wished not to join swimming beneath her, the working class, and a class she wished she could join soaring above, the nobility. This precariousness was aggravated by her being a woman, which disqualified her from whatever work a member of the middle class might decently do: the clergy, the medical profession, the military. So all Austen's female characters worry endlessly about financial security, yet have only a single way of achieving it: marriage. Hungry for status and material goods, but unwilling (because unable) to earn them, always on the hunt for wealthy husbands, yet having only stuffiness, rigidity and pretence to offer—I suspect that if we met the female members of Jane Austen's class today, with our modern sensibilities, we would find them deeply disagreeable. There is this exchange between two female characters in *The Watsons*, the latest book I am sending you:

"To be so bent on marriage, to pursue a man merely for the sake of situation is a sort of thing that shocks me; I cannot understand it. Poverty is a great evil, but to a woman of education and feeling it ought not, it cannot be the greatest. I would rather be teacher at a school (and I can think of nothing worse) than marry a man I did not like."

"I would rather do anything than be teacher at a school," said her sister. "*I* have been at school, Emma, and know what a life they lead; *you* never have. I should not like marrying a disagreeable man any more than yourself, but I do not think there *are* many very disagreeable men; I think I could like any good-humoured man with a comfortable income."

How sad to have the most important profession in the world thought of as worse than what has facetiously been called the oldest profession in the world. Thankfully, things have changed. Today, the middle class in Canada has expanded to absorb all other classes, so that practically everyone is of the working class, the class that works, and the sinking and the soaring is called mobility, and it is a triumph of our time that women can avail themselves of that mobility (though still not as much as men—there's still some liberating work that needs doing).

But back to Jane Austen: boxed in, left only to play card games, look forward to the next ball and keep an eye out for eligible bachelors, surrounded by green pastures and rolling hills, does this strike you as promising grounds for great art?

Well, in the case of Jane Austen, it was. Because she had the great and good luck of having a loving and intellectually lively family, and she was blessed with a keen and critical sense of observation, as well as an inherently positive disposition.

So though limited by class and by sex, Jane Austen was able to transcend these limitations. Her novels are marvels of wit and perspicacity, and in them she examined her society with such fresh and engaging realism that the English novel was durably changed.

The Watsons is easily Jane Austen's least-known work. But I selected it for you for two reasons: it is short, and it is unfinished. Its shortness will I hope make you want to read some of Austen's longer novels, *Pride and Prejudice* or *Emma* perhaps.

And though it is unfinished, an abandoned draft, there is more perfection in it than in many a completed novel. Austen abandoned *The Watsons* in 1805 as a result of personal difficulties: the death of a good friend, and right afterwards the illness and death of her own father, which left her and her sister and her mother in uncertain circumstances. Eventually, four years later, her brother Edward was able to provide his mother and sisters with a cottage, and Austen began writing again.

She let go and then started up again, able to produce novels that marked the English novel forever. In that, there is something instructive. There is so much we must leave unfinished. How hard it is to let go.

Yours truly,
Yann Martel

JANE AUSTEN (1775–1817) was an English novelist whose realist works offer strong female characters and biting social commentary. She never married, and lived with her family until her death at the age of forty-one. Several of her novels have been adapted for the screen. Her novels are still popular today, and *Pride and Prejudice* has inspired modern spoofs including *Bridget Jones's Diary* by Helen Fielding, the Bollywood film *Bride & Prejudice* directed by Gurinder Chadha, and *Pride and Prejudice and Zombies*, adapted from Austen's original novel by Seth Grahame-Smith.

BOOK 12:

MAUS
BY ART SPIEGELMAN
September 17, 2007

To Stephen Harper,
Prime Minister of Canada,
This most disturbing and necessary book,
From a Canadian writer,
With best wishes,
Yann Martel

Dear Mr. Harper,

I am sorry but you will have to endure this time a letter written
in my terrible handwriting. I didn't manage to find a printer in
Oświęcim, the small Polish town where I'm staying at the moment.

Oświęcim is better known by the name the Germans gave it:
Auschwitz. Have you been?

I am here trying to finish my next book. And it also explains
my choice of the latest book I am sending you: the graphic novel
Maus, by Art Spiegelman. Don't be fooled by the format. This
comic book is *real* literature.

Some stories need to be told in many different ways so that
they will exist in new ways for new generations. The story of the
murder of nearly six million of Europe's Jewish people at the hands
of the Nazis and their criminal accomplices is just the sort of story
that needs renewing if we don't want a part of ourselves to fall
asleep, like grandchildren nodding off after hearing grandfather
repeat the same story of yore one time too many.

I know I said I would send you books that would increase your "stillness." But a sense of peace and calm focus, of what Buddhists call "passionate detachment," must not fall into self-satisfaction or complacency. So a disturbance—and Auschwitz is profoundly disturbing—can be the right way to renew one's stillness.

Maus is a masterpiece. Spiegelman tells his story, or, more accurately, the story of his father and mother, in a bold and radical way. It's not just that he takes the graphic form, thought perhaps by some to be a medium only for children, to new artistic heights by taking on such a momentous topic as exterminationist genocide. It's more than that. It's how he tells the story. You will see. The narrative agility and ease of it. And how the frames speak large. Some, small though they are, and in black and white, have an impact that one would think possible only with large paintings or shots from a movie.

And I haven't even mentioned the main device, which explains the title of the book: all the characters have the heads of one kind of animal or other. So the Jews have the heads of mice, the Germans of cats, the Poles of pigs, the Americans of dogs, and so on.

It's brilliant. It so takes you in, it so rips you apart. From there you must make your own tricky way back again to what it means to be human.

Yours truly,
Yann Martel

ART SPIEGELMAN (b. 1948) is a Swedish-born American comic artist who was part of the underground comics movements of the 1960s and '70s, contributing to several publications and co-founding *Arcade* and *Raw*. He was a co-creator of garbage candy and Garbage Pail Kids trading cards. Named one of *TIME* magazine's "Top 100 Most Influential People" in 2005, he has won multiple awards for his work, including the Pulitzer Prize in 1992 for *Maus* and its sequel, *Maus II*. He continues to publish new work and promote the comic medium, and in 2004 published a large board book, *In the Shadow of No Towers*, about the September 11, 2001, terrorist attacks on New York City.

BOOK 13:

TO KILL A MOCKINGBIRD
BY HARPER LEE
October 1, 2007

To Stephen Harper,
Prime Minister of Canada,
From a Canadian writer,
With best wishes,
Yann Martel

Dear Mr. Harper,

In an interview some years ago Mavis Gallant mentioned an operation she underwent. She awoke from general anaesthesia in a state of mental confusion. For several minutes she couldn't remember any details of her identity or of her life, not her name or her age or what she did, not where she was nor why she was there. An amnesia that was complete—except for this: she knew she was a woman and that she was thinking in English. Inextricably linked to the faintest glimmer of consciousness were those two identity traits: sex and language.

Which says how deep language goes. It becomes part of our biology. Our lungs need and are made for air, our mouths and stomachs need and are made for nutrition; our ears and noses can hear and smell and, lo, there are things to be heard and smelled. The mind is the same: it needs and is made for language, and, lo, there are things to be said and understood.

I am no champion of any particular language. Every language, from Afrikaans to Zulu, does the job it is required to do: map the world with sounds that conveniently identify objects and concepts. Given a little time, every living language spoken by a sufficient number of people will match any new object or concept with a new word. Have you heard the notion of how the Inuit are supposed to have twenty-six words for snow, while we in English have only the one, "snow"? Well, that's nonsense. Ask avid English-language skiers and they'll come up with twenty-six words or compounds to describe snow.

Just as there are many cuisines on this earth, many styles of dress and many understandings of the divine, each of which can keep the stomach content, the body smartly covered and the soul attuned to the eternal, so there are many different kinds of sounds with which we can make ourselves understood. Each language has its own sonority, cadence, specialized vocabulary, and so on, but it all evens out. Each of us can be fully human in any language.

But since you are a native English speaker, let me champion English in this letter as an introduction to the latest semi-monthly book I am sending you. The English language has by far the largest vocabulary of any language on earth, well over 600,000 words. French, by comparison, is said to have 350,000 words and Italian, 250,000. Now right away, before I get jumped upon by those from my native province and all my Italian-speaking friends, this exuberance of vocabulary is largely irrelevant. Just 7,000 words represent 90 percent of the root vocabulary the average English speaker uses.

And let's not forget: the voluble Italians showed no reticence in launching—and thoroughly enjoying—their *Renascimento* with their fewer words while the reserved Britons sat in their dark and dank island idling away the hours of pouring rain by wondering whether they should adopt the Italian word for that explosion of optimism and sunshine or call it the *Rebirth* or the *Renaissance*.

How did a local-yokel language spoken on an island—truly, an insular language—come to span the globe? The explanation can be summarized in two words: *invasions* and counter-invasions; that is, *colonialism*. The Germanic language of the Anglo-Saxons was immeasurably enriched by a number of invasions. In linguistic terms, the Christianization of Britannia was a beachhead, the Norman invasion of 1066 was a flood, and the Renaissance was a flourish. After that, the verbally empowered English set out to conquer the world, a great plundering that made them wealthy, not only with other people's gold but also with other people's words.

English is a hot stew of many ingredients. In it can be found words that have their origin in Arabic, Breton, Czech, Danish, Finnish, Gaelic, Hindi, Inuit, Japanese, Latin, Malay, Norwegian, Polish, Russian, Spanish, Turkish, Welsh, to mention only a selection. And that's only vocabulary. English usage—how people speak their English—is also extraordinarily varied.

And that's the reason for my gift to you this time: *To Kill a Mockingbird*, by Harper Lee. It's a modern classic, a great story, one that will make you love lawyers, but it's for the usage that I chose it. Rural Alabama English of the 1950s as spoken by children is something else. And yet it is English, so you will understand it without a problem. That is the rare privilege of those who speak English: in reading untranslated books from every continent they can feel both at home and abroad.

Bonne lecture!

Yours truly,
Yann Martel

HARPER LEE (b. 1926) is an American writer, best-known for her Pulitzer Prize–winning novel *To Kill a Mockingbird*. This novel, which is frequently taught in schools to this day, was made into an Academy Award–winning film starring Gregory Peck as Atticus Finch. Many autobiographical elements are present in the novel, and the character of Dill is based on Lee's lifelong friend Truman Capote. After publishing her book to instant acclaim and long-lasting success, Lee retreated from public life. To date, *To Kill a Mockingbird* is the only work she has published beyond the scope of magazines.

BOOK 14:

LE PETIT PRINCE
BY ANTOINE DE SAINT-EXUPÉRY
October 15, 2007

To Stephen Harper,
Prime Minister of Canada,
Ce livre en français,
From a Canadian writer,
With best wishes,
Yann Martel

Cher Monsieur Harper,

Vous parlez le français. Vous avez fait de grands et fructueux efforts pour apprendre et parler cette langue depuis que vous êtes premier ministre. Vous espérez ainsi apprivoiser les Québécois.

Par ailleurs, la dernière fois, je vous ai beaucoup entretenu de l'anglais. Alors cette fois-ci je vous envoie un livre en français. Il est très connu. C'est *Le Petit Prince*, de l'écrivain français Antoine de Saint-Exupéry. Vous l'avez peut-être lu au cours de vos études mais il saura vous être encore assurément très utile, non seulement pour maintenir votre français, mais aussi pour vous aider auprès des Québécois, puisque *Le Petit Prince* c'est aussi l'histoire d'un apprivoisement, dans ce cas-ci, d'un renard.

Le renard fait cadeau d'une très importante leçon au Petit Prince, mais je ne vais pas la répéter. Je vous laisse la redécouvrir.

Le vocabulaire est simple, les scènes claires à comprendre, la morale évidente et attachante. C'est en fait un conte chrétien.

Vous allez soupirer, "Si seulement les Québécois étaient aussi faciles à apprivoiser que les renards."

Mais nous sommes plutôt, nous Québécois, comme la fleur du Petit Prince, avec notre orgueil et nos quatre épines.

Cordialement vôtre,
Yann Martel

[TRANSLATION]

Dear Mr. Harper,

You speak French. You've made great and fruitful efforts to learn the language since you became Prime Minister. You hope in this way to tame Quebeckers.

In my last letter, I discussed the English language. So this time I'm sending you a book in French, one that is very well known. It's *The Little Prince*, by the French writer Antoine de Saint-Exupéry. You perhaps read it during your French-language studies, but I'm certain it will still be of use to you, not only to help you maintain your French, but also to help you with Quebeckers, since *The Little Prince* is also the story of a taming, in this case of a fox.

The fox teaches the Little Prince a very important life lesson, but I won't divulge it here. I'll leave it for you to find it.

The vocabulary is simple, the scenes easy to understand, the moral obvious and endearing. It's a Christian tale.

You'll sigh, "If only Quebeckers were so easy to tame."

But we Quebeckers are rather like the Little Prince's flower, with our pride and our four thorns.

Yours truly,
Yann Martel

ANTOINE DE SAINT-EXUPÉRY (1900–1944), a French novelist and artist, is most famous for his illustrated philosophical novella, *Le Petit Prince* (*The Little Prince*). This story is so beloved that Saint-Exupéry's drawing of the Little Prince was printed on the French 50-franc note until the introduction of the euro. Saint-Exupéry was an aviator and, in most of his works, including *Night Flight* and *Wind, Sand and Stars*, he drew on his experiences as a pilot. He worked as a pilot for the postal service for years. During World War II, he flew reconnaissance missions for the Allies. On one of these flights he went missing and was presumed dead.

BOOK 15:

ORANGES ARE NOT THE ONLY FRUIT
BY JEANETTE WINTERSON

October 29, 2007

To Stephen Harper,
From an English writer,
With best wishes,
Jeanette Winterson
(Sent to you by a Canadian writer, Yann Martel)

Dear Mr. Harper,

The great thing about reading books is that it makes us better than cats. Cats are said to have nine lives. What is that compared to the girl, boy, man, woman who reads books? A book read is a life added to one's own. So it takes only nine books to make cats look at you with envy.

And I'm not talking here only of "good" books. Any book—trash to classic—makes us live the life of another person, injects us with the wisdom and folly of their years. When we've read the last page of a book, we know more, either in the form of raw knowledge—the name of a gun, perhaps—or in the form of greater understanding. The worth of these vicarious lives is not to be underestimated. There's nothing sadder—or sometimes more dangerous—than the person who has lived only his or her single, narrow life, unenlightened by the experience, real or invented, of others.

The book I am sending you today is a perfect instance of a story that offers you another life. It is a *Bildungsroman* (from the German, literally a "novel of education"), a novel that follows the moral development of its main character. Because it's told in the first person, the reader can easily slip into the skin, see through the eyes, of the person speaking. Jeanette Winterson's *Oranges Are Not the Only Fruit* is a brief 170 pages, but during those pages you become "Jeanette," the main character. Jeanette is a young woman who lives in small-town England a few decades ago. Her mother loves the Lord in a big way, and so does Jeanette. But the problem is, the problem becomes, that Jeanette also loves women in a big way. And those two—loving the Lord and loving women when you are yourself a woman—are not compatible, at least according to some who love the Lord and take it upon themselves to judge in His name.

Written in sparkling prose, *Oranges* is the sad, funny, tender tale of a young woman who must break into two pieces and then choose which of the two she wants to become. And that, having to make hard choices, having to choose between competing loves and lives, having to lose oneself so that one might find oneself, is instructive—besides highly entertaining—not only to adolescent Lancashire lesbians, but to me, to you, to everyone who is interested in making the most of life.

So enclosed, a fifteenth book, a fifteenth life.

Yours truly,
Yann Martel

P.S. Note the dedication. A book signed by the author herself. I had the good luck of meeting Jeanette Winterson in England recently and she kindly inscribed a copy of her book to you.

JEANETTE WINTERSON (b. 1959) is a British author and journalist. She shot to fame with the publication of her first novel, *Oranges Are Not the Only Fruit*, which won the 1985 Whitbread Prize for a First Novel. Since then, her novels have continued to push the boundaries of gender roles, sexual identity and imagination. Her continued contribution to British literature has earned her an Order of the British Empire. In addition to writing, Winterson owns a fine-food emporium, Verdes, in London.

BOOK 16

LETTERS TO A YOUNG POET
BY RAINER MARIA RILKE

Translated from the German by M. D. Herter Norton

November 12, 2007

To Stephen Harper,
Prime Minister of Canada,
These lessons from a wise and generous writer,
From a Canadian writer,
With best wishes,
Yann Martel

Dear Mr. Harper,

Rainer Maria Rilke's *Letters to a Young Poet*, the sixteenth book I am sending you, is a rich lode. These ten letters, written between 1903 and 1908 by the great German poet to a young man by the name of Franz Xaver Kappus, might be considered a precursor of creative writing instruction. They are useful to all of us who aspire to write. They have helped me, and I have no doubt that they will help you in the writing of your book on hockey.

For example, in the very first letter, Rilke asks the young poet to ask himself the vital question "Must I write?" If there is not that unstoppable inner necessity, then one should not even attempt to write, suggests Rilke. He also makes much of the need for solitude, for that quiet sifting of impressions from which comes good, true writing and which can occur only when one is on one's own.

However, if Rilke's letters were no more than technical advice on artful writing, I don't think I would have sent them to you. Of what interest is a trade manual to someone who practices another trade? But these letters are much more than that, because what holds for art also holds for life. What illuminates the first illuminates the second. So, self-knowledge—must I write?—is useful not only in writing but in living. And solitude bears fruit not only for the one who aspires to write poetry but for anyone who aspires to anything. Whereas, to take a counter-example, I think it's rare that advice to do with commerce has much use beyond commerce. Our deepest way of examining life, of getting to our existential core, is through the artistic. At its best, such an examination has nearly a religious feel.

Take this passage towards the end of Letter Four, in which Rilke advises the Young Poet to wrap himself in solitude:

Therefore, dear sir, love your solitude and bear with sweet-sounding lamentation the suffering it causes you. For those who are near you are far, you say, and that shows it is beginning to grow wide about you. And when what is near you is far, then your distance is already among the stars and very large; rejoice in your growth, in which you naturally can take no one with you, and be kind to those who remain behind, and be sure and calm before them and do not torment them with your doubts and do not frighten them with your confidence or joy, which they could not understand. Seek yourself some sort of simple and loyal community with them, which need not necessarily change as you yourself become different and again different; love in them life in an unfamiliar form and be considerate of aging people, who fear that being-alone in which you trust. Avoid contributing material to the drama that is always stretched taut between parents and children; it uses up much of the children's energy and consumes the love of their elders, which is effective and warming even if it does not comprehend. Ask no advice from them and count upon no understanding; but believe in a love that is being stored up for you like an inheritance and trust that in this love there is a strength and a blessing. . . .

Doesn't this sound like a passage that Paul the Apostle might have written in one of his letters to the Corinthians?

Rilke's letters overflow with understanding, generosity and wise advice. They shine with loving kindness. Not surprising then that Franz Xaver Kappus wished so ardently to pass them on to posterity.

Yours truly,
Yann Martel

RAINER MARIA RILKE (1875–1926) was a poet and writer of lyrical prose. He was born in Prague, and studied in Germany. His works were heavily influenced by his studies in philosophy and his knowledge of Classic literature, and focus primarily on the themes of solitude and anxiety. Some of his most famous works include the *Sonnets to Orpheus*, the *Duino Elegies*, *Letters to a Young Poet* and *The Notebooks of Malte Laurids Brigge*. He was an avid traveller, and his journeys to France, Sweden and Russia, and the relationships he formed in those countries, marked his work. He died of leukemia.

BOOK 17:

THE ISLAND MEANS MINAGO
BY MILTON ACORN

November 26, 2007

To Stephen Harper,
Prime Minister of Canada,
A book from an Island revolutionary,
From a Canadian writer,
With best wishes,
Yann Martel

Dear Mr. Harper,

Growing up, I was aware of the title that was popularly given to Milton Acorn: the People's Poet. I assumed that this was because his poetry was down-to-earth, the language plain, the meaning reaching into the accessible depths of common experience. What I hadn't realized until much later was that the People's Poet also had a political edge. That edge is made abundantly clear in the book that accompanies this letter, Acorn's *The Island Means Minago*, a varied collection of poems, personal essays and short plays. If you turn to the last pages of the book, you will find information on the publisher:

> NC Press is the Canadian Liberation publisher. It is truly a people's publishing house, distributing books on the struggle for national independence and socialism in Canada and throughout the world.

On the next page, towards the bottom, there's also the follow-ing information:

NC Press is the largest Canadian distributor of books, periodi-cals, and records from the People's Republic of China.

An address is given for the organization behind both NC Press and its companion newspaper, New Canada:

Canadian Liberation Movement
Box 41, Station E, Toronto 4, Ontario

Was a revolutionary Canada ever a real possibility? Well, some people, way back in 1975, thought it was. Since then, I imagine the Canadian Liberation Movement has vanished, at least formally under that name, or if it still exists, that Box 41 is a peephole onto a lonely place.

But any revolution that uses poetry as one of its weapons has at least one correct thing going for it: the knowledge that artistic expression is central to who and how a people are. I wonder if the Fraser Institute has ever thought of publishing poetry to make its point, and if it hasn't, why not?

The portrait that Milton Acorn draws of Prince Edward Island, his native province, will likely be unfamiliar to you, as will be his reading of Canadian history. Let that be a reminder to you that the past is one thing, but what we make of it, the conclusions we draw, is another. History can be many things, depending on how we read it, just as the future can be many things, depend-ing on how we live it. There is no inevitability to any historical occurrence, only what people will allow to take place. And it is by dreaming first that we get to new realities. Hence the need for poets.

So Milton Acorn was, of necessity as a poet, a dreamer (a tough one, mind you). He dreamt of a Canada that would be better, fairer, freer. He could not abide what he felt were the American shackles of capitalism and economic colonialism that held us down. He was an Island revolutionary. One might be inclined to smile at the extent to which some people's dreams are delusions. But better to dream than just to endure. Better to be bold than just to be told. Better to imagine many realities and fight for the one that seems best than just to shrug and retreat further into oneself.

The Island Means Minago represents yet another thing a book can be: a time capsule, a snapshot, a museum shelf of old dreams—that is, a reminder of a past future that never became (but is perhaps still worth dreaming about).

I'm making it sound as if *Minago* (Minago is the name the Mi'kmaq gave to P.E.I.) were nothing more than a political tract, which it is not. It is a book of poetry, a cry far richer than a tract. So I'll finish this letter the proper way, with one of Acorn's poems:

> Bump, Bump, Bump Little Heart
>
> Bump, bump, bump, little heart
>   along this journey
>   we've gone together,
>   you piping all the fuel.
>   You're fistsize, and fistlike
>   you clench and unclench,
>   clench and unclench
>   keeping this head upright
>   to batter its way
>   through the walls of the day.

Yours truly,
Yann Martel

MILTON ACORN (1923–1986), known as the People's Poet, had a seminal influence on Canadian literature. He was born in Charlottetown, and spent most of his life travelling between the growing literary scenes of Montreal, Toronto and Vancouver. He worked with many famous Canadian writers including Irving Layton, bill bissett, Al Purdy, Dorothy Livesay and Margaret Atwood. Acorn was a poetry-workshop instructor and founder of the *Georgia Straight*. He won the Canadian Poet's Award and the Governor General's Literary Award for *The Island Means Minago*. Other famous works include *Dig Up My Heart* and *Jawbreakers*.

BOOK 18:

METAMORPHOSIS
BY FRANZ KAFKA

Translated from the German by Michael Hofmann

December 10, 2007

To Stephen Harper,
Prime Minister of Canada,
A cautionary tale of sorts,
From a Canadian writer,
With best wishes,
Yann Martel

Dear Mr. Harper,

The book that accompanies this letter is one of the great literary icons of the twentieth century. If you haven't already read it, you've surely heard of it. The story it tells—of an anxious, dutiful travelling salesman who wakes up one morning transformed into a large insect—is highly intriguing, and therefore entertaining. The practical considerations of such a change—the new diet, the new family dynamic, the poor job prospects, and so on—are all worked out to their logical conclusion. But that Gregor Samsa, the salesman in question, nonetheless remains at heart the same person, the same soul, still moved by music, for example, is also plainly laid out. And what it all might mean, this waking up as a bug, is left to the reader to determine.

Franz Kafka published *Metamorphosis* in 1915. It was one of his few works published while he was alive, as he was racked by doubts about his writing. Upon his death in 1924 of tuberculosis, he asked his friend and literary executor, Max Brod, to destroy all his unpublished works. Brod ignored this wish and did the exact opposite: he published them all. Three unfinished novels were published, *The Trial*, *The Castle* and *Amerika*, but in my opinion his many short stories are better, and not only because they're finished.

Kafka's life, and subsequently his work, was dominated by one figure, his domineering father. A coarse man who valued only material success, he found his son's literary inclinations incomprehensible. Kafka obediently tried to fit into the mould into which his father squeezed him. He worked most of his life, and with a fair degree of professional success, for the Workers' Accident Insurance Institute of the Kingdom of Bohemia (doesn't that sound like it's right out of, well, Kafka?). But to work during the day to live, and then to work at night on his writings so that he might feel alive, exhausted him and ultimately cost him his life. He was only forty years old when he died.

Kafka introduced to our age a feeling that hasn't left us yet: angst. Misery before then was material, felt in the body. Think of Dickens and the misery of poverty he portrayed; material success was the road out of that misery. But with Kafka, we have the misery of the mind, a dread that comes from within and will not go away, no matter if we have jobs. The dysfunctional side of the twentieth century, the dread that comes from mindless work, from constant, grinding, petty regulation, the dread that comes from the greyness of urban, capitalist existence, where each one of us is no more than a lonely cog in a machine, this was what Kafka revealed. Are we done with these concerns? Have we worked our way out of anxiety, isolation and alienation? Alas, I think not. Kafka still speaks to us.

Kafka died seven months into the public life of Adolf Hitler—the failed Munich Beer Hall Putsch, in which the ugly

Austrian corporal had prematurely tried to seize power, took place in November of 1923—and there is something annunciatory about the overlap, as if what Kafka felt, Hitler delivered. The overlap is sadder still: Kafka's three sisters died in Nazi concentration camps.

Metamorphosis makes for a fascinating yet grim read. The premise may bring a black-humoured smile to one's face, but the full story wipes that smile away. One possible way of reading *Metamorphosis* is as a cautionary tale. So much alienation in its pages makes one thirst for authenticity in one's life.

Christmas is fast approaching. I'll see with the next book I send you if I can't come up with something cheerier to match the festive season.

Yours truly,
Yann Martel

FRANZ KAFKA (1883–1924) was born in Prague, Bohemia (now the Czech Republic), and is considered one of the most influential authors of the twentieth century. Much of Kafka's work is disturbing, dealing with nightmarish situations and dark themes including alienation, dehumanization and totalitarianism, a literary style now known as "Kafkaesque." He is best known for his novella *Metamorphosis* as well as for two of his novels, *The Trial* and *The Castle*, which were published posthumously. He earned a doctorate in law and wrote in his spare time, spending most of his working life at an insurance company.

THE BROTHERS LIONHEART
BY ASTRID LINDGREN
Translated from the Swedish by Jill M. Morgan

IMAGINE A DAY
BY SARAH L. THOMSON AND ROB GONSALVES

THE MYSTERIES OF HARRIS BURDICK
BY CHRIS VAN ALLSBURG

December 24, 2007

To Stephen Harper,
Prime Minister of Canada,
Three books to make you and your family dream,
From a Canadian writer,
With best wishes,
Yann Martel
P.S. Merry Christmas

Dear Mr. Harper,

It is Christmas tomorrow, and we live in a country where the first-mentioned fundamental freedom in the Charter of Rights is the freedom of conscience and religion. It is a time to celebrate. But curious how, despite the vast, lawful liberty that is ours to enjoy, we Canadians are so constricted in our religious expression. So "Merry Christmas!" is fast disappearing from public greetings, replaced by formulations such as "Happy Holidays" or "Holiday Greetings," which are held to be safely generic, the original meaning of holiday—holy day—being conveniently forgotten.

Yet "Merry Christmas" is just a blessing being offered. Does it offend? Would you or I be offended, actually offended, if someone shouted to us, "Happy Diwali!" or "Happy Hanukkah!" or "Happy Eid!" with a smile and a wave of the hand? Wouldn't we rather be gratified by the well-wisher's kind intentions, even if we are not Hindu, Jewish or Muslim? Similarly, when we gift a "Merry Christmas" to a stranger—and how good it is to reach out to strangers—is our intention not kind? Our spiritual stomach is full, so to speak, and we are offering blessed food to another. If that person should reply, "Thank you! Blessed be your Baby, my Prophet thought most highly of him," we don't take offence that their stomach is already full. In fact, we are happy for them. Better an abundance of food than a lack, no?

I love it that one religious group stops working, halts the making of money, to celebrate the birth of a Baby. We tend to forget babies too much, I think. We tend to neglect magical thinking.

Most of our compatriots take their religious freedom as meaning they are free not to practice any religion, and they address life with big questions and big myths they get else-where. That's fine. To each his or her own path.

But it's Christmas tomorrow, I repeat, and by all accounts you are a Christian, and rightly entitled to say "Merry Christmas," though you are far more discreet about your Christianity than your predecessor as party leader, the Honourable Stockwell Day. It made people uncomfortable, his liberal use of his constitution-ally given religious freedom. You are more savvy and cautious. You seem to be somewhat of a closet Christian, not speaking much or sharing much of Jesus of Nazareth.

Still, it's Christmas tomorrow and there's a Baby to be celebrated.

So, in the spirit of the occasion, I offer you this time not one book, but three, and books not to be read alone, like an adult, but to be shared with children. *The Mysteries of Harris Burdick*, by Chris Van Allsburg, and *Imagine a Day*, written by Sarah L. Thomson and illustrated by Rob Gonsalves, are picture books of contagious magic. You will look at them, at each page, and marvel. *The Brothers Lionheart* (pardon the terrible cover—it's the only edition I could find), by Astrid Lindgren, of the famous Pippi Longstocking series, is a novel for children with fewer illustrations, and black and white, but it is just as magical. I hope you and your family enjoy all three books.

Merry Christmas, Mr. Harper. May your heart be the manger in which the newborn Baby lies.

Yours truly,
Yann Martel

ASTRID LINDGREN (1907–2002) was a Swedish author best remembered for her contributions to children's literature, particularly the beloved Pippi Longstocking and Karlsson-on-the-Roof series. Her stories have been translated into dozens of languages and are read around the world. During her career, she received the Hans Christian Andersen Award and the Right Livelihood Award. After her death, the government of Sweden created an award in her name to honour outstanding achievement in children's and youth literature.

SARAH L. THOMSON was formerly a senior editor at HarperCollins Children's Books. After publishing her first book, *The Dragon's Son*, she resigned from her editorial position in order to pursue writing full-time. To date she has written twenty children's titles and won several awards, including the 2005 Oppenheim Toy Portfolio Gold

Seal Award for *Amazing Tigers!* and a Bank Street College of Education Best Book of the Year award for *Amazing Gorillas!*

ROB GONSALVES (b. 1959) is a Canadian painter whose style is described as both surrealist and magical realist. His art is characterized by fantastical and detailed optical illusions, transforming the ordinary into the extraordinary. He has worked as an architect, muralist and theatre painter, experiences that are reflected in his paintings of buildings and landscapes. Though he is not primarily a children's illustrator, he has worked on the children's books *Imagine a Day*, *Imagine a Night* and *Imagine a Place*.

CHRIS VAN ALLSBURG (b. 1949) is an American author and illustrator of children's books, most notably *Jumanji* and *The Polar Express*. His fantastical stories are set in incredible places and feature magical, dangerous or mysterious objects. Van Allsburg is known for exploring themes in his stories that are darker than those usually associated with children's literature. He has also collaborated as an illustrator with other authors, including illustrated editions of C. S. Lewis's *Chronicles of Narnia*. He has won the Caldecott Honor Medal several times.

BOOK 20:

THE EDUCATED IMAGINATION
BY NORTHROP FRYE

January 7, 2008

To Stephen Harper,
Prime Minister of Canada,
A book that defends the essential,
From a Canadian writer,
With best wishes,
Yann Martel

Dear Mr. Harper,

I hope you and your family had a good Christmas and that you are returning to work with your mind and heart refreshed. I suspect 2008 will be a busy year for us. I have a book to finish and you have a government to run. We both hope to get good reviews for our respective labours.

I was in Moncton in late November last year, doing a series of special events organized by the Northrop Frye Literary Festival, which runs every year in April. Someone asked me, in a lovely Acadian accent, "As-tu lu *The Educated Imagination* de Northrop Frye?" ("Have you read . . .")

I hadn't read Frye's *The Educated Imagination*. Or anything else by him. Northrop Frye—and I'm educating myself as I tell you what follows, catching up—lived between 1912 and 1991, spending his early formative years in Moncton (hence the name of the festival) and most of his adult years at the University of Toronto, where he was a great light. Frye was a world-class literary critic who wrote such books as *Fearful Symmetry: A Study of William Blake*, *Anatomy of Criticism* and *The Great Code: The Bible and Literature*. He led a thrilling life of the mind, most of it fed by literature, and he gave much to his students and readers. He was a great thinker, teacher, Canadian.

I should explain why I have never until now read Frye. It wasn't intellectual sloth. It was rather a conscious decision. Frye, as I've just said, was a literary critic. He looked at literature, he looked *through* literature, seeing in it recurring symbols, underlying structures, overarching metaphors. All of which is no doubt fascinating—but not to the young man I was when I started writing. Self-knowledge is often a good thing—it teaches you your limits—but too much of it too soon can ruin the incipient artist in you if it gives you the sense that you have no original core, that you are just dough in a pre-established mould. Then, as now, I just wanted to write, to create, to invent. I wasn't interested in being told what I was doing, whom I was repeating, what convention I was adhering to. Why become self-conscious if it meant I wouldn't dare to write? So I avoided literary criticism, those words and books that might snuff out my wavering creative flame. Trope was tripe to me.

However, right after being asked the question by the person with the lovely Acadian accent, I was presented by her with the book in question, Northrop Frye's *The Educated Imagination*. She thought of it because of the small book club you and I have going. She wondered if you might not enjoy it (you may be interested to know that I get suggestions of books to send you all the time). I felt it would be rude not to read so considerate a gift. And surely, with three books completed and a fourth one nearly done, I could withstand a literary critic suddenly turning a mirror on me.

Well, I'm happy to report that I read the book and I'm still standing. *The Educated Imagination* was interesting to me, and I think it might be even more interesting to you. Frye, in this short, oral book—he delivered it in six parts as the 1962 Massey Lectures—speaks about the role of literature in education and society, about whether the first is needed by the other two.

It certainly is needed, Frye argues persuasively. It all comes down to language and the imagination. Frye explains that no matter what use we are making of language, whether it's for practical self-expression, to convey information or self-consciously to be creative, we must use our imagination. As he puts it: "Literature speaks the language of the imagination, and the study of literature is supposed to train and improve the imagination. But we use our imagination all the time: it comes into all our conversation and practical life: it even produces dreams when we're asleep. Consequently we have only the choice between a badly trained imagination and a well-trained one, whether we ever read a poem or not." Imagination is not just for writers. It's for everyone. At another point, Frye says, "The fundamental job of the imagination in ordinary life . . . is to produce, out of the society we have to live in, a vision of the society we want to live in." This statement has obvious political implications. You see why I said this book might be of interest to you.

One of the classic dualities of existence is that of the head and the heart, of thinking and feeling, of reason and emotion. It's not untrue, but I do wonder how useful this division is. One might suppose that a mathematician hard at work is being entirely reasonable while someone crying at the scene of a terrible accident is being entirely emotional, but otherwise can we so clearly delineate between the two? Frye believed that these are rather different ways of using one's imagination, that the imagination underpins them both. And the better, the more fertile our imagination, the better we can be at being both reasonable and emotional. As broad and deep as our dreams are, so can our realities become. And there's no better way to train that vital part of us than through literature.

The imagination, then, is where is all starts, both for you and for me.

Happy New Year.

Yours truly,
· Yann Martel

NORTHROP FRYE (1912–1991) was one of Canada's most respected literary critics and theorists. He gained international notoriety for his first book, *Fearful Symmetry*, and continued to establish his reputation with *Anatomy of Criticism* and *The Stubborn Structure*. Frye was a member of the Royal Society of Canada and a Companion of the Order of Canada. During his lifetime, he won several awards including the Lorne Pierce Medal, the Pierre Chauveau Medal and the Governor General's Literary Award. Apart from his significant contributions to Canadian literature, his name is also a frequent crossword puzzle clue and he is honoured each year at a literary festival in Moncton.

BOOK 21:

THE CELLIST OF SARAJEVO
BY STEVEN GALLOWAY

January 21, 2008

To Stephen Harper,
Prime Minister of Canada,
A whole-person work,
From a Canadian writer,
With best wishes,
Yann Martel

Dear Mr. Harper,

You may have asked yourself on occasion what process I go through to select the books I have been sending you. Why don't I answer that question in this letter.

Any book adheres to one convention or another—be it that of the Novel or the Biography—and all sentences are either conventionally grammatical or conventionally ungrammatical. It's the rare, very rare writer who is genuinely unconventional, and usually their revolution is at one level only, affecting, say, point-of-view, while following the herd when it comes to punctuation. A writer who is unconventional on too many levels runs the risk of losing the reader, who can't manage to get a solid footing on so much new territory and gives up the effort. *Finnegans Wake*, by the Irish writer James Joyce, is an example of such arduous total newness.

A book is a convention, then, as are the categories of thinking that produce books: Art, History, Geography, Science, and so on. That's how we like it, we humans. We like orderly sentences and orderly books in much the same way we like orderly streets and orderly governments. Which is not to say that we are not bold creatures. We are; in fact, there is no bolder creature on Earth. To give you a non-literary example: in the late 1960s, the Americans marshalled together the conventions of science, engineering, management and financing, and as a result achieved the highly unconventional goal of popping two of their citizens onto the Moon.

Back to books. They are products of convention, but there are many conventions. I mentioned two already, the Novel and the Biography, which flow from two other conventions, Fiction and Non-fiction. Within each, there are sub-conventions, categories, genres. I have tended to send you books of fiction rather than non-fiction because fiction is a more worked-through interpretation of life. What do I mean by that? I mean that fiction is both more personal and more synthesized than non-fiction. Fiction is more whole-person. A novel is about Life itself, whereas a history remains about a specific instance of Life. A great Russian novel—remember the Tolstoy I sent you—will always have a more universal resonance than a great history of Russia; you will think of the first as being about you on some level, whereas the second is about someone else.

So that's the first rule: a work of fiction. Now, there are many *kinds* of fictions. There is the literary novel, the thriller, the murder mystery, the satire, and so on. As you haven't yet communicated to me your literary interests, and since it's not for me to judge what you should read, I have not excluded any genre. Whatever book I send you must only be good; that is, once you've read it, you must feel wiser, or at least more knowledgeable. Or to put it another way, as I did many months ago, it must increase your sense of *stillness*.

The other considerations are simple:

1) I send you short books, generally under two hundred pages. You are probably busier than most people, and you probably feel that you are more importantly busy. I believe that's an illusion. As a friend once told me, the only thing that will really go down in history is how we raise our children. The life of the Canadian people is determined and built by each and every Canadian, one small act at a time. There are twenty-four hours in a day and each one of us chooses how to fill those hours. No one's hour is more important than anyone else's. Nonetheless, it's harder to follow an eight-hundred-page tome in fifteen-minute snatches than it is a slim novel.

2) For the same reason that you likely don't give yourself stretches of hours in which to wrap your mind around a convoluted story, I send you books that speak plainly.

3) I send you books that are varied, that will show you all that the word can do. At the rate of one book every two weeks, this is a harder requirement to satisfy. There are *so* many good books out there, Mr. Harper. But I must pace myself. I am starting with older books, aiming to be foundational, and from there I will build up to books from our comparatively young nations of Canada and Quebec.

Within those broad criteria, I choose the books I send you in a spontaneous, nearly random way, just whatever strikes me as possibly of interest to you. I also listen to the suggestions of others, as I did two weeks ago with Frye's *The Educated Imagination.* (Did you enjoy it, by the way?)

But some rules are meant to be broken, and this week's book is an example of that. Steven Galloway's novel *The Cellist of Sarajevo* speaks plainly, but it's a little too long by our criteria (fifty-eight pages over the limit), it's Canadian and it's so recent that it qualifies as prenatal: it hasn't even been published yet. It's supposed to come out in April of this year. The unadorned paperback you have in your hands is what publishers call an advance reading copy. It's sent out to booksellers, journalists and book clubs to drum up interest and excitement in a book prior to its publication—sort of like politicians doing the summer barbecue circuit before an election. The general reading public does not normally see an advance reading copy. What you are holding in your hands is a rare item.

And it's also a grand and powerful novel about how people retain or reclaim their humanity when they are under extreme duress. I'm sure you will hear about *The Cellist of Sarajevo* from other people than just me. It's set during the brutal siege of the Bosnian city of Sarajevo in the early 1990s. That story was in the news for years, yet I think most of us just took it in dumbly, wondering how people could do that to each other. Well, Galloway's novel explains how. It does the work of a good fiction: it transports you to a situation that might be alien to you, makes it familiar, and so brings understanding. That's what I meant when I said fiction is "whole-person." While reading *The Cellist of Sarajevo* you are imaginatively there, in Sarajevo, as the mortar shells are falling and snipers are seeking to kill you as you cross a street. Your mind's eye sees, your moral sense is outraged: your full humanity is being exercised.

Yet *The Cellist* is a directed and digested take on reality, it's not journalism. There is subtle intent woven into the realistic narrative of its three main characters. You will see that when you read the last line of the novel, which is magnificent.

Yours truly,
Yann Martel

Steven Galloway (b. 1975) is a Canadian novelist whose work has been translated into more than twenty languages. Besides *The Cellist of Sarajevo*, he has written the novels *Finnie Walsh* and *Ascension*. Galloway teaches creative writing at Simon Fraser University and the University of British Columbia.

BOOK 22:

MEDITATIONS
BY MARCUS AURELIUS
Translated from the Greek by Maxwell Staniforth
February 4, 2008

To Stephen Harper,
Prime Minister of Canada,
A book from a fellow head of government,
From a Canadian writer,
With best wishes,
Yann Martel

Dear Mr. Harper,

Like you, Marcus Aurelius was a head of government. In AD 161, he became Emperor of Rome, the last of the "five good emperors"—Nerva, Trajan, Hadrian, Antoninus Pius, Marcus Aurelius—who ruled over an eighty-four-year period of peace and prosperity that lasted from AD 96 to 180, the Roman Empire's golden apogee.

The case of Rome is worth studying. How a small town on a river became the centre of one of the mightiest empires the world has known, eventually dominating thousands of other small towns on rivers, is a source of many lessons. That Rome was mighty is not to be doubted. The sheer size the empire achieved is breathtaking: from the Firth of Forth to the Euphrates, from the Tagus to the Rhine, spilling over into Northern Africa, for a time the Romans ruled over most of the world known to them. What they didn't rule over wasn't worth having, they felt: they left what was beyond their frontiers to "barbarians."

Another measure of their greatness can be found in the Roman influences that continue to be felt to this day. Rome's local lingo, Latin, became the mother language of most of Europe, and Italian, French, Spanish and Portuguese are still spoken all over the world. (The Germanic hordes beyond the Rhine, meanwhile, have managed to sponsor only one international language, albeit a successful one, English.) We also owe the Romans our calendar, with its twelve months and 365-and-a-quarter-day years; three days in our week hark back to three Roman days—Moonday, Saturnday and Sunday; and though we now use the Roman number system (i, ii, iii, iv, v, vi . . .) only occasionally, we use their 26-letter alphabet constantly.

Despite their power and might, another lesson about the Roman Empire forces itself upon us: how it's all gone. The Romans reigned far and wide for centuries but now their empire has vanished entirely. A Roman today is simply someone who lives in Rome, a city that is beautiful because of its clutter of ruins. Such has been the fate of all empires: the Roman, the Ottoman, the British, the Soviet, to name only a few European empires. Which will be the next empire to fall, the next to rise?

The interest in reading Marcus Aurelius's *Meditations*, the book I am sending you this time, lies as much in their content as in the knowledge of who wrote them. European history has got us used to seeing one monarch after another reach the throne for no reason other than direct filial relation, with talent and ability playing no role. Thus the unending line of mediocre personalities—to put it charitably—who came to rule and mismanage so many European nations. This was not Marcus Aurelius's route to power. Although he inherited the throne from Emperor Antoninus Pius, he was not Pius's biological son.

Nor was he elected. He was rather selected. Roman emperors did pass on their emperorship to their sons, but this linkage was rarely directly biological. They instead designated their successors by a system that was authoritarian yet flexible: adoption. Marcus Aurelius became emperor as a result of being adopted by the reigning emperor. Each emperor chose whom he wanted as his successor from among the many capable and competing members of Rome's diverse elite class. Members of that class were often related, but they still had to prove themselves if they wanted to move up in the world.

In that, Roman society was much like the modern democracies of today, with an educated, principled elite that sought to perpetuate the system and, with it, itself. The Rome of then, in some ways, doesn't seem so different from the Ottawa, Washington or London of today. After the alien abyss, frankly, that is much European history, with the Europeans thinking and behaving in ways that are close to unfathomable by contemporary standards, it is a surprise to see, nearly two thousand years ago, a people who thought and fought and squabbled and had principles which they squandered, and so on—why, a people seemingly just like us. Hence the endless interest of Roman history.

So Marcus Aurelius was a man of great ability selected to be Roman emperor. In other words, he was a politician, and, like you, a busy one; he spent much of his time battling barbarian hordes on the frontiers of the empire. But at the same time, he was a thinking man—with a penchant for philosophy—who put his thoughts down on the page. He was a writer.

Emperor Marcus Aurelius was a Stoic and some of his pronouncements are on the gloomy side: "Soon you will have forgotten the world, and soon the world will have forgotten you," is a fairly typical pronouncement of his. There is much made in these meditations on the ephemerality of the body, of fame, of empires, of pretty well everything. Over and over, Marcus Aurelius exhorts himself to higher standards of thinking and behaving. It's bracing, salutary stuff. In many ways, it's the perfect book for you, Mr. Harper. A practical book on thinking, being and acting by a philosopher-king.

It's also not the sort of book one reads right through from page 1 to page 163. It has no continuous narrative or developing argument. The *Meditations* are rather self-contained musings divided into twelve books, each book divided into numbered points that range in length from a single sentence to a few paragraphs. The book lends itself to being dipped into at random. My suggestion is that each time you open and read it, you put a dot next to the meditations you read. That way, over time, you will read all of them.

Yours truly,
Yann Martel

MARCUS AURELIUS (121–180 CE) wrote his *Meditations* in Greek while on military campaigns during 170–180 CE. In them, he stresses the importance of government service, duty, endurance, abstinence, surrendering to Providence and achieving detachment from things beyond one's control.

BOOK 23:

ARTISTS AND MODELS
BY ANAÏS NIN
February 18, 2008

To Stephen Harper,
Prime Minister of Canada,
Hot stuff,
From a Canadian writer,
With best wishes,
Yann Martel

Dear Mr. Harper,

Valentine's Day was just a few days ago and we've had a long cold snap here in Saskatchewan—two good reasons to send you something warming.

Anaïs Nin—such a lovely name—lived between 1903 and 1977 and she was the author of a number of novels that remain unknown to me: *Ladders to Fire*, *Children of the Albatross*, *The Four-Chambered Heart*, *A Spy in the House of Love* and *Solar Barque* form a five-volume *roman-fleuve* entitled *Cities of the Interior* (1959). She also published the novels *House of Incest* (1936), *The Seduction of the Minotaur* (1961) and *Collages* (1964), and a collection of short stories, *Under a Glass Bell*. The only pleasure these have given me has been to wonder what they are about. What story would a novel called *Solar Barque* tell? What was the *Albatross* and who were her *Children*?

Nin is better known for her published diaries, which covered every decade of her life except the first (and she missed that one only by a year, since she started her diary when she was eleven years old). She was born in France, lived in the United States for many years, she was beautiful and cosmopolitan, and she came to know many interesting and famous people, the writer Henry Miller among them, all of whom she discussed and dissected in her diary. Her diary's importance lies in the fact that female voices have often been silenced or ignored—still are—and an extended female monologue covering the first half of the twentieth century is rare.

And Anaïs Nin also wrote erotica. Hot stuff. Kinky stuff. Pages full of women who are wet not because it's raining and men who are hard not because they're cruel. *Artists and Models*, which contains two stories from her collections of erotic writings *Delta of Venus* and *Little Birds*, is the latest book I'm sending you. It may leave you cold, Mr. Harper, reading about Mafouka the hermaphrodite painter from Montparnasse and her lesbian roommates or about the sexual awakening of a painter's model in New York, but it bears noting that while covering our loins and our hearts with clothes is often useful—it's minus 23 degrees Celsius outside as I write these words—there is the risk that they are also hiding, perhaps burying, an essential part of us, one that does not think but rather feels. Clothes are the commonest trappings of vanity. When we are naked, we are honest. That is the essential quality of these lustful stories of Nin, embellished or wholly invented though they may be: their honesty. They say: this is part of who we are—deny it, and you are denying yourself.

Yours truly,
Yann Martel

ANAÏS NIN (1903–1977) was born in Paris, raised in the United States and identified herself as a Catalan-Cuban-French author. Nin was a prolific novelist, short story writer and diarist, best known for her multi-volume *Diary*. She was also one of the greatest writers of female erotica, and is famous for her affairs with notable individuals including Henry Miller and Gore Vidal.

BOOK 24:

WAITING FOR GODOT
BY SAMUEL BECKETT
March 3, 2008

To Stephen Harper,
Prime Minister of Canada,
A modernist masterpiece,
From a Canadian writer,
With best wishes,
Yann Martel

Dear Mr. Harper,

Curiously, the book that I am sending you this early March, a play, only the second dramatic work I've sent you, is one that I don't actually like. It has always irked me. Which is not to say that it is not a good play, indeed, a great play. In fact, that it continues to irk me confirms its greatness in a way, because if I said to you confidently, "This is a masterpiece," that would imply I had a settled view of it, a fixed understanding, and that the play stood for me like a statue on a pedestal: lofty, staid and undisturbing. Samuel Beckett's *Waiting for Godot* is none of these.

To further confirm that I'm wrong in my view of *Godot*, I'll say that despite being written in the late 1940s, the play will not feel dated when you read it. This is a significant achievement. Plays, to state the obvious, are made up of dialogue. There is no surrounding prose to supply context. You might think the setting of a play would be the equivalent of the description in a novel that sets up the story, but that is not the case. Many historical plays and operas are restaged in settings that their playwrights and composers would never have imagined, and no meaning is lost. Shakespeare's *Macbeth* does not need a castle in the background to make sense to theatregoers. The meaning and development of a play is entirely carried on the shoulders of its dialogue. But the way we speak changes over time, and quickly words and expressions that were current to the playwright sound old-fashioned to us today.

Moreover, plays are exclusively concerned with relationships, with the feelings between characters, revealed in what they say to each other and how they behave, and some relationships have also changed over the course of history. Lastly, plays are precisely, literally situated, the actors wearing costumes and moving about settings that we actually see, as opposed to imagining them in prose. How these last two points make most plays a more perishable product than most prose will be made clear if you think back to old television shows. Do you remember the 1970s American television series *Bewitched*, Mr. Harper, about a witch named Samantha who lives in suburbia with her husband, Darrin, and their daughter, Tabitha? I lapped it up when I was a kid. A few years ago I happened to see an episode again—and I was appalled. The sexism struck me as egregious, what with Darrin always trying to prevent Samantha from using her magic and Samantha, being the good, docile housewife, always trying to comply. And the way they dressed and their hairdos—that at least was innocently laughable. You get my point. What was fresh and funny then is now old and embarrassing. Women are now more free to use their magic, and we dress differently. By capturing so exactly a time, a place and a lingo, many plays are as fleeting as newspapers.

It is a mighty playwright who manages to speak to his or her time and also to ours. Shakespeare does it, toweringly. That a student doesn't know what a "thane" is, that kings don't rule in 2008 the way they ruled in 1608 in no way affects the power and meaning of the Scottish play today. *Waiting for Godot* has also managed to speak to all times, so far. Despite premiering in 1953, the antics, musings and worries of Vladimir and Estragon will likely strike you as funny, puzzling, insightful, maddening and still current.

The play is about the human condition, which in Beckett's pared-down vision of it means that the play is mostly about nothing. Two men, the ones just mentioned, Didi and Gogo familiarly, wait around because they believe they have an appointment with a certain Godot. They wait around and talk and despair, are twice interrupted by two crazies by the names of Pozzo and Lucky, and then they go back to waiting around, talking and despairing. That's pretty well it. No plot, no real development, no final point. The setting is also mostly nothing: just a single, solitary tree along an empty country road. The only props of note are boots, bowler hats and a rope.

Essentially, two hours of nothing that's good and deep, pessimistic and funny. Beckett meant to strip away at the vanities of our existence and look at the elemental. Therein lies what makes *Waiting for Godot* both great and eye-rolling as far as I'm concerned. There is this line, for example, said by I can't remember which character: "We give birth astride a grave." I suppose that's true. Death interrupting life, what value can life have? If we must eventually let go of everything, why take hold of anything to start with? This sort of pessimism is the burden of those who have witnessed terrible times (Beckett lived in France during the German occupation) and the delight of undergraduates in the throes of youthful angst. I realize that my life is no more durable than a leaf's, but between when I'm fresh and gloriously atop a tree and when I'll be yellow and raked away by Time, there are some good moments to be had.

Samuel Beckett was with the same woman, Suzanne Beckett, *née* Deschevaux-Dumesnil, for over fifty years. And he was apparently an avid fan and player of tennis. In these two attachments, I see a contradiction between what the man wrote and how he lived. If he had the joy and energy to whack a bouncy yellow ball over a net, if he had the joy and comfort of knowing that someone was there for him at the end of each day, what was he so desperate about? A wife and tennis—how much more did he expect from life? And this is aside from exploring the ideas of those who dismiss death as a mere threshold, just a gap you have to mind between the train of life and the platform of the eternal.

Still, I know *Waiting for Godot* is a great play. You'll see that when you read it. It's a masterpiece. It does what no play did before it.

Yours truly,
Yann Martel

SAMUEL BECKETT (1906–1989) was an Irish author, playwright and poet, and is considered one of the last modernists or possibly one of the first post-modernists. Beckett's writing was characterized by minimalism and black humour. He lived in France, and worked as a courier in the French Resistance during World War II. He was awarded the Nobel Prize in Literature in 1969. His best-known novels are *Molloy*, *Malone Dies* and *The Unnamable*.

BOOK 25:

THE DRAGONFLY OF CHICOUTIMI
BY LARRY TREMBLAY
March 17, 2008

To Stephen Harper,
Prime Minister of Canada,
This play to defeat silence,
From a Canadian writer,
With best wishes,
Yann Martel

Dear Mr. Harper,

It's about time I sent you the work of a writer from English Canada's twin solitude. It's a play again, the second in a row, the third in all. And for the second time—*Le Petit Prince* was the first—I am sending you a book in French. Mind you, the French of Larry Tremblay's *The Dragonfly of Chicoutimi* is a bit peculiar. Not that it's *joual*, or any other variation of Quebec French; that wouldn't be peculiar, it would be expected from a Québécois play. Rather, if you glance at the text, you will think it's just English, plain and simple. Well, it's not. Tremblay's play is a play written in French—that is, thought, felt, ordered, and expressed by a French mind—only using English words.

What's the point of that? Is this a bit of stand-up comedy, some party trick drawn out into a play? It's not. The cover of the book will tell you as much. Do you recognize the man on it? It's Jean-Louis Millette, the great actor who died just a few years ago, far too soon. His arms are raised, his face expresses anguish, the background is black: this play is no joke, says the cover. *The Dragonfly of Chicoutimi* is indeed a serious work of art, premiered and reprised by a master.

Is the point of writing a play that is French in its nature but English in its appearance political? The answer to that question might be yes, but a tenuous yes, in that any work of art can be taken to have political implications. In this case, to read the play politically I think diminishes its scope. Larry Tremblay's play is both far too personal—it's the monologue of a man opening up his heart about a private matter—and far too universal to be reduced to a political tract about the survival of the French language in Quebec.

I think Tremblay means to signal the political neutrality of his play when Gaston Talbot, the man who is opening up his heart, says of himself:

> once upon a time a boy named Gaston Talbot
> born in Chicoutimi
> in the beautiful province of Quebec
> in the great country of Canada
> had a dream . . .

In describing both entities, and with adjectives of equal banality—if not cliché in the case of Quebec, officially "La Belle Province"—my guess is that Tremblay sought to place his play's linguistic dualism beyond a merely political interpretation. The dream mentioned, by the way, is not a political dream, but a dream about Gaston Talbot's mother, whose love he seeks.

So what has Gaston Talbot from Chicoutimi got to say, and why is he saying it in French rendered in English?

I would suggest that *The Dragonfly of Chicoutimi* is a play about suffering and redemption, about what we have to do to get back to ourselves. Gaston Talbot is an adult French-speaking man struck with aphasia who, when we meet him, suddenly begins to speak again, only in English rather than in his native tongue. And what he recounts is how, long ago, he was a sixteen-year-old boy in love with a twelve-year-old boy by the name of Pierre Gagnon-Connally and how the two went by the river bank to play and Pierre asked Gaston to be his horse and Pierre

> . . . catches me
>> with an invisible lasso
>> inserts in my mouth an invisible bit
>> and jumps on my back
>> he rides me guiding me with his hands on my hair
>> after a while he gets down from my back
>> looks at me as he never did before
>> then he starts to give me orders in English
> I don't know English
>> but on that hot sunny day of July
>> every word which comes
>> from the mouth of Pierre Gagnon-Connally
>> is clearly understandable
> Get rid of your clothes
>> Yes sir
>> Faster faster

And then something happened, it's not clear what, an accident, an inexplicable burst of violence, and Pierre Gagnon-Connally dies and Gaston Talbot falls into silence.

The play is a web of self-confessed lies and inventions. The first thing Gaston Talbot says is "I travel a lot." Later, he admits that he hasn't travelled anywhere. In recounting a dream, he first says that he had one face, a "Picasso face," then admits that it was another face. Gaston Talbot holds these lies up like a shield, and with them he edges forward towards the truth. English words are thus just one more of these truth-revealing lies that allow him to address what pushed him into the worst abyss of all: silence.

As I did for the fourth book I sent you, *By Grand Central Station I Sat Down and Wept*, by Elizabeth Smart, I would suggest that you read *The Dragonfly of Chicoutimi* aloud. Even better: that you read it silently a first time, as if you were Gaston Talbot before the start of the play, and then read it a second time aloud, as if you were Gaston Talbot gasping for expression.

The play of course raises the question of language and identity, of what it means to speak in one language rather than another. Languages obviously have cultural reference points, but these can change. Witness English, spoken, taken on fully, by so many people around the world who are not of English culture. But the play puts the question on a more personal level. Gaston Talbot manages to reach back into his painful past and say what he has to say thanks to a bilingual subterfuge. That is the startling and moving conclusion of the play: the sight of truth found through a mask.

Yours truly,
Yann Martel

LARRY TREMBLAY (b. 1954), born in Chicoutimi, is a Québécois poet, novelist, non-fiction writer, playwright, stage director, actor and teacher. His plays often explore psychic and social violence, and show-case his use of vivid imagery and his signature crisp, rhythmic style.

BOOK 26:

BIRTHDAY LETTERS
BY TED HUGHES

March 31, 2008

To Stephen Harper,
Prime Minister of Canada,
This collection of great poems to celebrate
the one-year anniversary of our book club,
From a Canadian writer,
With best wishes,
Yann Martel

Dear Mr. Harper,

We are celebrating a birthday, you and I. The book that accompanies this letter is the twenty-sixth that you have received from me. Since I have been sending you these literary gifts every two weeks, that means that our cozy book group is celebrating its first anniversary. How have we done? It's been a most interesting odyssey, taking more of my time than I expected, but the pleasure has kept me keen and motivated. The result, so far, is a folder with copies of twenty-six letters for me and a shelf with twenty-eight slim books for you (a discrepancy owing to the fact that I sent you three books for Christmas). If we look over your new, growing library, we see:

13 novels
3   collections of poetry

3 plays
4 books of non-fiction
4 children's books, and
1 graphic novel

written (or, in one case, edited) by:
1 Russian
5 Britons
7 Canadians (including 1 Québécois)
1 Indian
4 French
1 Colombian
2 Swedes
3 Americans
1 German
1 Czech
1 Italian, and
1 Irish

of whom:
16 were men
9 were women, with
2 books authored by both sexes, and
1 book authored by writers of unknown sex (though my guess is that the *Bhagavad Gita* was written by men)

Too many novels, too many men, not enough poetry, why haven't I sent you a Margaret Atwood or an Alice Munro yet—at the rate of a book every two weeks, it's hard to be representative and impossible to please everyone. But we're getting there. Glenn Gould once said, "The purpose of art is the lifelong construction of a state of wonder." There is time yet.

It seemed appropriate on this anniversary occasion to offer you a book entitled *Birthday Letters*. It has the celebratory word in the title, even if the tone of the book does not exactly evoke a cake with a small lit candle on it.

The facts are as follows. In 1956, a twenty-six-year-old Englishman named X married a twenty-three-year-old American woman named Y. They had two children. Their relationship proved fraught with tensions, made worse by X's affair with a woman named Z, and in 1962 X and Y separated. In 1963, Y, mentally unstable since her teenage years, committed suicide by gassing herself. Six years later, in 1969, Z, who by then had a child with X, a little girl nicknamed Shura, also killed herself, unpardonably taking Shura with her. Two last facts: first, by virtue of being still married to Y when she died, X became her testamentary executor, and, second, X was constant throughout his life in his infidelities.

The amount of pain contained within these anonymous facts—the torment, the heartache, the sorrow, the shame, the regret—is barely conceivable. What life would not be over-whelmed, utterly destroyed, by such pain? And would that pain not be made worse if it were displayed for the whole world to see and comment upon?

X was Ted Hughes, Y was Sylvia Plath and Z was Assia Wevill, and their collective pain, the terrible mess that was their lives, would have been lost and forgotten had not the first two been superb and well-known poets who gave expression to that pain. Further notoriety was added by the fact that sides could easily be taken with this tragedy. Why does tragedy so often make us take sides? I guess because strong emotions move us, and we move to one side or another, so to speak, as if fleeing a car that is out of control, and it takes the passage of time, the examination of memory, for us to look back with calm sorrow, standing steadily, no longer so inclined to move and take sides. At any rate, it doesn't take a lawyer to detect conflict of interest in Hughes being the literary executor of Plath, her pained posthumous collections of poetry and her pained journals being edited by the very man who caused a good deal of her pain, some say editing her works with an eye to improving his reputation. That he furthermore destroyed the last volume of her journal, the one chronicling the last months of their relationship, only makes the charge against him more credible. And what to think of his incessant promiscuity? Who could imagine that shame and regret would so little curb libido?

Sides were taken, vociferously. Hughes was scorned and hated until his death by feminists and Plath-lovers, and I doubt the controversy of their relationship will ever slip from public interest. What stands in Hughes's defence? That question has an easy answer. His poetry.

That the author of *Birthday Letters* might be portrayed as a callous philanderer, arrogant and remorseless, is irrelevant in the face of the magnificence of his poetry. It reminds one of the fact that great art is, in its essence, not moral but testimonial, bearing witness to life as it is honestly lived, in its glorious heights as well as in its turpitudinous depths.

Great poetry tends to shut up the novelist in me. It takes so many words to make a novel, reams and reams of sentences and paragraphs, and then I read a single great poem, not even two pages long, and all my prose feels like verbiage. You will see what I mean when you read these poems. They are narrative poems, the tone intimate, usually an "I" speaking to a "you," the language quicksilver, extraordinarily concise, simple words arranged in an original and forceful way, and the result, poem after poem, is not only a clear image but an unforgettable impression. Take "Sam," or "Your Paris," or "You Hated Spain," or

"Chaucer," or "Flounders," or "The Literary Life," or "The Badlands," or "Epiphany," or "The Table."

The evidence from *Birthday Letters* is clear: X really did love Y, so if art can redeem, here is redemption.

Yours truly,
Yann Martel

TED HUGHES (1930–1998) was a children's writer, dramatist, short story writer, critic and acclaimed poet, holding the position of British Poet Laureate from 1984 until his death. Hughes's earlier poetry, including his first collection, *Hawk Roosting*, focused on beauty and violence in nature, while his later collections, like *Crow*, were existential, satirical and cynical. He wrote more than ninety books, and received a Guggenheim fellowship, the Whitbread Prize for Poetry and the Order of Merit.

BOOK 27:

TO THE LIGHTHOUSE
BY VIRGINIA WOOLF
April 14, 2008

To Stephen Harper,
Prime Minister of Canada,
From a Canadian writer,
With best wishes,
Yann Martel

Dear Mr. Harper,

Your classic this week is a somewhat harder read than most of the other books I have sent you. Many books are direct and frontal in their approach; immediately upon starting them, a reader senses what the author wants to talk about. To take an example from the books on your shelf, we are immediately familiar with the setting of George Orwell's *Animal Farm*, even if we've never lived on a farm, and we see right away his allegorical intent. We appreciate that a real event, the tragedy of Soviet Russia under Stalin, is going to be examined by means of a fable set on an imaginary farm. Armed with that understanding, animated by certain expectations, we read on.

Books such as these, the majority of books I'd say, create a subtle interplay of familiarity and strangeness. The familiar brings the reader onboard, and then the strange takes that reader somewhere new. The two elements are necessary. A book that proves to be entirely familiar is boring. Even the most formulaic of genre fiction attempts to convey some feeling of uncertainty and then, only at the very end, reassures the reader that every-thing is as he or she would wish it to be, the boy getting the girl or the detective catching the murderer. Conversely, a book can't be entirely strange, otherwise the reader would have no entry point, would flounder and give up.

Virginia Woolf's *To the Lighthouse*, published in 1927, will have you floundering a bit. Please don't give up. For me, it starts working, it takes you in, on about the twentieth page (that is, on page 29 of the edition I'm sending you). Before that, you'll be puzzled, perhaps even vaguely annoyed. So many char-acters coming and going, no clear plot in sight, tangents and digressions aplenty—where is the clarity and pace of good old Victorian literature? What is Woolf up to?

Well, it's anyone's guess—good literature is forever open to interpretation—but by my reckoning Woolf is exploring at least two things here:

1) She is exploring the mind, how consciousness interacts with reality. Woolf's experience of it, one that I'm sure will be familiar to you, is of intent buffeted by intrusion, like a salmon swimming upstream. Her characters think, but their thinking is constantly interrupted by events that are either external in their origin—other characters coming up—or internal, the mind distracting itself from its own thinking. I'm sure you've heard of the term "stream of consciousness," Woolf's narrative technique is like that. What she is exploring in *To the Lighthouse* isn't so much an ordered series of events—although those are present in the novel—as the mind filtering those events.

2) She is exploring time, the effect and experience of it, which explains why the novel is given its cadence not by

the regular, objective tick-tock of a clock, but instead by the subjective reactions of the characters to time, which goes by slowly when the characters are engrossed, and then seems to leap forward years in a blink. Isn't that how time is for all of us, both crawling and leaping, like a frog's progress. Those two animal images might help you as you read the book. Try to recognize the salmon and the frog in *To the Lighthouse*.

Woolf's prose is dense, detailed and repetitive, but in a mesmerizing way. Not surprisingly, another of Woolf's novels is called *The Waves*. Her novel is like that, lulling and mysterious.

It's always nice to know a little about the author of a book. Virginia Woolf was English. She was born in 1882 and she died in 1941 by suicide. She was mad at times and mad most of the time; that is, she was periodically plagued by mental illness and she was always angry at the limitations placed upon women. Virginia Woolf was a bold, experimental writer and a feminist figurehead of great importance.

One indication both of Woolf's literary approach and of her character is her fondness for the semi-colon. The period is final and unsubtle, might be termed masculine. The comma, on the other hand, is feminine as some men might want women to be, indefinite and subservient. Woolf instead favours the punctuation mark that most resembles where she wanted to be as a writer and as a woman, a mark like a sluice gate, one that is more open than the period but more in control than the comma, a feminist punctuation mark. Woolf famously wrote an essay called *A Room of One's Own*, in which she describes the difficulties of being a female writer in a field dominated by men. Well, her prose is like that, full of thoughts that are related but wouldn't fit in the oppressive big room of a single sentence;

they rather inhabit the many smaller rooms of a sentence punctuated by semi-colons.

I invite you to enter slowly, mindfully, taking your time, the many rooms of Virginia Woolf's prose.

Yours truly,
Yann Martel

VIRGINIA WOOLF (1882–1941) was a prolific British writer, publishing over five hundred essays and dozens of novels, short stories and non-fiction books. *A Room of One's Own*, her most famous non-fiction composition, discusses the issue of women writing in a male-dominated society and why few women in her time were successful novelists. Other celebrated works include *To the Lighthouse*, *The Waves* and *Orlando*. She was married to the writer Leonard Woolf, and together they founded and operated the Hogarth Press, which published works by T. S. Eliot, Katherine Mansfield and John Maynard Keynes, and introduced British readers to Sigmund Freud's work on psychoanalysis. Woolf committed suicide when she was fifty-nine, most likely because of undiagnosed bipolar disorder.

BOOK 28:

READ ALL ABOUT IT!
BY LAURA BUSH AND JENNA BUSH

April 28, 2008

To Stephen Harper,
Prime Minister of Canada,
A book from two pillars of society,
From a Canadian writer,
With best wishes,
Yann Martel

Dear Mr. Harper,

This is an unusual book I am sending you, for a number of reasons. For starters, it's fresh off the press. I bought it the day it was published. None of that pleasing, comforting worn-ness to it, like an old friend coming for a visit. Instead, a shiny, spine-cracking, new-smelling newness. And it's a children's book, not something I'd normally send to an adult.

What won me over to this book was its theme and the profession of its authors. *Read All About It!* is about the appeal and the importance of reading. Tyrone Brown, the protagonist, a student at Good Day Elementary School, is good at math, good at science, good at sports, but he doesn't like reading. When Miss Libro brings the kids to the school library to read to them, Tyrone is soooooo bored. He'd rather daydream. But one day, when Miss Libro is reading from a book about an astronaut, he pays attention—and he's taken in. Suddenly his world changes. It becomes populated by ghosts and dragons and historical figures like Benjamin Franklin (this is an American book) and, most endearingly, by a pig. Tyrone comes to realize that books are a fantastic way to dream. I won't tell you the rest of the story. You'll have to read all about it yourself.

The authors, Laura Bush and Jenna Bush, a mother-daughter team, are teachers and, according to their bios on the backflap, "passionate about reading."

A word about teachers. I love teachers. I always have. If I were not a writer, I'd be a teacher. I cannot think of a more important profession. It has always struck me as odd that lawyers and doctors should have such high standing—reflected not only in their salaries but in their social prominence—when, in the course of a normal, happy, healthy life, one should only exceptionally have to consult either. But teachers—we've all met and needed teachers. Teachers shaped us. They came into our dark minds and lit a light. They taught us both explicitly and by example. To teach is a magnificent verb, a social verb, implying someone else, whereas the verbs to earn, to buy, to want are lonely and hollow.

I could name so many of the teachers who marked my life. In fact, I will. Miss Preston and Mrs. Robinson were two of my early homeroom teachers. Mr. Grant taught me biology. Mr. Harvey taught me Latin. Mr. McNamara and Sister Reid taught me mathematics. Mr. Lawson and Mr. Davidson taught me English. Mr. Van Husen and Mr. Archer taught me history. The amazing Mr. Saunders taught me geography. And so on. Three decades have gone by, and still I remember these people. Where would I be without them, what frustrated, angry soul would I be? There is only so much parents can do to form us. After that, our fate lies with teachers.

And when we are no longer full-time students, there are all the informal teachers we meet as adults, the men, women and children who know better and who show us how to do better, how to be better.

Pity, then, that we live in a society that so little values teachers and schools. We have, alas, Mr. Harper, fallen upon times in which the common thinking seems to be that societies should be run as if they were corporations, with profitability as the guiding imperative. In this corporatist view of society, those who do not generate dollars are deemed undesirable. So it is that rich societies become unkind to the poor. I see this mean attitude in my own beloved province of Saskatchewan, where the new government is waging, as I've heard it put, a "war on the poor," and this, at a time of unprecedented prosperity [which is ongoing in Saskatchewan, despite the global economic crisis; we are a "have" province]. As if the poor will just disappear if ignored enough. As if there will be no broader consequence to the poor becoming poorer. As if the poor aren't citizens too. As if some of the poor aren't helpless children.

Well, in this race in which they are left behind, the poor are joined by students. Because investing in the education of a six-year-old, with a return that will be seen only in fifteen years or so, once that student has got a job and has started paying taxes, is not an investment worth making if one is looking to make quick money. And so we fund our schools minimally, burdening university students with levels of debt that neutralize their ability to be wealth-generating citizens. How can you buy a car, a house, appliances, how can you contribute to the economy, if you're crushed by a massive debt? The corporatist agenda is thus defeated by its own ideology.

Teachers are at the forefront of resisting this negative trend. With whatever means they are given, until they burn out, as they too commonly do, they continue their effort to produce intelligent, knowledgeable, caring citizens. Teachers are pillars of society.

Most teachers are women, certainly at the elementary school level, just as most readers are women. Laura Bush and Jenna Bush, teachers and readers both, are in that way typical. One is left wondering: while wives and daughters are teaching and reading, what are husbands and fathers doing? In our society, does the left hand know what the right hand is doing?

Yours truly,
Yann Martel

LAURA BUSH (b. 1946), wife of former president George W. Bush, taught elementary school and worked as a school librarian. She is a founder of the National Book Festival, and honorary chair of the Laura Bush Foundation for America's Libraries. During her husband's presidential terms, she was honoured by the Elie Wiesel Foundation for Humanity and the American Library Association. Her daughter JENNA HAGER (née Bush) (b. 1981) is also an elementary school teacher. In 2007, Jenna wrote *Ana's Story: A Journey of Hope*, chronicling her experiences with UNICEF in South America.

BOOK 29:

DROWN
BY JUNOT DÍAZ
May 12, 2008

To Stephen Harper,
Prime Minister of Canada,
A bottle with ten genies in it,
From a Canadian writer,
With best wishes,
Yann Martel

Dear Mr. Harper,

The book that accompanies this letter was heartily recommended to me by a bookseller. I'd never heard of it or of its author. I thought to myself, Well, why not? An obscure book that moved at least one reader. That makes it as valid as a book that moved a million. A little later, I mentioned my choice to a friend and she said, "Oh, he just won the Pulitzer Prize two days ago."

So much for the obscurity of Junot Díaz. I'm sending you *Drown*, his first book, a collection of short stories. It came out in 1996. It took Díaz eleven years to write his second book, the novel *The Brief Wondrous Life of Oscar Wao*, for which he won, just a month ago, the Pulitzer.

That's one of the good things about literary prizes. They bring attention to books or authors that might otherwise be missed by readers. The life of the literary writer is mostly invisible, like the movement of lava under the surface of the earth. Poems, short stories and novels are published, they are reviewed here and there, sales are modest, the world forgets, the writer writes on. It sounds dull, it's generally financially impoverishing, but hidden from view is the intoxication of being creative, the wrestling with words, the heaven of good writing days, the hell of bad ones, with at the end of it the sense that one has proven King Lear wrong, that something *can* come of nothing. A book is a bottle with a genie inside it. Rub it, open it, and the genie will come out to enchant you. Imagine being the one who put the genie in the bottle. Yes, it's terribly exciting work.

However, the world is strewn with such bottles, and many don't get much rubbing. Sometimes that's right, sometimes it's unfair. Only time will tell. Meanwhile, the writer continues to labour.

Then, one day, you are told that five readers liked your book. And they're the right readers, because they're on the jury of a prize. In fact, they've decided to give you the prize. Suddenly the clouds of the book world part and you hear a booming voice say, "This is my son, whom I love; with him I am well pleased." You're ceremoniously hauled out of obscurity. It's not an unpleasant experience, far from it. I'm grateful for every nod I've ever received.

But if I won, doesn't it mean that someone lost? That's the less appealing part of it, the feeling that you've become a racehorse, that you are competing, that there are winners and losers. History may decree that it is so, but it's not how it feels on the inside. On the inside, you're alone in your shop with your bottle and your genie.

Back to Junot Díaz. *Drown* is a collection of ten short stories, ranging in length from six to thirty-nine pages. These are the first short stories I've sent you. You'll find the experience quite different from reading novels. You'll be changing gears more often, so to speak. Díaz is a Dominican-American and his stories cover what it means to have a hyphen in one's identity, the potential for it to be a gulf, a dream, a strain, a loss. The English is peppered with Spanish, the tone is oral and informal, the characters profane and touching. It's a world of kids left to themselves, where there's no money and no father, no jobs and no prospects, only streets and harried mothers, drugs and fickle relations.

Now how will these stories expand your stillness, you might ask, the stillness with which life is properly examined? The answer might be found in the following quote from the story "Boyfriend," about a couple breaking up. The man comes by a few times to pick his stuff up:

> She let him fuck her every time, maybe hoping that it would make him stay but you know, once someone gets a little escape velocity going, ain't no play in the world that will keep them from leaving. I would listen to them going at it and I would be like, Damn, ain't nothing more shabby than those farewell fucks.

The toughness is surface. Beneath it is hurt and questioning. People are people, just trying to get by and make sense of things. No matter the language or the posing, the yearning for stillness is the same.

Yours truly,
Yann Martel

JUNOT DÍAZ (b. 1968) is a Dominican-American novelist and short story writer. He and his family moved to New Jersey when he was six years old. His first novel, *The Brief Wondrous Life of Oscar Wao*, is his best-known work; it has earned him several awards including the National Book Critics Circle Award and the 2008 Pulitzer Prize, and has been optioned for film. Díaz currently teaches creative writing at MIT and is the fiction editor at the *Boston Review*.

BOOK 30:

THE KREUTZER SONATA
BY LEO TOLSTOY

Translated from the Russian by Aylmer Maude

May 26, 2008

To Stephen Harper,
Prime Minister of Canada,
Music, both beautiful and discordant,
From a Canadian writer,
With best wishes,
Yann Martel

Dear Mr. Harper,

Tolstoy again. Sixty weeks back I sent you *The Death of Ivan Ilych*, if you remember. This week it's *The Kreutzer Sonata*, published three years later, in 1889. A very different book. As much as *Ilych* is an artistic gem, the realism seemingly effortless, the characters fully incarnate yet universal, the emotions finely expressed, the lyricism simple and profound, the portrayal of life and its fleetingness dead on, so to speak—in sum, as much as *Ilych* is perfect, *The Kreutzer Sonata* is imperfect. For example, the setting—a long train ride in which two passengers converse—comes off poorly because nearly the entire novella is taken up by the endless discourse of the main character, Pozdnyshev. Our nameless narrator just sits there, stunned into listening and memorizing the seventy-five-page tirade directed at him. It's as clunky a device as one of Plato's dialogues—without the wisdom, for the most part. *The Kreutzer*

Sonata is a long rant about love, sex and marriage, with side-swipes at doctors and children, leading up to a vivid portrayal of insane jealousy, all of it told by an unconvicted murderer. Imagine that, a man telling you on a train, "I killed my wife. Let me tell you about it, since we've got all night." I guess I wouldn't interrupt him, either.

Imperfect art, then. So why the interest? Because it's still Tolstoy. Simple people lead simple lives. Complex people lead complex lives. The difference between the two has to do with one's openness to life. Whether determined by misfortune—a congenital deficiency, a stunting upbringing, a lack of opportunity, a timid disposition—or determined by will—by the use and abuse of religion or ideology, for example—there are many ways in which life, one's portion of it, can be regulated and made acceptably simple. Tolstoy was unregulated. He lived in a manner unbridled and unblinkered. He took it all in. He was supremely complex. And so there was much of life in his long life, life good and bad, wise and unwise, happy and unhappy. Thus the interest of his writings, because of their extraordinary existential breadth. If the earth could gather itself up, could bring together everything upon it, all men, women and children, every plant and animal, every mountain and valley, every plain and ocean, and twist itself into a fine point, and at that fine point grasp a pen, and with that pen begin to write, it would write like Tolstoy. Tolstoy, like Shakespeare, like Dante, like all great artists, is life itself speaking.

But whereas *Ilych* elicits consonance in the reader, *The Kreutzer Sonata* elicits dissonance. In it, love between men and women does not really exist but is merely a euphemism for lust. Marriage is covenanted prostitution, a cage in which lust unhappily fulfills itself. Men are depraved, women hate sex, children are a burden, doctors are a fraud. The only solution is complete sexual abstinence, and if that means the end of the human species, all the better. Because otherwise men and women will always be unhappy with each other, and some men may be driven to killing their wives. It's a bleak, excessively scouring view of the relations between the sexes, a reflection of Tolstoy's frustration at the social constrictions of his times, no doubt, but nonetheless going too far, wrong-headed, objectionable. And so its effect, the scandal upon its publication, and the reaction it has to this day. Tolstoy does indeed go too far in *The Kreutzer Sonata*, but in it are nonetheless expressed all the elements—the hypocrisy and the outrage, the guilt and the anger—that were at the core of that greatest revolution of the twentieth century: feminism.

As an aside, this second book by Tolstoy was a last-minute choice. There's such a world of books out there to share with you that I thought one book per author as introduction was enough. After that, if you were interested, you could look up for yourself any given author's other books.

Only I wanted a book this week that touched on music. (I've forgotten to explain the title of Tolstoy's novella. Pozdnyshev's wife is an amateur pianist. The couple meets an accomplished amateur violinist by the name of Trukhashevsky, a man. The wife and he become, in all innocence, friends because of their mutual fondness for music. They decide to play Beethoven's Kreutzer Sonata, for piano and violin, together. In the wings, her husband grows angrier.) Why a book on music? Because serious music, at least as represented by new and classical music, is fast disappearing from our Canadian lives. I have belatedly learned of the latest proof of this: the CBC Radio Orchestra is to be disbanded. Already our public radio's fare of music has been paltrified. There was once, Mr. Harper, a show called *Two New Hours* on CBC, hosted by Larry Lake. It played Canadian new music. Its last slot, surely the least desirable for any show, was on Sundays between 10 p.m. and midnight, too late for the early birds, too early for the night owls. Airing at that time, no surprise that few people managed to listen to it. When I did, though, I was grateful. New music is a strange offering. It is, as far as I can tell, music that has broken free. Free of rules, forms, traditions, expectations. Frontier music. New world music. Anarchy as music. Which might explain the screechy violins, the pianos gone crazy, the weird electronic stuff.

I have intense memories of listening to *Two New Hours* and doing nothing but that. Because really, it's impossible to read while your radio is sounding like two tractors mating. I suppose I'm more jaded when it comes to writing—jaded, jealous, bored, whatever. But I listened to *Two New Hours* out of pure curiosity. And I was surprised, moved and proud that there were creators out there responding to our world in such fresh and serious ways. Because it was clear to me: this was serious stuff, strange as it sounded. This was music that, under whatever guise, was the voice of a single person trying to communicate with me. And I listened, thrilled at the newness of it. That is, I listened until the show was cancelled.

And now the CBC Radio Orchestra, the last radio orchestra in North America, is to be similarly cancelled. No more, "That was _____, played by the CBC Radio Orchestra, conducted by Mario Bernardi," as I heard for years. Who will play us our Bach and Mozart now, our R. Murray Schafer and Christos Hatzis?

It amazes me that at a time when Canada is riding the commodities wave to unprecedented wealth, with most levels of government experiencing budgetary surpluses, that we are ridding ourselves of a piddly little orchestra. If this is how we are when in fortune, how will we be when in misfortune?* How much culture can we do *without* before we become lifeless, corporate drones?

I believe that both in good and bad times we need beautiful music.

Yours truly,
Yann Martel

---

* The CBC Radio Orchestra was indeed disbanded at the end of November 2008. It is now trying to survive as the National Broadcast Orchestra, on a budget of one million dollars a year, peanuts compared to the money Western economies have lost thanks to incompetent bankers and politicians. We are now poorer in every way, with less classical music coming to us from the radio and less money in our pockets.

BOOK 31:

THEIR EYES WERE WATCHING GOD
BY ZORA NEALE HURSTON

June 9, 2008

To Stephen Harper,
Prime Minister of Canada,
An incandescent novel,
From a Canadian writer,
With best wishes,
Yann Martel

Dear Mr. Harper,

Some voices are barely heard. They are left to speak among themselves, worlds within worlds. Then someone listens, gives them artistic expression, and now the loss is lesser, because those voices have become eternal. Such is the achievement of the American writer Zora Neale Hurston (1891–1960) with her masterpiece *Their Eyes Were Watching God*. You will notice the language right away. There are two voices in the novel. One is the narrative voice that frames the story. It is lyrical, metaphor laden and formal. Take the first two paragraphs of the novel:

> Ships at a distance have every man's wish on board. For some they come in with the tide. For others they sail forever on the horizon, never out of sight, never landing until the Watcher turns his eyes away in resignation, his dreams mocked to death by Time. That is the life of men.

Now, women forget all those things they don't want to remember, and remember everything they don't want to forget. The dream is the truth. Then they act and do things accordingly.

The other voice is that of the characters, and it's something else. They speak in the African-American vernacular, and you'll hardly believe that English can do such things. A random example:

> "Well, all right, Tea Cake, Ah wants tuh go wid you real bad, but,—oh, Tea Cake, don't make no false pretense wid me!"
> "Janie, Ah hope God may kill me, if Ah'm lyin.' Nobody else on earth kin hold uh candle tuh you, baby. You got de keys to de kingdom."

It's not cute, it's not folkloric, it's not patronizing. The effect is rather of a renewal of language. You read—you hear—as if you were hearing for the first time. And what you will hear is the story of Janie Crawford, a black woman whose voyage of self-discovery, with its hard-earned lessons, is told through her three marriages.

The most significant element in the life of Zora Neale Hurston—even greater than that she was a woman—was that she was black. It is inconceivable that her writing—consisting of four novels, two books of folklore, an autobiography and more than fifty shorter pieces—would have been the same had she been white. She was black in a white society that for two hundred years had held blacks in slavery. She was black in a society that was, at best, racial in its thinking, and, at worst, racist. I imagine that every day of her life there was some glance, some exchange, some limitation that reminded Hurston of the colour of her skin and what that was held to mean.

Now, it's hard, when you are perpetually made aware of one single element of your identity, be it the colour of your skin, the shape of your body, your sexual orientation, your ethnic heritage, whatever, not to linger and dwell on that element, not to become twisted and bitter as a result. Yet the miracle of Hurston's art is that it manages not to linger and dwell, not to be twisted and bitter. *Their Eyes Were Watching God* is not a diatribe about racist America, though examples of racism are easily found in it. It is instead an incandescent novel about a character whose full humanity and destiny is explored—and she happens to be black.

I suspect that if you read the first chapter of *Their Eyes Were Watching God*, you'll read the other nineteen. You will read about Janie and Tea Cake, about love and muck, about happiness and disaster. And the worth of that—other than that you will have been entertained—is that for the duration of a story you will have entered the being of an African-American woman. You will have heard voices that you might otherwise never have heard.

Yours truly,
Yann Martel

P.S. One of the joys of buying secondhand books is the unexpected treasures they sometimes contain. Case in point: a colour photo slipped out of your copy of Their Eyes *when I opened it. A group shot. Nothing written on the back. Nine people camping: five women, three men, and one girl in a lifejacket. Though no doubt casually taken, note what an excellent photo it happens to*

be, how the way the people are arranged is aesthetically pleasing, the eye moving in an easy circle from the seated woman on the left to the girl on the right, how the group is slightly off-centre so that the feel of the shot is unstudied, how the peripheral elements are unobtrusive yet revealing. It struck me that the group is shaped in the form of an eye. We think we're looking at them, but, in fact, they are an eye looking out at us, winking. Perhaps that's why they're smiling, amused at the trick they're playing on us, the viewer being viewed. I wonder what the story of these people is. Clearly they're a family. Was this their book? Who among them read it? What stories do they have, what voices?

ZORA NEALE HURSTON (1891–1960) was part of the Harlem Renaissance of the 1920s. She published four novels, two books of folklore, an autobiography and more than fifty essays, articles, short stories and plays. Her most famous novel, *Their Eyes Were Watching God*, is written in a fluid and expressive vernacular, a bold stylistic choice that gave new literary voice to African-Americans. There was a revived interest in her work following a 1975 article published in *Ms. Magazine* by Alice Walker about Hurston's writings.

BOOK 32:

THE REZ SISTERS
BY TOMSON HIGHWAY

June 23, 2008

To Stephen Harper,
Prime Minister of Canada,
From a Canadian writer,
With best wishes,
Yann Martel

Dear Mr. Harper,

So far, if there is one thing that your administration has done
that will stand the test of time, it is the formal apology to the
victims of the Canadian government's Native residential school
system. Policies come and go, are changed and forgotten, but an
apology stands. An apology changes the course of history. It is
the first step in true healing and reconciliation. I congratulate
you on this important symbolic gesture.

Since your mind was recently on Canada's original
inhabitants—and since National Aboriginal Day was just
two days ago—it's appropriate that I should send you Tomson
Highway's play *The Rez Sisters*. It too is of historical importance.
Of the author, there's an unusually long bio at the start of the
book, a full four pages, so you can read there about the life of
Tomson Highway, at least until 1988, when the play was published.

What is not mentioned in the bio is the synergy that developed
in the Aboriginal cultural world in Toronto in the mid-1980s.
Suddenly then—the time was right—some Natives came together

and did what they had hardly done until then: they spoke. The production company Native Earth Performing Arts was founded in 1982 to give voice to Aboriginal theatre, dance and music. Before that, with the exception of Inuit prints and sculptures and Maria Campbell's memoir *Half-Breed*, the Canadian cultural scene was practically bare of Native expression. That would change with Native Earth. Along with Tomson Highway, the company fostered the careers of such writers as Daniel David Moses and Drew Hayden Taylor.

When *The Rez Sisters* opened in November 1986, the cast had to go out into the streets and beg passersby to come in and see the play. Well, those first people liked what they saw and word of mouth did the rest. *The Rez Sisters* became a hit. It drew large audiences, toured the country, was produced at the Edinburgh Theatre Festival.

Like your last book, Zora Neale Hurston's *Their Eyes Were Watching God*, the force of *The Rez Sisters* lies with its characters. Seven women—Pelajia Patchnose, Philomena Moosetail, Marie-Adele Starblanket, Annie Cook, Emily Dictionary, Veronique St. Pierre and Zhaboonigan Peterson—live on the Wasaychigan Hill Indian Reserve, on Manitoulin Island. Life there is as life is everywhere, with its ups and downs. But then comes momentous news: THE BIGGEST BINGO IN THE WORLD is being organized in Toronto. And do you know what kind of a jackpot THE BIGGEST BINGO IN THE WORLD would have? Something BIG. The dreams that winning that jackpot might fulfill is at the heart of the play. It's a comedy, the kind that makes you laugh while also delivering a fair load of sadness. Stereotypes are set up and then mocked, but it's not an overtly political play, hence its universal resonance. We may not be Native women on a reserve, we may not be bingo aficionados, but we all have dreams and worries.

There is a last character in the play who must be mentioned. Nanabush, in his various incarnations, is as important in Native mythology as Christ is in the Christian world. But there's a playful element to Nanabush that is absent in our portrayal of Christ. In *The Rez Sisters*, he appears in the guise of a seagull or a nighthawk. He dances and prances and pesters. Marie-Adele, who has cancer, and Zhaboonigan, who was brutally raped, are the only ones who explicitly interact with him. He is the angel of death, but also the spirit of life. He hovers over much of the play.

Yours truly,
Yann Martel

TOMSON HIGHWAY (b. 1951) is a Cree author and playwright who is best known for his plays *The Rez Sisters* and *Dry Lips Oughta Move to Kapuskasing*, both winners of the Dora Mavor Moore Award. He is also the author of the bestselling novel *Kiss of the Fur Queen*. Highway's writing features Native characters living on reserves and incorporates Native spirituality. He continues to advocate for Native issues and expose the injustices and challenges faced by the Native Canadian population. Highway is a talented concert pianist and an entertaining stage presence, and is currently producing his third play, *Rose*.

BOOK 33:

PERSEPOLIS
BY MARJANE SATRAPI

Translated from the French by Mattias Ripa

July 7, 2008

To Stephen Harper,
Prime Minister of Canada,
This armchair trip to the Islamic Republic of Iran,
From a Canadian writer,
With best wishes,
Yann Martel

Dear Mr. Harper,

In the mid-1990s, I travelled to Iran with a young woman. In the two months we were there, we met maybe twenty Western travellers, all of them with transit visas and all speedily making their way along the central corridor that passes through Iran from the border of Turkey to the border of Pakistan. We were specifically interested in Iran, not in getting from Europe to Asia, so we had managed to get tourist visas. We wandered all over the country, visiting not only Teheran, Esfahan and Shiraz, cities you will have heard of, but others, too: Tabriz, Rasht, Mashhad, Gorgan, Yazd, Kerman, Bandar Abbas, Bam, Ahvaz, Khorramabad, Sanandaj. (Sorry for the long list of names; they may mean nothing to you, but each one opens up a volume of memories in me.) We also visited Zoroastrian fire temples in the desert. We climbed an ancient ziggurat. We took ferries to islands. We rested in oases.

I've often found that, excluding war zones, a foreign place is never so dangerous as when you are far away from it. The closer you get to it, the more the distortions caused by fear and misunderstanding dissipate, so that, to take the case at hand, the image we had of the Islamic Republic of Iran, that terrifying place that brought the world full-on religious fanaticism, with oppressed women going about dressed from head to toe in black and people flagellating themselves in public and fountains spewing blood-red water, disappeared once we entered the country and was replaced by this or that friendly individual standing in front of us, eyeing us with curiosity, wanting to be kind but uncertain of his or her English.

If Iran was challenging, it was in the way it challenged our expectations. For example, in all our time there, talking freely to men and women of all social classes, from the rural poor to the urban middle class, from the devout to the secular, we never met, not once, a person who complained about living in an Islamic republic. A government has to be a mirror into which its people can look and recognize themselves. Well, the Iranians we met recognized themselves in their Islamic democracy. The only complaint we heard, and often, was about the state of the economy. Iranians complained about lacking money, not lacking freedom.

There wasn't much to do in Iran in the way of leisure then. It was, by Western standards, and probably still is, an arid society, with little space or money given over to cinemas, concert halls, sports complexes and the like. And there were no bars or discos, of course. Iran was a sober place, both literally and metaphorically. So Iranians did the only thing they could easily: they socialized. As a result, they are a people with the most graceful and sophisticated social skills I've ever seen, a people who, when they meet you, really meet you, turning their full attention to you. The Iranians we met were open, curious, generous, extraordinarily hospitable and endlessly chatty.

And the horrors of fundamentalism? The people who brought us Salman Rushdie's fatwa? The oppression of women? That's all true, too. But what place is above censure? People in Iran are like people anywhere: they want to be happy and live in peace, with a modicum of material well-being. The rules of their society, their values—the means by which they hope to become happy—are different from Canada's, but what of that? They have their problems, we have ours. Let them muddle through theirs, as we hope to muddle through ours. Progress can't be jump-started; it must arise organically from within a society, it cannot be imposed from without.

Such eye-opening travel as I had the luck of doing isn't a possibility for everyone. Work, family and inclination may prevent one from ever visiting this or that foreign place. Which is where books come in. The armchair traveller can be as well informed as the backpacker roughing it, so long as he or she reads the right books. Travel, whether directly with one's feet or vicariously through a book, humanizes a place. A people emerge in their individual particularity, miles away from caricature or calumny.

And so *Persepolis*, by Marjane Satrapi. It's a graphic novel, the second I've sent you after *Maus*, by Art Spiegelman. It's charming, witty, sad and illuminating. The point of view is that of a ten-year-old girl named Marjane. She's like all ten-year-olds the world over, living in her own half-imaginary universe—only it's 1979 and she lives in Iran. A revolution is afoot, one that will be welcomed at first by her middle-class family because it will bring down the odiously corrupt and brutal regime of the Shah, but later will be hated because of the excesses that followed. It's a story that has the ring of truth to it because it's the story of an individual telling it as she saw it.

I invite you to read *Persepolis* and get a hint of the Iran I visited some years ago. If you enjoy it, you should know that there's a *Persepolis 2*, which continues Marjane's story, and there's also a movie.

Yours truly,
Yann Martel

MARJANE SATRAPI (b. 1969) is a multi-talented Iranian-French author. She is primarily a graphic novelist but also writes and illustrates children's books. She is best known for her popular autobiographical graphic novel *Persepolis*, and its sequel, *Persepolis 2*. In these books, she recalls her childhood growing up in Iran and her adolescence studying in Europe. *Persepolis* won the Angoulême Coup de Coeur Award and was later adapted into an animated film recognized at the Cannes Film Festival. Satrapi studied illustration in Strasbourg and lives in France.

BOOK 34:

THE BLUEST EYE
BY TONI MORRISON
July 21, 2008

To Stephen Harper,
Prime Minister of Canada,
From a Canadian writer,
With best wishes,
Yann Martel

Dear Mr. Harper,

Oh, the mess that the heart wreaks. The pity of it all when so much was possible. Toni Morrison's novel *The Bluest Eye* is unbelievably short—a mere 160 pages—considering all that it carries of pain, sadness, anger, cruelty, dashed hopes, of descriptions, characters, events, of all that makes a novel great. Once again, like many of the books I have sent you, you might be inclined to think at first, "This story won't speak to me." After all, a story set in Lorain, Ohio, in the early 1940s, mostly told from the point of view of children; a cast of characters who are poor and whose blackness makes them not just a skin colour removed from you and me but a world removed; a perspective that is innately feminist—there is much in this story that starts where you and I have never been.

And yet it will speak to you. Read, read beyond the first few pages, plunge into the story the way you might dive into a chilly lake—and you will find that it's warmer than you expected, that in fact you're quite comfortable in its waters. You will find that the characters—Claudia, Frieda, Pecola—are not so unfamiliar, because you were once a child yourself, and you will find that the cruelty, the racism, the inequality are not so alien either, because we've all experienced the nastiness of the human heart, either in being the one lashed or the one lashing out.

The making of art, as I may have mentioned to you before, involves a lot of work. Because of that, it is implicitly constructive. One doesn't work so hard merely to destroy. One rather hopes to build. No matter how much cruelty and sadness a story may hold, its effect is always the opposite. So a glad tale is taken gladly, and a cruel tale is taken ironically, with feelings of pity and terror, pushing one to reject cruelty. Art then is implicitly liberal; it encourages us towards openness and generosity, it seeks to unlock doors. I suspect this will be the effect of *The Bluest Eye* on you, with its many lives blighted by poverty, stifled by racism, dashed by random cruelty. You will feel more keenly the suffering of others, no matter how different you thought they were from you at first.

Yours truly,
Yann Martel

TONI MORRISON (b. 1931), born Chloe Anthony Wofford, is an American author of novels, short stories, children's literature and non-fiction. Some of her most famous publications include *The Bluest Eye*, *Song of Solomon* and *Beloved*. She is a member of the American Academy of Arts and Letters and has won multiple awards, including a Pulitzer Prize and, in 1993, the Nobel Prize in Literature. Beyond her career as an author, she has been a literary critic, lecturer, editor, professor and chair at several universities.

BOOK 35:

UNDER MILK WOOD
BY DYLAN THOMAS

August 5, 2008

To Stephen Harper,
Prime Minister of Canada,
From a Canadian writer,
With best wishes,
Yann Martel

Dear Mr. Harper,

Your latest book will be late this week. I'm sorry about that. The delay is not due to the long weekend. Like most self-employed workers, I'm willing to work on weekends and during holidays because if I don't do the job, no one will do it for me. The problem lies elsewhere. The book that accompanies this letter, *Under Milk Wood*, by the Welsh poet Dylan Thomas (1914–1953), is such a lyrical work that it demands not only to be read but to be heard. So I thought I'd send you an audio version in addition to the text. There is a famous performance recorded in New York with Dylan Thomas himself reading several of the parts, done hardly two months before his death, and my family owns an LP of that recording, but I'm not willing to part with it, and even if I were, I doubt you have a record player at hand. The more recent performance that I've found for you, on CD, is a BBC production and it's been slow to arrive in the mail. Hence the delay.

A word about audiobooks. Have you ever listened to one? I went on a road trip to the Yukon a few years ago and brought some along to give them a try. I thought I'd dislike having a voice insistently whispering me a story while Canada's majestic northern landscape surged before my eyes. A three-minute pop song I can handle—but a twelve-hour story? I thought it would drive me crazy. I was wrong. Be forewarned: audiobooks are totally addictive. The origin of language is oral, not written. We spoke before we wrote, as children but also as a species. It's in being spoken that words achieve their full power. If the written word is the recipe, then the spoken word is the dish prepared, the voice adding tone, accent, emphasis, emotion. As I'm sure you will agree, the quality of oratory in Canadian and American public life has deteriorated in the last few years. Barack Obama is where he is, on the cusp of the US presidency, in part, I believe, because of his skill in making his words lofty, inspirational and convincing. His ability is unusual. Most public speakers nowadays are plodding. Actors are the great exception. Their public speaking is superb because it is the very basis of their trade. And it's actors who read the stories on audiobooks. The combination of a writer's carefully chosen words and an actor's carefully calibrated delivery makes for a package that is spellbinding. Time and again on my trip to the Yukon I wouldn't get out of the car until a chapter had ended. And then the next morning I couldn't wait to get on with the next. As soon as one story was done, I hastened to start another. Every time I go on a car trip now, I stop by the public library to pick up a selection of audiobooks.

There's talk of an election this fall. That means a lot of travelling for you. I suggest you pack a few audiobooks for those long bus and airplane trips you will have to endure. My only advice is to avoid abridged versions. Otherwise, select as you please. Murder mysteries are particularly effective—as is poetry.

Which brings us back to *Under Milk Wood*. Dylan Thomas is no doubt one of the world's most famous poets. He had a rare quality among modern bards: a persona. His aura as a hard-drinking, hard-living writer—one who died young, to boot; always a boon to one's immortality—has helped his poetry, which is of genuine quality, achieve a cult status. His poems are endlessly anthologized. You've no doubt heard of "Do Not Go Gentle into That Good Night."

Under Milk Wood is a radio play. That might make you think it's a tight, fast-paced affair in which a few distinctive voices are aided by clear sound effects. Not at all. There's no plot to speak of, just a day in the life of a Welsh village named Llareggub. Read that name backwards and you'll get an idea of what Dylan Thomas thought there was to do in Welsh villages. But life is still good, and that's what *Under Milk Wood* is at heart, a celebration of life. With an astounding sixty-nine different voices, it's symphonic in effect. What carries the whole piece, its melody so to speak, is Dylan Thomas's gift for language. His words describe, imitate, bubble, scintillate, run, stop, amuse, surprise, enchant. This is verbal beauty at its purest.

Beauty—the word is much bandied about. But like many words that we use all the time—*good*, *fair*, *just*, for example—if we look a little closer, we find that behind the cliché lies a philosophical odyssey that goes as far back as human thinking. Clearly, beauty moves us, motivates us, shames us, shapes us. I won't in this letter even try to define what beauty is. Best to leave you to think on it, or to look it up. If you are serious in your curiosity, you'll find yourself following a strand of Western philosophy that goes as far back as Pythagoras (who associated beauty with symmetry), and of course all of visual art concerns itself in one way or another with beauty. There's much there for the mind that wants to study, a lifetime's worth of material.

I'll limit myself to a much narrower focus, and that is the question of beauty and the prose writer. A writer has many tools to tell a story: characterization, plot and description are some of the obvious ones. Tell a gripping story with full-blooded characters in a convincing setting and you've told a good story. Depending on the writer, one element may prevail more than another. So John Grisham or Stephen King will have much plot to show, with some description, but the characters may be there mainly to serve a narrative purpose. A writer like John Banville, on the other hand (do you know him? Irish, an extraordinary stylist), will tend to be less driven by plot, but will have characters and descriptions that are startling in their richness. And so on. Every writer, depending on his or her strengths and interests, will bring some different ratio of ingredients to the making up of a story.

One notion that is constant in all writers, though, is that of beauty. Every writer, in some way, aspires to literary beauty. That might mean a beautiful plot device, elegant in its simplicity. Or it might mean an ability to paint with words, to create such vivid portraits of people or settings that readers feel that they are "seeing" what the writer is describing. More commonly, the writer of serious ambition aspires to beautiful writing; that is, to writing that by dint of apt vocabulary, happy syntax and pleasing cadence will make the reader marvel. I promise you, if one day you are glad-handing and you end up shaking the hand of a writer and you're at a lost for words, if you say, "You're a beautiful writer," you will please that writer. They will know exactly what you mean, that you're not talking about their shoes or their tie or their complexion, but that you're talking about how they lay their words on the page, and they will glow, they will beam, they will nearly wilt under your praise.

But—there's always a but—one has to be careful about beauty. In all walks of life. In our overly visual society, we tend to be too easily won over by beauty, whether it be in a person, in a product or even in a book. A beautifully written book, like a beautiful person, may not have much to say. The beauty of substance often loses out to the beauty of appearance. A good writer knows that beautiful writing can't substitute for having something to say. The best beauty is that in which beauty of form is held up by beauty of content.

Beauty, in another words, can be a mask hiding a vacuum, hiding falsehood, even hiding ugliness.

No danger here, with *Under Milk Wood*. The lyricism of the language rests solidly on Dylan Thomas's gut knowledge that life is good, however bad it may be at times. It is said that Dylan Thomas wrote *Under Milk Wood* in reaction to the atomic bombing of Hiroshima. I doubt that's factually true. It sounds too conveniently perfect. But opposing a radiant symphonic poem against the darkness of a mass killing of civilians does hark to a spiritual truth: that beauty can be a road back to goodness.

Yours truly,
Yann Martel

DYLAN THOMAS (1914–1953) was a Welsh poet, prose writer and playwright. His poems were characteristically dense, lyrical and exuberant, often reflecting on the themes of unity in the natural world and the cyclical nature of life and death. His most famous works include the short story *A Child's Christmas in Wales* and the poem "Do Not Go Gentle into That Good Night." After World War II, he went to the United States on a series of celebrated reading tours, during one of which, while in New York City, he died of a drinking overdose.

BOOK 36:

EVERYTHING THAT RISES MUST CONVERGE
BY FLANNERY O'CONNOR
August 18, 2008

To Stephen Harper,
Prime Minister of Canada,
From a Canadian writer,
With best wishes,
Yann Martel

Dear Mr. Harper,

The work now in your hands is the quintessential used book. The cover looks old, both in style and in condition. A number, a price, has been written directly on the cover: $4.50. Someone put a line of tape along the spine to keep the cover from falling off. There's the dash of a black marker along the bottom of the book, the telltale sign of a used book. The pages inside are yellowed with age along their outside edges. You'll notice a further yellow mark along the left side of the first pages; it looks like the book was accidentally soaked once and a watermark has remained. The book unmistakably shows its venerable age. The edition now yours, a first paperback printing, was published forty-one years ago, in 1967. I was four years old, you were nine. Not bad for an assemblage of flimsy elements: cheap paper and thin cardboard.

The book has lasted this long for two reasons: it is good, and so it has been treated well. Inexpensive in price, it has glowed with value in the eyes of all who owned it, and so they handled it with care. As I mentioned to you in an earlier letter, the used book is economically odd: despite age and lack of rarity, it does not depreciate with age. In fact, it is the contrary: if you take good care of this book, in a few years, because it is a first paperback printing, it will go up in value.

That undiminishing richness is of course due to a paperback's inner wealth, all those little black markings. They inhabit a book the way a soul inhabits a body. Books, like people, can't be reduced to the cost of the materials with which they were made. Books, like people, become unique and precious once you get to know them.

That cultural glory, the used paperback, is perfectly represented here by Flannery O'Connor. Neither new nor aged, but rather enduring, she is the typical glittering treasure to be found in a used bookstore. Imagine: for $4.50 I got you her collection of short stories *Everything That Rises Must Converge*. The discrepancy between price and value is laughably out of whack. What it really says is this: the object you are now holding is of such worth that to give it any price is ridiculous, so here, to emphasize the nonsense of the notion, we'll charge you $4.50.

Flannery O'Connor was American. She was born in 1925 in Georgia and she died there in 1964 of lupus. She was only thirty-nine years old. She was religious, devoutly Catholic to be exact, but her faith was not a set of blinkers. Rather, it charged the world with God's grace and made apparent to her the gap between the sacred and the human. By my reckoning, what O'Connor wrote about, over and over, was the Fall. Her stories are about the ruination of Paradise, about the cost of listening to snakes and reaching for apples. They are moral stories, but there's nothing pat about them. By virtue of good writing, fine dark humour, rich characterization and compelling narrative, they sift through life without reducing it.

And so their effect. Each story feels, has the weight, of a small novel. And with no dull literariness, I assure you. You'll see for yourself. Start on any one of them and a character will quickly reach out from the page, grab you by the arm and pull you along. These stories are engrossing. After each, you will feel that you have lived longer, that you have a greater experience of life, that you are wiser. They are dark stories. In every one, either a son hates his mother or a mother despairs over her useless sons, or it might be a grandfather or a father who is despairing. And the end result, besides highly entertaining, is invariably tragic. Hence the wisdom given off. It's nearly a mathematical equation: reader + story of folly = wiser reader.

I especially recommend to you the stories "Greenleaf," "A View of the Woods" and "The Lame Shall Enter First."

I have another matter I would like to raise with you. The cancellation of PromArt was recently announced. The program, administered by the Department of Foreign Affairs, helps cover some of the travel costs of Canadian artists and cultural groups going abroad to promote their work. The grants to individuals are small, often between $750 and $1,500. The budget of the entire program is only $4.7 million. That's about 14 cents a year per Canadian. For that small sum, Canada shows its best, most enduring quality to the nations of the earth. To remind you of what I'm sure you already know, a country cannot be reduced to the corporations it happens to shelter. Businesses come and go, following their own commercial logic. No one feels deep, patriotic feelings for a corporation, certainly not its shareholders. They will vote where the money leads them. So while Canadians can feel proud about such global players as Bombardier and Alcan and hosts of others, we should not pin our identity to them. Canada is a people, not a business. We shine because of our cultural achievements, not our mercantile wealth. So to cut an international arts promotion program is to vow our country to cultural anonymity. It means foreigners will have no impressions of Canada, and so no affection.

The PromArt program is a vital part of our foreign policy. I ask you to reconsider the decision to shut it down. The value-added worth of this modest program is akin to, well, the value-added worth of a paperback.

Yours truly,
Yann Martel

FLANNERY O'CONNOR (1925–1964) was an American essayist, novelist and short story writer whose work is often called grotesque, disturbing and typical of Southern Gothic literature. Her writing is characterized by blunt foreshadowing, irony and allegory, and generally explores questions of religion and morality. Among her best-known works are her novels *Wise Blood* and *The Violent Bear It Away*, and her short story collections *Everything That Rises Must Converge* and *A Good Man Is Hard to Find*. After spending time in New York City and at an artists' colony, she was diagnosed with lupus and returned to her family farm, where she lived for the last fourteen years of her life, raising peacocks and writing. She was posthumously awarded the National Book Award for *The Complete Stories of Flannery O'Connor*.

BOOK 37:

A MODEST PROPOSAL
BY JONATHAN SWIFT

September 1, 2008

To Stephen Harper,
Prime Minister of Canada,
A cookbook of sorts,
From a Canadian writer,
With best wishes,
Yann Martel

Dear Mr. Harper,

So, more cuts in arts funding. In my last letter I mentioned only the PromArt program, not having got wind yet of the other cuts. Nearly $45 million in all. That will bite, that will hurt, that will kill. With less art in the future, I wonder what you think there will be more of. What does $45 million buy that has more worth than a people's cultural expression, than a people's sense of who they are?

This calls for a special book. How we administer ourselves— the people we elect, the laws they enact—finds itself reflected in art. Politics is also culture. *A Modest Proposal*, by the Irish writer Jonathan Swift (1667–1745), is a good example of an artistic reflection upon politics. It is a piece of satire, admirable for its humorous ferocity and brevity. At a mere eight pages, it is the shortest work I've ever sent you.

The key paragraph, enunciating Swift's suggested solution to Ireland's poverty, the modest proposal in question, goes like this:

I have been assured by a very knowing American of my acquaintance in London, that a young healthy child well nursed is at a year old a most delicious, nourishing, and wholesome food, whether stewed, roasted, baked or boiled; and I make no doubt that it will equally serve in a fricassee or a ragout.

The question is simple and pertinent, Mr. Harper: are you preparing a ragout?

Yours truly,
Yann Martel

JONATHAN SWIFT (1667–1745) was an Irish satirist and essayist, and a founding member of the Martinus Scriblerus Club, whose members included Alexander Pope and Thomas Parnell. Swift was politically involved, writing pamphlets first for the Whigs, then for the Tories, before championing Irish concerns. He studied in Ireland and England, earning an MA from Oxford, and was an ordained Anglican minister. Swift's style is playful and humorous while being intensely critical of the objects of his satire. His best-known works include *Gulliver's Travels*, *A Modest Proposal* and *The Battle of the Books*.

BOOK 38:

ANTHEM
BY AYN RAND
September 15, 2008

To Stephen Harper,
Prime Minister of Canada,
Ayn Rand wanted us to be selfish,
but democracy asks us to be generous.
From a Canadian writer,
With best wishes,
Yann Martel

Dear Mr. Harper,

You've called an election. Appropriate then to send you Ayn (rhymes with Pine) Rand, whose books are highly political. It's very easy to dislike Ayn Rand, not only the writer, but even the person behind the writing, and many readers and intellectuals do indeed dislike her, intensely. However, more than a quarter century after her death (she lived from 1905 to 1982), Ayn Rand still has her dogged followers, a cult nearly, and her books continue to sell in great numbers. There is clearly something both attractive and off-putting about her writing. Her brief novel *Anthem*, just 123 pages, is a useful work to discuss in the context of an election. You will see in what follows that I fall on the side of those who dislike Ayn Rand.

Anthem, first published in 1938, is a dystopia with a utopian heart, a portrayal of a future where everything has gone wrong but where the reader is shown how things can be made right. The novel starts well. The language is simple, the writing understated, the cadence engaging. The story is told entirely from the point of view of the main character, whose name is Equality 7–2521. (Ayn Rand gives her characters names that clearly indicate the notions, the ideals, she wishes to debunk.) Equality 7–2521 does not live in good times. He has no significant freedoms. He has chosen neither where to live nor what to do for a living. He has no family and no real friends. In that, he is like every other man he knows, living a life of rigid conformity that is socially useful but grinding. The reader accepts this premise willingly because of a clever and effective linguistic device on Ayn Rand's part: the complete absence of singular personal pronouns. Equality 7–2521 does not speak as an "I," nor is anything ever his with a "my" or a "mine." Such individualistic concepts are banned from his society and he is a "we," as is everyone else, and all are at the service of the collectivity. As Equality 7–2521 says:

> We strive to be like all our brother men, for all men must be alike. Over the portals of the Palace of the World Council, there are words cut in the marble, which we repeat to ourselves whenever we are tempted:

> "We are one in all and all in one.
> There are no men but only the great WE,
> One, indivisible and forever."

Union 5–3992 and International 4–8818, fellow street sweepers, manage to endure such conformity, but:

> There are Fraternity 2–5503, a quiet boy with wise, kind eyes, who cry suddenly, without reason, in the midst of day or night, and their body shakes with sobs they cannot explain.

There are Solidarity 9–6347, who are a bright youth, without fear in the day; but they scream in their sleep, and they scream: "Help us! Help us! Help us!" into the night, in a voice which chills our bones . . .

As for Fraternity 9–3452, Democracy 4–6998, Unanimity 7–3304, International 1–5537, Solidarity 8–1164, Alliance 6–7349, Similarity 5–0306, and especially Collective 0–0009 (they are a nasty one), they are the oppressive system's prime defenders, and they will collide with Equality 7–2521, who is pushed irresistibly to think on his own and pursue his ideas, no matter where they lead him.

There are women. They live separately. Only once a year, for a single night during the "Time of Mating," do men and women come together, in pairs matched by the "Council of Eugenics." It is not then, but earlier, on the City's limits one work day, that Equality 7–2521 meets Liberty 5–3000. He falls in love with her, committing "the great Transgression of Preference." He calls her—they call them—"The Golden One."

This love of his, combined with his independent thinking, eventually forces Equality 7–2521 to flee the City for the Uncharted Forest. The Golden One joins him there. Far from dying in the forest, as he had expected, they find pastoral relief from the oppression of their urban lives. Better yet, they come upon an abandoned house in mountains beyond the forest and they find happiness. They find it because of books left in that house, relics from the ancient times before the "Great Rebirth." Equality 7–2521 begins to read and he comes upon a word, a concept, a philosophy, that gives expression to all the confused mental yearning he has been going through, the word "I."

That discovery—it is revealed on page 108 in the edition I am sending you, fifteen pages before the end of the book, the very beginning of Chapter 11, starting with the words "I am. I think. I will"—is where *Anthem* goes to pot. The point of Ayn Rand's fiction, as I'm sure you will have seized, is a critique of collectivism, typified at its most terrible by the horrors of communism under Stalin in Russia, the country of Rand's birth (she became an American citizen in 1931). And there, the reader, certainly this reader, is with her. Bloodthirsty dictatorships are repulsive to every sane human being. But Ayn Rand makes two mistakes in her allegory of life in the Soviet Union. First, she sees only the worst in collectivism, throwing out wholesale the good with the bad. To her, the Gulag and socialized health care, for example, were instances of one and the same evil. Second, in rejecting Stalin and his damnable system, she goes to an absurd opposite libertarian extreme. Rand posited that humanity would be happiest if we lived as autarkic individuals, beholden to no one, unbounded, unfettered, free, free, free. The virtue of self-ishness, that's what Ayn Rand is all about. It's even the title of one of her books. No wonder Rand appeals mostly to two disparate groups of readers: adolescents in the throes of carving out their individuality, and right-wing American capitalists bent on making and keeping too much money.

Back to the novel. Equality 7–2521, on page 108, has bust free thanks to the word "I." What follows is an orgy of I-ism, of me, me, me, mine, mine, mine:

My hands . . . My spirit . . . My sky . . . My forest . . . This earth of mine . . .

You know you're in trouble when someone claims to own the sky. As much as Equality 7–2521 was appealing when he was oppressed, once he is free he becomes annoying, pretentious, repelling. While his strange speech in the City—we this, we that—came off as noble and incantatory, his free speech in the mountains is dull and pompous. The struggling hero whom we cheered on has become just another self-righteous, domineering male who thinks he knows everything. We sympathized with his plight, but now we shudder at his solution:

> I wished to know the meaning of things. I am the meaning. . . . Whatever road I take, the guiding star is within me; the guiding star and the loadstone which point the way. They point in but one direction. They point to me. . . . I owe nothing to my brothers, nor do I gather debts from them. I ask none to live for me, nor do I live for any others. . . . And now I see the face of god, and I raise this god over the earth, this god whom men have sought since men came into being, this god who will grant them joy and peace and pride.
>
> This god, this one word:
> "I."

You are a religious man, Mr. Harper. You will know that the essence of every religion, of every god, is precisely the opposite of what Ayn Rand is speechifying about: God is about the abandonment of the self, not its exaltation. But that is an aside, a minor point. The main problem with Rand's libertarianism, this über-Nietzschean cult of the heroic individual standing on a mountaintop, is that it makes not only society unworkable, but even simple relations. An example jumps out in Rand's own novel. Equality 7–2521, now drunk with his own uniqueness, has naturally tired of his name. He says to the Golden One:

> "I have read of a man who lived many thousands of years ago, and of all the names in these books, his is the one I wish to

bear. He took the light of the gods and he brought it to men, and he taught men to be gods. And he suffered for his deed as all bearers of light must suffer. His name was Prometheus."

Prometheus, the nice guy formerly known as Equality 7–2521, goes on:

"And I have read of a goddess who was the mother of the earth and of all the gods. Her name was Gaea. Let this be your name, my Golden One, for you are to be the mother of a new kind of gods."

What if the Golden One rather fancied herself as a Lynette or a Bobbie-Jean? Who is this Prometheus to tell her what her name should be? And what if she doesn't want to be the mother of a screaming gaggle of kids? What if one child will do, and a girl if possible, thank you very much?

But, headstrong as Liberty 5–3000 seemed to be in the City, as Gaea she is passive and submissive, doing as she is told, because nothing and no one should get in the way of Ayn Rand's romantic Superman, especially not his woman.

And what does Prometheus intend to do with his new-found freedom? He'll raid the City for "chosen friends" and conquer the world!

Here, on this mountain, I and my sons and my chosen friends shall build our new land and our fort. . . . And the day will come when I shall break all the chains of the earth, and raze the cities of the enslaved, and my home will become the capital of a world where each man will be free to exist for his own sake.

Well, what does he want, does he want to be free and unfettered or a bustling capital?

The novel ends, with trumpeting triumphalism, as follows:

And here, over the portals of my fort, I shall cut in the stone the word which is to be my beacon and my banner. . . . The word which can never die on this earth, for it is the heart of it and the meaning and the glory.

The sacred word:

EGO

Just the kind of neighbour we all want, the loud, overbearing oaf with the poor, mousy wife who has the word EGO carved over his door.

That is the paradox and failure of Ayn Rand's vision. Her response to the excesses of collectivism is an excessive and simplistic egoism. The more realistic challenge in life is to be oneself amidst others, to heed one's own needs and at the same time satisfy the demands of one's community. It is not easy. Life, and not only politics, is the art of compromise.

That push and pull between the needs of the individual and the needs of the collectivity is at the heart of an election. If every voter votes strictly according to self-interest, then the collectivity, the nation, will be riven by discord and divisions and will risk falling apart. But if the collective We is overfed, then its constituent elements are starved. Every politician, and you first and foremost, Mr. Harper, must balance personal interest with what is good for the nation. If you divide and conquer too much, if you heed too little, then the country will suffer, as will your reputation in history. Enlightened statesmanship is required by all, both voters and politicians. But that's a risky sell, isn't it, trying to peddle a better future to voters worried about their immediate present? The best is demanded of all of us. I can only hope we will get it.

Since we have an election on our hands, let me make my personal appeal. Don't worry, it won't cost anything. I won't bay about arts funding or the centrality of art in our lives or even, more cravenly, about the profitability of the arts industry in Canada (what was the sum I read recently, $47 billion in 2007 alone, more than the profits from the mining industry? Not that I buy that argument. The essential is inherently profitable, existentially. The individual who is artless is poor, no matter how much money he or she may have). No, I only want to give you for free an idea, the following:

What if a reading list were established for prospective prime ministers of Canada, to ensure that they have sufficient imaginative depth to be at the helm of our country? After all, we expect a prime minister to have a fair knowledge of the history and geography of Canada, to know something about economics and public administration, about current events and foreign affairs, the financial assets of a prime minister are accountable to us, so why shouldn't his or her imaginative assets also be accountable?

Because that has been the whole point of our literary duet, hasn't it? If you haven't read, now or earlier, any of the books I have suggested, or books like them, if you haven't read *The Death of Ivan Ilych* or any other Russian novel, if you haven't read *Miss Julia* or any other Scandinavian play, if you haven't read *Metamorphosis* or any other German-language novel, if you haven't read *Waiting for Godot* or *To the Lighthouse* or any other experimental play or novel, if you haven't read *Artists and Models* or any other erotica, if you haven't read the *Meditations* of Marcus Aurelius or *The Educated Imagination* or any other philosophical inquiry, if you haven't read *Under Milk Wood* or any other poetic prose, if you haven't read *Their Eyes Were Watching God* or *Drown* or any other American novel, if you haven't read *The Cellist of Sarajevo* or *The Island Means Minago* or *The Dragonfly of Chicoutimi* or any other Canadian novel, poem or play—then what is your mind made of? What materials went into the building of the dreams you have for our country? What is the colour, the pattern, the rhyme and reason of your imagination? These are not questions one is usually entitled to ask, but once someone has power over me, then, yes, I do have the right to probe your imagination, because your dreams may become my nightmares.

This Prime Minister's Reading List could be administered by the Speaker of the House of Commons, an impartial figure, perhaps benefiting from recommendations not only from Members of Parliament but from all Canadian citizens. It would be a hard list to set up, that's for sure. How to represent concisely all that the written word has done, here and abroad, in English and French and other languages? The Prime Minister's Reading List couldn't be too long; we wouldn't want you sitting around reading novels your whole mandate. And it would be subject to regular updates, of course, to reflect changing times and tastes. How to implement the list would be another challenge. Would it be a yearly reading list, or just one at the beginning of each term? And how to check that you've actually read the books and not had an assistant summarize them for you? Would you have to write an exam, pen an essay, face a committee, answer questions during a Question Period exclusively devoted to the matter?

"I have no time for this nonsense," you might feel like shouting. But as I said to you in my very first letter, there is a space next to every bed where a book can be lying in wait. And I ask you again: what is your mind made of?

So, would that be an idea, to set up a Prime Minister's Reading List? What is your position on this vital issue?

I await your answer.

Yours truly,
Yann Martel

AYN RAND (1905–1982) was a Russian-born American novelist, playwright and screenwriter. Her most famous novels are *The Fountainhead* and *Atlas Shrugged*. Within two weeks of arriving in Hollywood to launch her screenwriting career, Rand was hired as an extra and then a script reader for director Cecil B. DeMille, and met her future husband, the actor Frank O'Connor, to whom she would stay married for fifty years. She was also politically active. Her works prominently reflect a belief in individualism, capitalism and basic civil liberties, as well as her staunch opposition to collectivist political structures.

BOOK 39:

MISTER PIP
BY LLOYD JONES

September 29, 2008

To Stephen Harper,
Prime Minister of Canada,
Words take you places.
Best wishes,
Lloyd Jones
September 21
Brisbane, Australia

Sent to you by
a Canadian writer,
With best wishes,
Yann Martel

Dear Mr. Harper,

Campaigning must be gruelling, especially when you are head
of a party. You work and travel constantly, you speak to people
morning, noon and evening, you must always be on your guard,
and all of it is very personal. The worst, I imagine, is the complete loss of privacy. Any time you might want for yourself
must be sacrificed to the demands of public life.

An excellent way to climb back into yourself is to read a
book. I suspect that reading is such a satisfying experience
because it is at one and the same time a dialogue —between
your mind and an external source of words—and an entirely

private experience. When you are reading, your guard needn't be up. You can be entirely yourself. Even better: you are totally free. You can read slowly or quickly, you can reread a section or skip it, why, you can even throw the book down and pick up another—it's all up to you. The freedom goes even further: what you experience while reading is also entirely your own affair. You can let yourself be engrossed by what you are reading, or you can let your mind wander. You can be a receptive reader, or, if you want, an obstreperous one. The freedom, I repeat, is total. When else do we have such a feeling? Is it not the case that in most every other activity, personal or social, we are hemmed in by rules and regulations, by the intrusions and expectations of others?

Reading is one of the best ways to bring on that essential condition for the thinking person, one that I mentioned at the start of our exchange: stillness. All the noise and confusion of the outer world falls away, is blocked off, when one is reading and one becomes still. Which is to say, one enters into dialogue with oneself, asking questions, coming up with replies, feeling and assessing facts and emotions. That is why reading is so fortifying, because in setting us free it allows us to re-centre ourselves, it allows the mind's eye to look at itself in a mirror and take stock.

What better book to bear witness to this process than *Mister Pip*, by the New Zealand writer Lloyd Jones. Your mind will travel far with this novel. For starters, the story takes place on the Pacific island of Bougainville, part of Papua New Guinea. But it also takes place, in a way, in Victorian England. There's a quieting appeal right there, isn't there? Who hasn't dreamed of spending time on an island in the Pacific, surrounded by blue sea and tropical greenery? And who doesn't like visiting Europe?

Mister Pip is a novel about a novel. The name Pip might be familiar to you. It's the name of the main character in *Great*

Expectations, the novel by Charles Dickens. This is no coincidence. *Great Expectations* is a character in Jones's novel, one might say. It is certainly the catalyst to much of the action in it.

On Bougainville, a white man, Mr. Watts, lives in a village of black people who accept him because he is married to one of them, Grace, who has gone crazy, but of whom Mr. Watts takes loving care. A rebellion shuts down the local mine and results in the evacuation of all the whites who work there. Only Mr. Watts stays on. He and the villagers are cut off from the rest of the world by a blockade. Mr. Watts agrees to become the schoolteacher. But he knows precious little. Chemistry is just a word, and history little more than a list of famous names. One thing he does know and love, though, is Charles Dickens's great novel. He reads it to the children. They are enchanted. They fall in love with Pip. But their parents and even more so the government troops that routinely descend upon the village to terrorize its inhabitants are suspicious of this Mr. Pip. Where is he hiding? Produce him or else, they warn.

Lloyd Jones's novel is about how literature can create a new world. It is about how the world can be read like a novel, and a novel like the world. If that sounds twee, be warned that there is also shocking meanness and violence in *Mister Pip*.

Does the violence make the fable-like element pale in comparison? Does "reality" come through and displace the "fiction"? Not at all. You will see. The novel argues that the imagination, whether religious or artistic, is what makes the world bearable.

I am also sending you *Great Expectations*. It's not necessary to have read it to understand *Mister Pip*, but it is such an enjoyable masterpiece that I thought I'd throw it in as an extra pleasure.

I had the pleasure of meeting Lloyd Jones just last week at the Brisbane Literary Festival. He kindly agreed to autograph your copy of his novel.

May you enjoy both *Mister Pip* and *Great Expectations*. Better still: may they bring you stillness.

Yours truly,
Yann Martel

LLOYD JONES (b. 1955) is a New Zealander who has been publishing books since 1985. His experiences as a journalist and travel writer have imbued his novels with a strong sense of realism. His most recent novel, *Mister Pip*, won the Commonwealth Writers' Prize for Best Book in 2007. Other well-known works by Jones include *Biografi*, *Here at the End of the World We Learn to Dance*, *Paint Your Wife* and *The Book of Fame*. Several of his novels have been successfully adapted for the stage. Jones has also written books for children, and edited an anthology of sports writing.

BOOK 40:

A CLOCKWORK ORANGE
BY ANTHONY BURGESS
October 13, 2008

To Stephen Harper,
Prime Minister of Canada,
"What's it going to be then, eh?"
From a Canadian writer,
With best wishes,
Yann Martel

Dear Mr. Harper,

Meet Alex. He's the nightmare of both citizens and govern-ments, the first because they are afraid of him and the second because they don't know what to do with him. Alex, you see, is a-lex, outside the law, from the Latin. He and his friends mug people, loot stores and invade homes, liberally dishing out extreme violence and routinely indulging in gang rape. And to think he's only fifteen. When he's caught, he rots in a juvenile home for a while until he's let out—and then what? Well, why stop when you're having such a good time? He gets back to the fun of "ultra-violence." Welcome to the world of *A Clockwork Orange*, a brilliant short novel by the English writer Anthony Burgess (1917–1993), published in 1962.

"What's it going to be then, eh?" That slightly bullying question appears at the beginning of each of the novel's three sections. It is asked not only of one or another of the story's characters; it is asked of us. What's it going to be with Alex then, eh? What are we to do with him? *A Clockwork Orange*, despite the great violence in it, in fact, because of it, is a morally preoccupied work.

When Alex is caught after his latest bout of thuggish mayhem, the authorities try a different approach. They try conditioning. If a dog can be conditioned to salivate upon hearing a bell tinkling, why can't a boy be conditioned to reject violence? Alex is subjected to the Ludovico Method, in which he is given injections that make him feel deathly nauseous at the same time as he is being shown extremely violent films. He thus learns to become sickened by violence, literally. Unfortunately, because of the soundtrack of some of the reels he is forced to watch, Alex is also accidentally conditioned to feel revulsion upon hearing classical music. This aggrieves him greatly because our Alex, despite his brutal tendencies, is a music lover (sounds historically familiar, doesn't it?).

A minor matter, the Minister of the Interior feels. Our main problem is solved. Now, when our boy sees violence, when he merely entertains thoughts of violence, he falls over helplessly, clutching his stomach and retching. If he also keels over when he hears Beethoven, so what? That's just a little collateral damage.

But if goodness is elected not by free choice but as a self-defence mechanism against nausea, is it morally valid goodness? "Is a man who chooses the bad perhaps in some way better than a man who has the good imposed on him?" the prison chaplain asks at one point. Burgess's answer is unequivocal: he chooses goodness as a free choice. And the reason why this answer is correct is given in the novel's key words, coming from Alex, dropped nearly casually in the middle of a long sentence:

I was still puzzling out all this and wondering whether I should refuse to be strapped down to this chair tomorrow and start a real bit of dratsing with them all, because I had my rights, when another chelloveck came in to see me.

I had my rights. Indeed, Alex does have his rights, as we all do. Ignore those rights, and the essential is lost: "When a man cannot choose he ceases to be a man."

A group of intellectuals opposed to the government decides to make use of Alex. They lock him in a room next to which they play loud classical music. Alex takes the only exit they've left him, an open window. The room is in an apartment block, several floors up. Alex plummets to the sidewalk—and straight into the hearts of citizens indignant at the brainwashing he's been subjected to. An election is in the offing and the Government is nervous about its prospects. At the hospital where he is recovering from his serious injuries, Alex's conditioning is hastily reversed. Alex is very happy about this. In the last scene of the penultimate chapter of the novel, we find him lying back, listening with renewed delight to Beethoven's Ninth. "I was cured all right," he says.

That line, if it were the last line of the book, would be fiercely ironic. Good that the boy's ears have been restored, but so has his moral compass. Its fine, trembling needle can now, once again, point as freely towards good as it can towards bad. Does that mean we citizens should start to tremble too? No worries, says Burgess in the last chapter of the book, Chapter 21. Alex's ordeal has eaten up over two years of his life. He's now eighteen and has matured. The joys of rape and pillage just aren't what they used to be. Alex is now more in the mood to find himself a nice girl, settle down and start a family. The novel ends with a softer, mellower Alex pining for a mate.

A weak ending, I'd say. Burgess successfully makes the case for the imperative of freedom at the level of the individual when making moral choices. But what are we to do at the level of a society? What choices does a society have in the face of citizens who are a-lex? Each of us must be free to be fully ourselves, granted, but how should a society balance the freedom of the individual with the safety of the group? Burgess avoids this difficult question by having Alex suddenly discover the peaceable joys of family life. To a social problem Burgess gives only an unpredictable individual solution. What if Alex had decided to continue with his life of violence?

The American edition of *A Clockwork Orange* was originally published without the last chapter. This editorial cut, which Burgess opposed, does throw the construction of the novel off balance. Nonetheless, Alex's uncertain claim at the end of Chapter 20 that he is cured is, I think, an ending more consistent with the material that has come earlier. It is this truncated version that Stanley Kubrick used to make his celebrated movie. He too clearly preferred a conclusion that wasn't so facilely optimistic.

What I've said so far may make you think that *A Clockwork Orange* is a blandly pious work, reducible to a few moral bromides. That's not the case. Just as a hockey game can't be reduced to its score, so a work of art can't be reduced to a summary. What makes *A Clockwork Orange* incompressible is its language. Alex and his friends speak a most peculiar English. Here's a sample, taken at random:

> I did not quite kopat what he was getting at govoreeting about calculations, seeing that getting better from feeling bolnoy is like your own affair and nothing to do with calculations. He sat down, all nice and droogy, on the bed's edge . . .

A mixture of English slang and words derived from Russian, delivered in cadences that sometimes sound biblical, at other times Elizabethan, it is this language, Nadsat, that makes *A Clockwork Orange* an enduring work of literature. It is the juice in the orange. The context makes the meaning of most Nadsat words clear, and the occasional befuddlement is not unpleasant.

Canadians go to the polls tomorrow. I offer you *A Clockwork Orange* the day before for a good reason. There's an element in the novel that is eerily familiar. The government under which Alex lives is democratically elected, yet it has recourse to policies that undermine the foundations of democracy. We have seen these kinds of policies for eight years now in the United States, a country morally bankrupted by its current president. You claim to have a solution for what to do with Alex. The experts disagree with you, as do the courts and the people; certainly the people in Quebec are resisting your ideas. But you think you know better.

Are you sure, Mr. Harper, that what you have up your sleeve aren't so many Ludovico Methods?

Yours truly,
Yann Martel

P.S. Have you seen Kubrick's classic adaptation? It's one of those rare cases where the movie is as good as the book. I'll try to find a DVD copy. When I do, I'll send it along.

ANTHONY BURGESS (1917–1993) was a prolific English novelist, poet, playwright, biographer, literary critic, linguist, translator and composer. His publications run the gamut from linguistically sophisticated literary novels like his Malayan trilogy, *The Long Day Wanes*, to criticism of works by James Joyce, to symphonies, to dystopian satires.

BOOK 41:

GILGAMESH
IN AN ENGLISH VERSION BY STEPHEN MITCHELL
October 27, 2008

To Stephen Harper,
Prime Minister of Canada,
The oldest story in the world, to celebrate your second minority,
From a Canadian writer,
With best wishes,
Yann Martel

Dear Mr. Harper,

Congratulations on your electoral win. You must be pleased
with your increased minority. What your continued tenure as
prime minister means, among other things, is that our book
club has survived. We can now really settle into this business
of discussing books. Since we have more time, why don't we
go back in time. Why don't we start where book talk probably started, along the banks of the river Euphrates. What has
become known as the standard version of the epic of *Gilgamesh*
was set down between the years 1300 and 1000 BCE in cuneiform
on twelve clay tablets in Babylonian, a dialect of the Akkadian
language. But earlier written fragments in Sumerian about the
heartbroken king of Uruk date from around 2000 BCE, and the
historical Gilgamesh, well, he died in about 2750 BCE, just a
couple of centuries shy of five thousand years ago.

Gilgamesh predates Homer and predates the Bible. It is the
cultural soil out of which these later texts emerged, which is

why some elements in the epic will sound familiar to you. Before the biblical Flood there was the Great Flood in *Gilgamesh*. Before Noah's Ark, there was the ship Utnapishtim built, crowded with animals. In *Gilgamesh*, there is an odyssey before the *Odyssey* and there is one who overcame mortality before Jesus of Nazareth overcame it. The theme of a terrible flood also finds itself echoed in the Hindu story of Matsya the fish, Vishnu's first avatar, and the theme of fear will perhaps remind you of the *Bhagavad Gita*, which I sent you last year. Remember Arjuna's fear before the battle? It is not dissimilar to Gilgamesh's fear before death. The inexorableness of fate might remind you of classical Greek thinking, just as the petulance of the Sumerian gods is much like that of the Greek gods. *Gilgamesh* is the mother of all stories. We, as literary animals, start with *Gilgamesh*.

That might make you think that reading the epic will be like staring into a display window of crude stone sculptures in an archaeology museum. Not so, I promise you, certainly not in the version of *Gilgamesh* that I'm sending you, by the American translator Stephen Mitchell. He's done away with scholarly encrustations and dull fidelity to disjointed fragments (though, if you care, there is a good introduction and lots of notes). Mitchell has sought to be faithful to the spirit of the original, more mindful of the needs of the English reader than the sensibility of the archaeologist.

The result is exhilarating. The prose is simple, vigorous and stately, the action thrillingly dramatic. I encourage you to read the epic aloud. It's an easy oral read, you will see. Your tongue will not trip, your mind will not stumble. Like the beating of a drum, the cadence of the beats and the repetition of some passages will hold you in thrall.

The mind can be immortal, living forever through ideas. An idea can leap from mind to mind, going down through the generations, forever keeping ahead of death. The mind of Plato, for example, is still with us, long dead though he is. But the heart? The heart is inescapably mortal. Every heart dies. Of Plato's heart, its share of things felt, we know nothing. *Gilgamesh* is the story of one man's heart and its breaking in the face of death. The emotional immediacy is palpable. Gilgamesh, king of great-walled Uruk, won't seem alien to you because that aggrieved voice pleading directly in your ear isn't from over four thousand years ago—it's the pulsing of your own perishable heart. Our only hope is that we might live as authentically as Gilgamesh and find a friend as loving and loyal as Enkidu.

There are some lovely lines. Keep an eye out for "A gust of wind passed," and "A gentle rain fell onto the mountains." They glow within their context. And there is a snake that does Gilgamesh a bad turn. That too will be biblically familiar to you. This snake, though, does not proffer; it takes. But the result is the same: unhappy Gilgamesh must accept his fate as a mortal.

Yours truly,
Yann Martel

STEPHEN MITCHELL (b. 1943) is a polyglot American translator known for his poetic, rather than literal, translations. He has translated works originally written in German, Hebrew, Greek, Latin, French, Spanish, Italian, Chinese, Sanskrit and Danish. His other translations include the Hindu text the *Bhagavad Gita* and the Buddhist *Tao Te Ching*. He has also published a collection of poetry, two novels, three works of non-fiction and several children's books.

BOOK 42:

GILGAMESH
IN AN ENGLISH VERSION BY DERREK HINES
November 10, 2008

To Stephen Harper,
Prime Minister of Canada,
Again, but made modern,
From a Canadian writer,
With best wishes,
Yann Martel

Dear Mr. Harper,

Gilgamesh again. But a very different *Gilgamesh*. The version I sent you two weeks ago took liberties, but the better to serve the original Sumerian classic. One senses that Stephen Mitchell took the broken clay tablets, fitted the pieces together and then adeptly filled in where the cracks made it hard to read. Our guide on that breathless trip across five thousand years to the banks of the Euphrates remained egoless and anonymous. Of Mitchell, we sensed nothing; in fact, we didn't even think to enquire about him.

With *Gilgamesh* as interpreted by the Canadian poet Derrek Hines, the time travel is in the opposite direction. It's Mesopotamia that's yanked into the present day, every speck of archaeological dust blown off. This version is all about liberties, and the clay tablets have been thrown out. Take the opening lines. In the Mitchell version, they go:

Surpassing all kings, powerful and tall
beyond all others, violent, splendid,
a wild bull of a man, unvanquished leader,
hero in the front lines, beloved by his soldiers—
fortress they called him, *protector of the people,*
raging flood that destroys all defences—
two-thirds divine and one-third human . . .

With Hines, we get:

Here is Gilgamesh, king of Uruk:
two-thirds divine, a mummy's boy,
zeppelin ego, cock like a trip-hammer,
and solid chrome, no-prisoners arrogance.

Get the picture? You don't want to read the versions in the wrong order. With the Mitchell, the scope, the vastness, the timelessness of an ancient epic is felt. With the Hines, you might wonder where the epic went. What's all this *riffing*? Well, that's it, the riffing is the point. Remember Ishtar's anger when Gilgamesh rejects her, how she goes to her father, the god Anu, wanting to borrow the Bull of Heaven so that she can unleash it on Uruk? This is what Hines makes of it, Ishtar speaking:

"I'll have the Bull of Heaven or I'll unzip Hell,
and free the un-dead to suck frost into the living."
Then, on a pulse, an actor's mood change—
she, pouting: "Darling Anu,
you know how I'm insulted;
I want, *want* the Bull of Heaven
to revenge my honour."

> She lifts a perfect foot to stamp,
> and the tiles of Heaven's floor in rivalry
> shift like a Rubik's cube to receive it.

It's *Gilgamesh* meets Naomi Campbell. Besides the Rubik's cube, there are a great many other un-Mesopotamian references in the text: atomic blasts, Brueghel, buildings in New York, CAT scans, event horizons, express trains, Marlene Dietrich, oxygen masks, paparazzi, Swiss bank accounts, X-rays, the Wizard of Oz, and so on. This joy in the anachronistic bears witness to the very different approach that Hines takes.

All things are met and understood through one mind, the one we have. Timelessness, transcendence, the evanescence of the ego—these are true, but they are not what we experience. They were neither felt by Gilgamesh, nor are they felt by us. We are not all one. We are just one, each on our own. You, me, him, her, six billion times over. Each one of us has a blip note of mortality. It's only when the blips are put together that we seem to hear a symphony throbbing down through time. Mitchell's version of *Gilgamesh* plays on that symphony. He makes the epic new, but it works because we know it's old. Hines wants none of this hand-me-down worth. He's a modern; this blip here and now will speak freshly for that old, fifty-century-old blip. With Hines you get the singularity of the living poet expressing himself in his own right, drawing attention to himself, saying "This is me, this is our language, this is our condition—whaddya think?"

I think it's very good. A harder read than the Mitchell, for sure. At times, the poetic pithiness requires work to unpack. Then in the next stanza, a startling image makes perfect sense. Which is why I would recommend that you read the Hines more than once. It's only sixty pages, and well spaced at that. The more familiar you are with it, the more it will make sense, and soon enough you will have furnished a beautiful room in your mind. It's a rich, exciting text, with some stabbingly brilliant lines. Take this, part of Gilgamesh's lament upon Enkidu's death:

> The complaisant dead inch away,
> dislocating the shared vanishing point
> of our perspective,
> and we struggle to repaint the picture.

A last example. Gilgamesh, after getting "snake-drunk" and losing the herb of eternal life, returns to Uruk to die. He has this to say:

> We are made and broken on a miracle
> we look on and cannot see—as though
> we had sold out instinct to thought
> blinding us to what the world is,
> the heart's gate to eternity.

That is a truth very old and, here, totally modern.

Yours truly,
Yann Martel

DERREK HINES is an award-winning Canadian poet best known for his reinterpretation of the epic *Gilgamesh*. By injecting modern images into his free verse retelling, Hines shrinks the gap of time between Sumerian origins and a contemporary audience, and recharges the tale's powerful effect. Hines has published two books of poetry. Raised in Southern Ontario, he now lives on the Lizard peninsula in Cornwall.

BOOK 43:

THE UNCOMMON READER
BY ALAN BENNETT

November 24, 2008

To Stephen Harper,
Prime Minister of Canada,
A short novel on a healthy addiction,
From a Canadian writer,
With best wishes,
Yann Martel

Dear Mr. Harper,

I can't think of a more delightful introduction to the republic of letters than Alan Bennett's short novel *The Uncommon Reader*. One day at the bottom of the Palace garden, parked next to the kitchen garbage bins, alerted by her corgis, the Queen discovers the City of Westminster's travelling library. She pops in to apologize for the barking dogs and, once there, impelled by a sense of duty rather than any real interest, she takes out a book. This simple act marks the beginning of Her Majesty's downfall, in a way. The irony in the story is as light as whipped cream, the humour as appealing as candy, the characterization as crisp as potato chips, but at the heart of it there's something highly nutritious to be digested: the effect that books can have on a life.

Upon finishing the book, you will think you know HM better, you will feel closer to her, you will like her. This is in part because of Bennett's skill in bringing his royal character to life. But it also has to do with the nature of books. In the republic of letters, all readers are equal. Unlike other retail outlets, bookstores don't really come in categories, be it luxury or low-end. A bookstore is a bookstore. Some specialize, but the restriction there has only to do with kinds of books—say modern languages or art—and not with classes of readers. Everyone is welcome in bookstores and all types rub shoulders in them, the wealthy and the poor, the highly educated and the self-taught, the old and the young, the adventurous and the conventional, and others still. You might even bump into the Queen.

Before I forget, one of our very own great Canadian writers, Alice Munro, makes a cameo appearance in *The Uncommon Reader*, on page 67.

Since I'm on the topic of bookstores, I thought I'd include a few snapshots of some that I've visited recently.

The Bookseller Crow on the Hill is in Crystal Palace, a

neighbourhood in the south of London where I've been staying recently. I'm standing next to John, the genial owner, and I'm holding in my hand the very book you now own, which I bought from John. The Crow is not a very big place in terms of square footage, but stand in front on any shelf—New Titles, Fiction, History, Philosophy, Poetry, Travel—and the mental space represented is as vast as the universe.

The next photo is of a small, venerable used bookstore on Milton Street in Montreal called The Word. It has served generations of students. I popped in to buy a novel by the English writer Ivy Compton-Burnett, whom Bennett mentions in his book and whom I'd never read. I found *A Family and a Fortune*, published in 1939. It cost me $3.95.

The last photo is of La Librairie du Square, a French bookstore also in Montreal. It was my father who taped the red poster you see on the glass door. It announces an event organized by PEN, Amnesty International and l'UNEQ to do with freedom of expression and imprisoned writers.

Independent bookstores are a vanishing breed, especially in North America. The ones who suffer the most from this disappearance are not necessarily readers, but neighbourhoods. After all, a large Chapters or Indigo or Barnes & Noble will hold more books than any reader could possibly read in a lifetime. But large chain stores tend to be fewer in number and are often accessible only by car. The Bookseller Crow, on the other hand, is in a row of small stores that includes a clothes store, a café, a pet store that specializes in fish, a shoe store, a real estate agent, a hairdresser, a newsagent, a bakery, a betting agency, a number of restaurants, and so on. The Word and La Librairie du Square are on streets along which thousands of people walk every day. Whenever an independent bookstore disappears, shareholders somewhere may be richer, but a neighbourhood is for sure poorer.

I'm sorry for writing such a busy letter, but there's one last matter I'd like to mention. A few weeks ago, on October 20 to be exact, I came upon an article in the *New York Times* on a man in Colombia who for the last decade has been travelling around his war-ravaged corner of the country with two donkeys—named Alfa and Beto—loaded with books. He stops in every remote pueblo to read to children and to lend books out. He started his Biblioburro, as he calls it, after seeing the positive effect that reading had on students growing up in a violent and uncertain environment. Ten years on, Luis Soriano remarks that his enterprise has become an obligation, and it is now considered an institution.

The City of Westminster's travelling library and the Biblioburro, the Bookseller Crow on the Hill and The Word—the rich life of the mind that these institutions offer makes joyful equals of us all, from monarchs to poor peasant children.

Yours truly,
Yann Martel

ALAN BENNETT (b. 1934) is an English author, actor, humorist and playwright. His first great success was co-authoring and starring in the comedy revue *Beyond the Fringe*. He then performed in innumerable stage, radio and television productions and wrote several short stories, novellas, non-fiction works and plays. Among his many acclaimed creations are the Academy Award–winning film adaptation *The Madness of King George*, and *The History Boys*, a play that won three Laurence Olivier Awards and was adapted for the screen.

BOOK 44:

THE GOOD EARTH
BY PEARL S. BUCK
December 8, 2008

To Stephen Harper,
Prime Minister of Canada,
A novel of fortunes made and lost,
From a Canadian writer,
With best wishes,
Yann Martel

Dear Mr. Harper,

One of the curious aspects of the life and work of Pearl Buck is the speed with which she rose to fame and then sank into comparative obscurity. Her first book was published in 1930. Eight years later, at the remarkably young age of forty-six, she was awarded the Nobel Prize in Literature, only the third American so rewarded, and this, principally on the basis of the three novels that form the trilogy *The House of Earth: The Good Earth* (1931), for which she won the Pulitzer Prize, *Sons* (1932) and *A House Divided* (1935). It is *The Good Earth* I am offering you this week.

Yet after this stellar start, despite continuing to produce quantities of books and fighting for many a good cause, Buck faded from the forefront of literature so that when she died in 1973 she was nearly a forgotten figure. The reasons for this are, I think, easy enough to discern. She wrote too many books—over eighty—and while a very able writer, she was no great experimenter. She didn't renew the novel or its language the way Faulkner and Hemingway did, fellow Americans who are still widely read and studied. Nor can her books—or at least the ones I'm familiar with—be stamped with the label "universal," which sometimes helps an author gain literary immortality. No, the books that made her name were remarkably local, even rooted. Pearl Buck was one of the first writers to bring to life for Western readers that country-civilization called China. It's a country she knew well for having spent a good part of her life there as the daughter of Christian missionaries and then as a missionary and teacher herself. Despite the hardships she endured there at times, China was a country she loved. She saw its people as just that, people, and she observed them with great sympathy and mixed with them and, eventually, wrote about them. She was the writer-as-bridge, and many people chose to cross the bridge she built.

You will see why when you read *The Good Earth*. From the first line—"It was Wang Lung's marriage day"—you slip into the skin of a Chinese peasant from pre-Communist times and you begin to live his life as he sees it and feels it. It's a harsh story, blighted by poverty and famine, and harsher still for the women in it, but it's also entirely engrossing. *The Good Earth* is the sort of novel you'll be itching to get back to whenever you have to put it down. After reading it, you'll feel that you know what it might mean to be Chinese at a certain time and in a certain part of China. Therein lies the passing nature of Buck's work. China has changed radically since *The Good Earth* was published. What was new and revelatory then is now hoary and out of date. The main appeal of Buck's work today is in the power of her stories rather than their currency.

Still, *The Good Earth* remains an excellent introduction to old China and a vivid parable on the fragility of fortune, how things gained can be lost, how what is built can easily be destroyed. This lesson will not be lost on you considering the political turmoil you are now going through. The fate of a politician is so terribly uncertain. Pearl Buck is a staple of every used bookstore. She is still widely read. Her name evokes fond memories. Whereas politicians, when they go, when they disappear from the stage, kicking and screaming sometimes, they really go, they vanish into oblivion so that quickly people scratch their heads, trying to remember when exactly they were in power and what they accomplished.

Yours truly,
Yann Martel

PEARL S. BUCK (1892–1973) was a Pulitzer Prize–winning American author and the first American woman to be awarded the Nobel Prize in Literature, in 1938. Born in the United States but raised in Zhenjiang, eastern China, Buck was an avid student of Chinese history and society, which contributed immensely to the vivid and detailed descriptions of Chinese life in her many novels. In addition to writing prolifically, Buck established Welcome House, the first international interracial adoption agency.

BOOK 45:

FICTIONS
BY JORGE LUIS BORGES

Translated from the Spanish by Andrew Hurley

December 22, 2008

To Stephen Harper,

Prime Minister of Canada,

A book you may or may not like,

From a Canadian writer,

With best wishes,

Yann Martel

Dear Mr. Harper,

I first read the short story collection *Fictions*, by the Argentinian writer Jorge Luis Borges (1899–1986), twenty years ago and I remember not liking it much. But Borges is a very famous writer from a continent with a rich literary tradition. No doubt my lack of appreciation indicated a lack in me, due to immaturity. Twenty years on, I would surely recognize its genius and I would join the legions of readers who hold Borges to be one of the great pens of the twentieth century.

Well, that change of opinion didn't take place. Upon rereading *Fictions* I was as unimpressed this time around as I remember being two decades ago.

These stories are intellectual games, literary forms of chess. They start simply enough, one pawn moving forward, so to speak, from fanciful premises—often about alternate worlds or fictitious books—that are then rigorously and organically developed by Borges till they reach a pitch of complexity that would please Bobby Fischer. Actually, the comparison to chess is not entirely right. Chess pieces, while moving around with great freedom, have fixed roles, established by a custom that is centuries old. Pawns move just so, as do rooks and knights and queens. With Borges, the chess pieces are played any which way, the rooks moving diagonally, the pawns laterally and so on. The result is stories that are surprising and inventive, but whose ideas can't be taken seriously because they aren't taken seriously by the author himself, who plays around with them *as if ideas didn't really matter*. And so the flashy but fraudulent erudition of *Fictions*. Let me give you one small example, taken at random. On page 68 of the story "The Library of Babel," which is about a universe shaped like an immense, infinite library, appears the following line concerning a particular book in that library:

> He showed his find to a traveling decipherer, who told him that the lines were written in Portuguese; others said it was Yiddish. Within the century experts had determined what the language actually was: a Samoyed-Lithuanian dialect of Guarani, with inflections from classical Arabic.

A Samoyed-Lithuanian dialect of Guarani, with inflections from classical Arabic? That's intellectually droll, in a nerdy way. There's a pleasure of the mind in seeing those languages unexpectedly juxtaposed. One mentally jumps around the map of the world. It's also, of course, linguistic nonsense. Samoyed and Lithuanian are from different language families—the first Uralic, the second Baltic—and so are unlikely ever to merge into a dialect, and even less so of Guarani, which is an indigenous language of South America. As for the inflections from classical Arabic, they involve yet another impossible leap over cultural and historical barriers. Do you see how this approach, if pursued relentlessly, makes a mockery of ideas? If ideas are mixed around like this for show and amusement, then they are ultimately reduced to show and amusement. And pursue this approach Borges does, line after line, page after page. His book is full of scholarly mumbo-jumbo that is ironic, magical, nonsensical. One of the games involved in *Fictions* is: do you get the references? If you do, you feel intelligent; if you don't, no worries, it's probably an invention, because much of the erudition in the book is invented. The only story that I found genuinely intellectually engaging, that is, making a serious, thought-provoking point, was "Three Versions of Judas," in which the character and theological implications of Judas are discussed. That story made me pause and think. Beyond the flash, there I found depth.

Borges is often described as a writer's writer. What this is supposed to mean is that writers will find in him all the finest qualities of the craft. I'm not sure I agree. By my reckoning, a great book increases one's involvement with the world. One seemingly turns away from the world when one reads a book, but only to see the world all the better once one has finished the book. Books, then, increase one's visual acuity of the world. With Borges, the more I read, the more the world was increasingly small and distant.

There's one characteristic that I noticed this time around that I hadn't the first time, and that is the extraordinary number of male names dropped into the narratives, most of them writers. The fictional world of Borges is nearly exclusively male unisexual. Women barely exist. The only female writers mentioned in *Fictions* are Dorothy Sayers, Agatha Christie and Gertrude Stein, the last two mentioned in "A Survey of the Works of

Herbert Quain" to make a negative point. In "Pierre Menard, Author of the *Quixote*," there is a Baroness de Bacourt and a Mme Henri Bachelier (note how Mme Bachelier's name is entirely concealed by her husband's). There may be a few others that I missed. Otherwise, the reader gets male friends and male writers and male characters into the multiple dozens. This is not merely a statistical feminist point. It hints rather at Borges's relationship to the world. The absence of women in his stories is matched by the absence of any intimate relations in them. Only in the last story, "The South," is there some warmth, some genuine pain to be felt between the characters. There is a failure in Borges to engage with the complexities of life, the complexities of conjugal or parental life, or, indeed, of any other emotional engagement. We have here a solitary male living entirely in his head, someone who refused to join the fray but instead hid in his books and spun one fantasy after another. And so my same, puzzled conclusion this time round after reading Borges: this is juvenile stuff.

Now why am I sending you a book that I don't like? For a good reason: because one should read widely, including books that one does not like. By so doing one avoids the possible pitfall of autodidacts, who risk shaping their reading to suit their limitations, thereby increasing those limitations. The advantage of structured learning, at the various schools available at all ages of one's life, is that one must measure one's intellect against systems of ideas that have been developed over centuries. One's mind is thus confronted with unsuspected new ideas.

Which is to say that one learns, one is shaped, as much by the books that one has liked as by those that one has disliked.

And there is also, of course, the possibility that you may love Borges. You may find his stories rich, deep, original and entertaining. You may think that I should try him again in another twenty years. Maybe then I'll be ready for Borges.

In the meantime, I wish you and your family a merry Christmas.

Yours truly,
Yann Martel

JORGE LUIS BORGES (1899–1986) was an Argentinian poet, short story writer, anthologist, critic, essayist and librarian. In his writings, he often explored the ideas of reality, philosophy, identity and time, frequently using the images of labyrinths and mirrors. Borges shared the 1961 Prix Formentor with Samuel Beckett, gaining international fame. In addition to writing and giving speaking engagements in the United States, Borges was the director of the National Library in Argentina, ironically gaining this position as he was losing his eyesight.

BOOK 46

BLACKBIRD SINGING:
POEMS AND LYRICS 1965–1999
BY PAUL McCARTNEY

January 5, 2009

To Stephen Harper,
Prime Minister of Canada,
Hey Jude,
From a Canadian writer,
With best wishes,
Yann Martel

Dear Mr. Harper,

Christmas crept up on me unnoticed this winter. Suddenly it was December 25 and I realized that I had committed that common, life-eating error: I had stopped paying heed to the flow of time. This lapse was reflected in the last book I sent you. Though original and imaginative, Borges's *Fictions* does not obviously fit with the original and imaginative books I sent you last Christmas (this is our *second* Christmas together, speaking of the flow of time). Those, if you remember, were three children's books: *The Brothers Lionheart*, *Imagine a Day*, and *The Mysteries of Harris Burdick*. They were suitably festive. Did you and your family enjoy them? Did they make you smile and laugh? This week I am sending you a book that I hope will genuinely please you, that you will unwrap, so to speak, and react to with surprise and delight. A real Christmas book, in other words.

I gather you are a Beatles fan. Here then is a selection of poems and lyrics by Paul McCartney. The songs he penned as a Beatle jumped out at me. I found it impossible to read "The Fool on the Hill" or "Eleanor Rigby" or "Lady Madonna" or "Maxwell's Silver Hammer" or "Lovely Rita" or "Rocky Raccoon" or "When I'm Sixty-Four," among others, in the hushed, even voice of normal prose. Instead, I sang along in my head, pausing at the right moments for the band to play its part. I'm not very familiar with McCartney's later career with Wings or as a solo artist, so those songs lay more quietly on the page for me, as did the poems. I could generally tell the lyrics from the poems because the former had more repetitions and something seemed lacking in them to give them independent literary life. It was in looking in the index that I would see that they were, most often, the words from a Wings song.

A song's lyrics, I realized, are inseparable from its melody. The melody supplies the *lift*, suspending one's disbelief and cynicism or giving one permission to entertain the forbidden, while the lyrics supply the *in*, inviting one to compare one's experience of life with what is being said in the song, or, even better, inviting one to sing along. The possibility of listening intelligibly and of singing along are essential to a song's appeal, because both involve the direct, personal participation of the listener. This participation, the extent to which one can mesh one's life and dreams with a song, explains why something so short—most of the Beatles' early songs are less than two minutes long—can go so deep so quickly. That's the beguiling illusion of a great song: it speaks to each of us individually, and with a magnetic voice, and so we listen intently, instantly drawn into an inner dream world. Who hasn't been moved to the core by a song, eyes closed and body shuddering with emotion? In that state, we address feelings we might be too shy to deal with in plain speech—raw, hungering lust, for example—or ones that cut deep but are so mundane we are embarrassed to talk about them: loneliness, yearning, heartbreak.

A good song is a hard trick to pull off. Classical musicians scoff at the crudeness of pop melodies, while more literary poets roll their eyes at the banality of pop lyrics, but there is a measure of envy in this resentment. What violinist or poet would not want a stadium full of rapt listeners? At any rate, Paul McCartney, with appealing lyrics and mesmerizing melodies, within the amazing creative synergy that was the Beatles, magisterially assisted by producer George Martin, pulled off that trick so well that every generation since the mid-sixties has fallen in love with his songs. But you already know that.

Yours truly,
Yann Martel

PAUL MCCARTNEY (b. 1942) has been a musical icon for nearly fifty years, penning songs, movie soundtracks and orchestral arrangements. He remains most famous as a member of the Beatles, for whom, with John Lennon, he wrote some of his best songs. His success continued after the breakup of the band in 1970. Performing with Wings, and as a solo artist, McCartney has maintained his status as one of the most prolific and talented musicians of all time. He is also known for his animal rights activism.

BOOK 47

THE LESSER EVIL:
POLITICAL ETHICS IN AN AGE OF TERROR
BY MICHAEL IGNATIEFF

January 19, 2009

To Stephen Harper,
Prime Minister of Canada,
A book for a leader by a leader,
From a Canadian writer,
With best wishes,
Yann Martel

Dear Mr. Harper,

Okay, back to work, for you and for me. I'm rewriting my next book, for the third and last time I hope, and a new session of Parliament is opening soon. We both face a busy winter.

I believe you said in an interview not long ago that you hadn't read much of Michael Ignatieff's work. It's obvious that you should, isn't it? After all, you will be facing him every day in the House of Commons this year—he may even take your job—so it would be to your advantage to get to know his mind. The man has an impressive c.v., I must say. Degrees from the University of Toronto, Oxford, Harvard; teaching positions at Cambridge, Hautes Études in Paris, Harvard; a career in broadcasting and journalism; sixteen books to his credit (including three novels)—I can't think of an aspiring Canadian prime minister with a resumé to match. There have been prime ministers who were well educated and prime ministers who have written books, but none to this extent. Does that mean he would make a peerless prime minister? Of course not. Leadership can't be reduced to academic credentials or books on a shelf. Personality, vision, instinct, people skills, practical knowledge, toughness, resilience, rhetorical flair, charisma, luck—there is much that goes into the making of a political leader besides grey matter.

Having said that, a formidable intellect can only help, especially if it has been tested in practical ways, as Mr. Ignatieff's has. There's been little of the proverbial ivory tower in the years before he was elected to Parliament. His concern for human rights and democracy are real, not theoretical. He has travelled to many troubled spots on this planet to try to answer that essential question: how best can a society govern itself? Should Mr. Ignatieff ever move into 24 Sussex Drive, the gain for Canadians will no doubt be public policy goals that are sound and enlightened. Will he be able to bring these goals about? Will he know when to listen, when to compromise, when to act decisively? Many a politician has come to power with set ideas on how to fix things, only to find reality either more complex or more resistant than they had anticipated. We'll find out in the coming months how Michael Ignatieff fares.

In the meantime, to help you not only in dealing with the new Leader of Her Majesty's Loyal Opposition but also as an aid in setting policy, I am sending you *The Lesser Evil: Political Ethics in an Age of Terror*, a more recent book by your fellow parliamentarian, published in 2004. The cover seems uninspiring. It was chosen for a good reason: it's a photograph of a staircase at Auschwitz. Up and down those stairs went people who were in the grip of political ethics gone terribly wrong. As I said, there's nothing abstract about Mr. Ignatieff's concerns. He looks at real-life political dilemmas and seeks to find out what went wrong and how those wrongs might be made right.

The Lesser Evil is a study on liberal democracies and terrorism. How do people who value freedom and dignity handle those who commit senseless violence against them? What is the right balance between the competing demands of rights and security? What can a democratic society allow itself to do and still call itself democratic? These are some of the questions that Mr. Ignatieff tries to answer. He looks at nations as diverse as Russia, the United Kingdom, the U.S., Germany, Italy, Spain, Sri Lanka, Chile, Argentina, Israel and Palestine, in their current state but also historically, to see how they have dealt with assaults by terrorists. He also makes literary references, to Dostoyevsky and Conrad, to Euripides and Homer. Throughout, the approach is open, fair and critical, the analysis is rigorous and insightful, the conclusions are wise. Last but not least, the style is engaging. Mr. Ignatieff has a fine pen. My favourite line in the book is this one, on page 121: "Liberal states cannot be protected by herbivores."

Mr. Ignatieff is a passionate yet subtle defender of liberal democracies and he finds that generally the tools they already have at their disposal will do in times of terrorist threat. Indeed, he argues that overreaction to a threat can do more long-term harm to a liberal democracy than the threat itself. The U.S. Patriot Act and Canada's Bill C-36 are two examples Mr. Ignatieff gives of well-meaning but redundant and misguided attempts to deal with terrorism. When the regular tools won't do, he acknowledges that the choices faced by liberal democracies are difficult. He makes the case that when a society that values freedom and human dignity is confronted with a threat to its existence, it must move beyond rigid moral perfectionism or outright utilitarian necessity and—carefully, mindfully, vigilantly—follow a path of lesser evil, that is, allow itself to commit some infringements of the part in order to save the whole. It is a position that seeks to reconcile the *realism* necessary to fight terrorism with the *idealism* of our democratic values. To work one's way through such treacherous ground, to get down to details and talk about torture and preemptive military action, to give just two examples, requires a mind that is tough, sharp and brave. I'm glad to say that Mr. Ignatieff has such a mind.

Yours truly,
Yann Martel

MICHAEL IGNATIEFF (b. 1947) was the leader of the Liberal Party of Canada from 2009 to 2011. Prior to his political career, Ignatieff held several prominent positions in academia and broadcasting. He has been on the faculty of the universities of Oxford, Cambridge and Toronto, and was the director from 2000 to 2005 of Harvard's Carr Center for Human Rights Policy. During his time in England, he worked as a documentary filmmaker and political commentator with the BBC. Ignatieff is the author of sixteen books, including a biography of Isaiah Berlin and three novels.

BOOK 48

GILEAD

BY MARILYNNE ROBINSON

February 2, 2009

To Stephen Harper,
Prime Minister of Canada,
An Obama pick,
From a Canadian writer,
With best wishes,
Yann Martel

Dear Mr. Harper,

Well, with a budget like that, you might as well be a socialist. Remarkable how much your government has vowed to spend. Your days as a radical Reformer, determined to shrink the government like a wool sweater in a hot water wash, must be from a former life. I wonder what your friends at the National Citizens Coalition think? (Why is there no apostrophe in the name of that organization? I checked their website and that's how they spell it. Are they so committed to free enterprise and fearful of social commitment that they won't put the Citizens in the possessive case?)

I gather Michael Ignatieff was amused to hear echoes of his own statements in the recent Speech from the Throne (I enclose a *Globe and Mail* article). Don't worry, you're not the only one echoing him. President Obama (I do like the ring of that), in explaining why he was closing down the detention camp at Guantanamo Bay and the CIA's secret overseas prisons and repealing other dubious counterterrorism measures taken by George W. Bush, used words that could have been Mr. Ignatieff's. How our liberal democratic ideals must be reflected in our actions, how we cannot lightly sacrifice rights for the sake of excessive security expediency, how we will triumph over our enemies by keeping faith with our ideals, not by abandoning them, and so on—it's all entirely in the spirit of the forty-seventh book in our library, *The Lesser Evil*. Clearly Mr. Ignatieff's views are shared by many, influenced by and feeding into a current of thought that is now becoming widely accepted, so you do well to open yourself to it.

Speaking of President Obama, it's because of him that I'm sending you the novel *Gilead*, by the American writer Marilynne Robinson. It's one of his favourite novels. It turns out Barack Obama is a reader, a big reader. And the books he has read and cherished have not only been practical texts that someone interested in governance would likely favour. No, he also likes poetry, fiction, philosophy: the Bible, Shakespeare's tragedies, Melville, Toni Morrison, Doris Lessing, the poets Elizabeth Alexander and Derek Walcott, the philosophers Reinhold Niebuhr and St. Augustine, and many more. They've formed his oratory, his thinking, his very being. He's a man-built-by-words and he has impressed the whole world.

I would sincerely recommend that you read *Gilead* before you meet President Obama on February 19. For two people who are meeting for the first time, there's nothing like talking about a book that both have read to create common ground and a sense of intimacy, of knowing the other in a small but important way. After all, to like the same book implies a similar emotional response to it, a shared recognition of the world reflected in it. This is assuming, of course, that you like the book.

That shouldn't be too hard. There is much to like in *Gilead*. It's a slow, honest novel, suffused with wonder and amazement (those two words come up often in the book), and surprisingly religious, practically devotional. There are no chapters, just entries divided by a blank line, as if it were a diary. The narration is leisurely and episodic, giving the impression of a ramble, but it's actually a carefully constructed novel, building in power as it goes along. There is no facile irony, no seeking to please by the easy recourse of humour. Instead, the tone is sober, gentle, intelligent. The story is told by John Ames, an aged preacher who is ill with a heart condition that will kill him soon enough. He has a seven-year-old son come to him late in life as a result of an autumnal marriage to a much younger, much loved woman. He wants his son to know something of his father, and of his father's father, and of his father's father's father—all of them named John Ames and all of them preachers—so he writes a long letter for his son to read when he is of age. The style is on the surface effortless, a plain, poetic speech with much about God and God's people and the meaning of it all, with a few references to baseball. Very American, then, a novel one could imagine Ralph Waldo Emerson having written if Emerson had written fiction. *Gilead* is a graceful work, suffused with grace, and it has the luminous feel of the profound. It's a book that aspires to be a church, quiet, sparely furnished, whitely lit, filled with Presence and steeped in the essential. If there's a novel that should give you a sense of stillness, it is this one.

I hope you like it. And if you don't, remember nonetheless that it is one of the keys that will let you into the mind of the current President of the United States.

Yours truly,
Yann Martel

MARILYNNE ROBINSON (b. 1943) is the American author of two works of non-fiction, *Mother Country* and *The Death of Adam*, and three novels. Her first novel, *Housekeeping*, won a Hemingway Foundation/PEN Award and earned her a nomination for the Pulitzer Prize for Fiction. Her second novel, *Gilead*, won several awards including the Pulitzer Prize for Fiction, the National Book Critics Circle Award for Fiction and the Ambassador Book Award. Robinson earned a Ph.D. from the University of Washington and at present teaches at the Iowa Writers' Workshop.

BOOK 49

THE OLD MAN AND THE SEA
BY ERNEST HEMINGWAY

February 16, 2009

To Stephen Harper,
Prime Minister of Canada,
From a Canadian writer,
With best wishes,
Yann Martel

Dear Mr. Harper,

The famous Ernest Hemingway. *The Old Man and the Sea* is one of those works of literature that most everyone has heard of, even those who haven't read it. Despite its brevity—127 pages in the well-spaced edition I am sending you—it's had a lasting effect on English literature, as has Hemingway's work in general. I'd say that his short stories, gathered in the collections *In Our Time*, *Men without Women* and *Winner Take Nothing*, among others, are his greatest achievement—and above all, the story "Big Two-Hearted River"—but his novels *The Sun Also Rises*, *A Farewell to Arms* and *For Whom the Bell Tolls* are more widely read.

The greatness of Hemingway lies not so much in what he said as how he said it. He took the English language and wrote it in a way that no one had written it before. If you compare Hemingway, who was born in 1899, and Henry James, who died in 1916, that overlap of seventeen years seems astonishing, so contrasting are their styles. With James, truth, verisimilitude, realism, whatever you want to call it, is achieved by a baroque abundance of language. Hemingway's style is the exact opposite. He stripped the language of ornamentation, prescribing adjectives and adverbs to his prose the way a careful doctor would prescribe pills to a hypochondriac. The result was prose of revolutionary terseness, with a cadence, vigour and elemental simplicity that bring to mind a much older text: the Bible.

That combination is not fortuitous. Hemingway was well versed in biblical language and imagery and *The Old Man and the Sea* can be read as a Christian allegory, though I wouldn't call it a religious work, certainly not in the way the book I sent you two weeks ago, *Gilead*, is. Rather, Hemingway uses Christ's passage on Earth in a secular way to explore the meaning of human suffering. "Grace under pressure" was the formulation Hemingway offered when he was asked what he meant by "guts" in describing the grit shown by many of his characters. Another way of putting that would be the achieving of victory through defeat, which matches more deeply, I think, the Christ-like odyssey of Santiago, the old man of the title. For concerning Christ, that was the Apostle Paul's momentous insight (some would call it God's gift): the possibility of triumph, of salvation, in the very midst of ruination. It's a message, a belief, that transforms the human experience entirely. Career failures, family disasters, accidents, disease, old age—these human experiences that might otherwise be tragically final instead become threshold events.

As I was thinking about Santiago and his epic encounter with the great marlin, I wondered whether there was any political dimension to his story. I came to the conclusion that there isn't. In politics, victory comes through victory and defeat only brings defeat. The message of Hemingway's poor Cuban fisherman is purely personal, addressing the individual in each one of us and not the roles we might take on. Despite its vast exterior setting, *The Old Man and the Sea* is an intimate work of the soul. And so I wish upon you what I wish upon all of us: that our return from the high seas be as dignified as Santiago's.

Yours truly,
Yann Martel

ERNEST HEMINGWAY (1899–1961) was an American journalist, novelist and short story writer. He is internationally acclaimed for his works *The Sun Also Rises*, *A Farewell to Arms*, *For Whom the Bell Tolls* and his Pulitzer Prize–winning novella, *The Old Man and the Sea*. Hemingway's writing style is characteristically straightforward and understated, featuring tightly constructed prose. He drove an ambulance in World War I, and was a key figure in the circle of expatriate artists and writers in Paris in the 1920s known as the "Lost Generation." Hemingway won the Nobel Prize in Literature in 1954.

BOOK 50:

JANE AUSTEN: A LIFE
BY CAROL SHIELDS

March 2, 2009

To Stephen Harper,
Prime Minister of Canada,
Our fiftieth book,
From a Canadian writer,
With best wishes,
Yann Martel

Dear Mr. Harper,

The gentle yet probing questioning, the lightness of touch, the accuracy of statement, the keen moral awareness, the constant intelligence—finally, it's only Jane Austen's irony that is missing from this excellent look at her life by Carol Shields, which is fitting since a fair-minded biography isn't the most suitable place for broad irony. Otherwise, without any attempt at imitation or pastiche, this book is so much in the spirit of its subject, so intimately concerned with the meaning of being a writer, that one can nearly imagine that one is reading *Carol Shields: A Life*, by Jane Austen. Not that Carol Shields intrudes on the text in an unseemly way. Not at all. Aside from the brief prologue, the personal pronoun *I* to designate the biographer never appears. This book is entirely a biography of Jane Austen. But the spirit of the two, of the English novelist who lived between 1775 and 1817 and of the Canadian novelist who lived between 1935 and 2003, are so kindred that the book exudes a feeling of friendship rather than of analysis.

The illusion of complicity is helped by the fact that not very much is known about Jane Austen, despite her being the author of six novels that sit with full rights in the library of great English literature. She wrote *Pride and Prejudice*, *Sense and Sensibility*, *Northanger Abbey*, *Mansfield Park*, *Emma* and *Persuasion* in unremitting rural obscurity. She became a published writer only six years before her death and the four novels that came out during her lifetime were published anonymously, the author being described only as "a Lady." And even when it became widely known after her death that the lady in question had been one Jane Austen, resident of the village of Chawton, in Hampshire, posterity didn't find out much more about her. Jane Austen never met another published writer, was never interviewed by a journalist and never moved in a literary circle beyond the completely personal one of her family, who were her first and most loyal readers. What we might have found out about her through her letters is partial, since many were destroyed by her sister Cassandra. In other words, Jane Austen lived among people who hardly took note of her, and I mean that literally: except for some few family members and friends, very little was written about Jane Austen during her lifetime that might have allowed us to become acquainted with her. A biography of such an elusive person will therefore have more the character of a spiritual quest than of a factual account. Therein lies the excellence of Shields's biography. It is not cluttered by facts. It is rather a meditation on the writerly existence of Jane Austen—and who better to do that than a writer who can be viewed as a modern incarnation of her? Carol Shields had a similar interest in the female perspective and was as comfortable as Jane Austen in exploring the domestic and the intimate, plumbing its depths until the universal was revealed. The intuitive rightness of her biography amply makes up for the dearth of hard facts.

The eleventh book I sent you was a Jane Austen novel, though a minor one because unfinished, *The Watsons*, if you remember. If that's the only Austen you've read, you don't have to worry that you will be left in the dark by this biography. It's called *Jane Austen: A Life*, after all, and not *Jane Austen: Her Books*. Of course, her books are discussed, but only to the extent that they shed light on their author. The reader doesn't have to have an intimate knowledge of them to appreciate what Shields is discussing.

This book is a real pleasure to read, I must emphasize that. It is intelligent in a most engaging way, not only making Jane Austen better known to us, but also bringing the reader in on the alchemical process of writing. Jane Austen, unlimited by her tightly circumscribed life, composed novels that still speak to readers today, whose lives, especially that of her female readers, have changed vastly. Carol Shields, for her part, unlimited by the poverty of source material, composed a biography that speaks to everyone, male or female, devoted Austen reader or neophyte. I hope you will enjoy it, this, the fiftieth book that we have shared.

In front of the Jane Austen Centre.

I was in Bath recently, where Jane Austen lived for a few years. She was miserable while there, but it's a lovely town nonetheless. I took a picture for you, which I include with this letter.

Yours truly,
Yann Martel

CAROL SHIELDS (1935–2003) was an American-Canadian poet, novelist, professor and critic. Her works include ten novels and two collections of short stories. During her literary career, Shields was a professor at the University of Ottawa, the University of British Columbia, the University of Manitoba and the University of Winnipeg, where she also served as chancellor. She is best remembered for her highly acclaimed novel *The Stone Diaries*, which won the Pulitzer Prize and the Governor General's Literary Award. Her biography of Jane Austen won the Charles Taylor Prize for Non-Fiction.

BOOK 51:

JULIUS CAESAR
BY WILLIAM SHAKESPEARE

March 16, 2009

To Stephen Harper,
Prime Minister of Canada,
S.O.S. (Save Our Shakespeare),
From a Canadian writer,
With best wishes,
Yann Martel

Dear Mr. Harper,

Yesterday was the Ides of March, and so *Julius Caesar*, by William Shakespeare. There is nothing sacred in or about Shakespeare, but one can lose and find oneself in his work the way one can lose and find oneself in the Bible. Both are full worlds, one secular, the other religious, and both have spawned generations of readers and scholars who can quote chapter and verse from any given book or play. If one were on a desert island with only the Bible or the complete works of Shakespeare, one would do all right. If one had both, one would do well.

There is everything in Shakespeare (including dullness in the history plays). The English language and the nature of drama were still on the anvil in the smithy when Shakespeare was around, which was between the years 1564 and 1616, and the formative beatings of his hammer mark to this day the English language, theatre, and our view of the world. To give you just two small examples: in Act I, towards the end of Scene II,

Cassius asks Casca if Cicero had anything to say about Caesar fainting. Cicero did, but in Greek. Casca deadpans, "It was Greek to me." Later, in Act III, Scene I, Caesar is making clear that his will is firm and that he is not easily put off his course. He is, he says, "constant as the northern star." These are but two of the many expressions that Shakespeare brought to the language he was working in. He brought more than that, of course. His plays, besides being vivid and dramatic, overflow with insights into the human condition. The adjective "Shakespearean" is a broad one. If that single man was a spring, we now all live in his delta.

Julius Caesar is a play about politics, more specifically about power. The potential power of one individual, the power of tradition, the power of principles, the power of persuasion, the power of the masses—all these powers clash in the play, to deadly effect. Shakespeare takes no sides. His play is a tragedy, but it is not only Caesar's tragedy. It is also the tragedy of Brutus and Cassius, of Portia and Calpurnia, of Cinna the Poet, of Rome itself.

Since *Julius Caesar* is about power and politics, we might as well talk about power and politics. Let me discuss concerns I have with two decisions your government recently announced.

My first concern is about the Social Sciences and Humanities Research Council. New money allocated to the Council is apparently to be spent exclusively on "business-related degrees." Don't you feel that there's a measure of contradiction between the libertarian, small-government ideals of your party and telling an arm's-length body how to spend its money? Aren't you making government bigger and more intrusive by doing so? But that's an aside. More troubling is the denaturing of SSHRC's role. I've never understood why public universities, funded by the taxpayer, should necessarily have business departments. Is making money really an academic discipline?

Don't get me wrong; there's nothing shameful about money, or the making of it, but we're losing sight of the purpose of a university if we think it's the place to churn out MBAs. A university is the repository and crucible of a society, the place where it studies itself. It is the brain of a society. It is not the wallet. Businesses come and go. Shakespeare doesn't. A university builds minds and souls. A business employs. The world would be a better place if rather than having business types infiltrating universities, we had Shakespeare types infiltrating businesses. I imagine this line of argument is falling on your deaf ear. Perhaps I've misunderstood. To paraphrase Antony speaking of Brutus, you are an honourable man and you must know what you're doing.

My second concern is the announcement by the Canadian Heritage Minister James Moore that funding from the new Canadian Periodical Fund might be restricted to those magazines that have a circulation greater than five thousand. That will pretty well kill off every single arts and literary magazine in Canada. "Good thing," you might be thinking. "Elitist little rags, who needs them?" Well, we all need them, because good things start small. I'll give you just one example: my own. I was first published by the *Malahat Review*, which comes out of Victoria, B.C. Their early support, when I was in my twenties, galvanized me. It made me want to write more and to write better. It's because I was published in the *Malahat* that I won my first literary award, that I met my literary agent, that I came to the attention of Toronto publishers. The *Malahat* is where I was born as a writer. If it goes, so does the next generation of writers and poets. But perhaps I've misunderstood. You are an honourable man and you must know what you're doing.

Turning SSHRC into an MBA funding agency and eliminating arts and literary magazines are incomprehensible measures to me. The sums involved are so small relatively, yet the purposes they serve so important. Is it really your aim to transform Canada into a post-literate society? As it is, many young people are post-historical and post-religious. If literacy is the next pillar to go, what will be left of our identity? But perhaps I've misunderstood. You are an honourable man and you must know what you're doing.

In Act III, Scene 3 of *Caesar*, you will meet Cinna the Poet. He is torn to pieces by the rabble, who mistake him for another Cinna, one of the conspirators. That is not the Canadian way. Here in Canada, at this time, it is the Canadian government that is attacking Cinna the Poet. But perhaps I've misunderstood. You are an honourable man and you must know what you're doing.

Yours truly,
Yann Martel

REPLY:

May 1, 2009

Dear Mr. Martel,

On behalf of the Right Honourable Stephen Harper, I would like to acknowledge receipt of your correspondence regarding the Social Sciences and Humanities Research Council (SSHRC) and the Canadian Periodical Fund. I would also like to thank you for the enclosure of *Julius Caesar*, by William Shakespeare.

Please be assured that your comments have been given careful consideration. I have taken the liberty of forwarding copies of your correspondence to the Honourable Tony Clement, Minister of Industry, and the Honourable James Moore, Minister of Canadian Heritage and Official Languages, so that they may be made aware of your concerns.

Once again, thank you for writing the Prime Minister.

Yours sincerely,
S. Russell
Executive Correspondence Officer

William Shakespeare (1564–1616) wrote plays and poems.

BOOK 52

BURNING ICE: ART & CLIMATE CHANGE
A COLLABORATION ORGANIZED
BY DAVID BUCKLAND
AND THE CAPE FAREWELL FOUNDATION

March 30, 2009

To Stephen Harper,
Prime Minister of Canada,
A book on a hot topic,
From a Canadian writer,
With best wishes,
Yann Martel

Dear Mr. Harper,

I had never heard of Cape Farewell, a British NGO, until an e-mail from them popped into my inbox. They were inviting me, thanks to funding by the Musagetes Foundation here in Canada, on a trip they were organizing to Peru. To explain their organization and its objectives, they offered to send me a book and a DVD. I was intrigued and so accepted. What did I have to lose? A few days later, said book and DVD arrived in the mail. I read the book, watched the DVD, checked out their website (www.capefarewell.com) and promptly wrote to Cape Farewell to accept their invitation.

Many people were first introduced to climate change by *An Inconvenient Truth*, the movie based on the touring presentation by Al Gore. Cape Farewell's mission is to move beyond that initial awareness and orchestrate a cultural response to climate change. To do that, they organize expeditions to the frontiers of climate change, those hot spots (literally) where the change is most apparent. Scientists are there too, doing their research, and so artists can see both climate change's theatre and some of its actors. The artists are then invited to respond, to become actors themselves. The DVD *Art from a Changing Arctic* documents the first three Cape Farewell expeditions to Svalbard, while *Burning Ice* records some of the responses by the artists.

It's a varied book, as you'll see. There is visual art, both photographic, pictorial and sculptural, there are essays, both scientific, giving a good recap about climate change, and personal, relating the reactions of individuals to that change. *Burning Ice* came out in 2006 and it's already out of date. In one essay, a scientist states that by 2050 there will be no more summer ice in the Arctic. Scientists are now predicting such a disappearance by 2013. Only three years on and matters have already gotten worse. It's easy to fall into pessimism when contemplating climate change. "Such a global calamity—what can I do?" The great quality of *Burning Ice* is that it shows what can be done: one can respond. Of course, a painting, a photograph, a string of words won't save the planet. But it's the beginning of coming to grips with the issue. Climate change on its own is an impersonal force, deeply disempowering. Art inspired by climate change, because the making of art is personally involving, a whole-person activity, is empowering, both for the maker and the spectator.

As I flipped through the pages of *Burning Ice*, gazing at the artwork, reading the essays, I marvelled and I was distressed: an odd mixture, but a step up from simply feeling distress. Whether the art that Cape Farewell generates, to be seen in books and exhibitions, turns out to be elegiac, a farewell to our planet, or the beginning of real change in the way we live, will only be seen in years to come. But one thing is certain: our response to climate change cannot be purely political. Politicians have been dragging their feet—you among them—because of the power of the carbon-fuel industrial complex. It is citizens who must move first, and art is an ideal way to help them do that. Art wrestles with its subject matter on a level that the individual, the man, woman, teenager and child on the street, can engage with and react to. Once citizens are involved in the vital issue of climate change, politicians will have to follow their lead.

You might as well get ahead of the wave. I hope you are both moved and alarmed by *Burning Ice*.

Yours truly,
Yann Martel

REPLY:

June 24, 2009

Dear Mr. Martel:

On behalf of the Right Honourable Stephen Harper, I would like to acknowledge receipt of your correspondence of March 30, which provided a copy of the book *Burning Ice: Art & Climate Change*.

Thank you for providing this material to the Prime Minister. Your courtesy in bringing this information to his attention is appreciated.

Yours sincerely,
P. Monteith
Executive Correspondence Officer

DAVID BUCKLAND is a British artist specializing in photography, portraiture, and set and costume design for theatrical productions. Many of his works have been exhibited in major galleries around the world, including the Centre Georges Pompidou in Paris and the Metropolitan Museum of Art in New York. Buckland is also the founder of the Cape Farewell Project, a community of artists, scientists and communicators committed to raising cultural awareness through artistic response to climate change.

BOOKS 53 AND 54:

LOUIS RIEL
BY CHESTER BROWN

AND

THE SAILOR WHO FELL FROM GRACE WITH THE SEA
BY YUKIO MISHIMA

Translated from the Japanese by John Nathan

April 13, 2009

for *Louis Riel*

To Stephen Harper,

Prime Minister of Canada,

A graphic novel on a key episode

in Canadian history,

From a Canadian writer,

With best wishes,

Yann Martel

for *The Sailor Who Fell from*
Grace with the Sea

To Stephen Harper,

Prime Minister of Canada,

A graphic novel of a different kind,

From a Canadian writer,

With best wishes,

Yann Martel

Dear Mr. Harper,

When I started sending you books, I said they would be books that would "inspire stillness." A book is a marvellous tool—in fact, a unique tool—to increase one's depth of reflection, to help one think and feel. It takes a long time and great effort to write a good book, whether of fiction or non-fiction. It's not only the preliminary research; there are also the weeks and months of thinking. When asked how long it took them to write a book, I've heard writers say, "My whole life." I know what they mean by that. Their entire being went into the writing of that book, and the few years it actually took to get it down on the page were only the tip of the proverbial iceberg. It's not surprising that such a lengthy process, akin to the maturing of a good wine, should yield a rich product worthy of careful consideration.

But the stillness that books can induce does not mean they are peaceable. Stillness is not the same thing as tranquility. You might have noticed that a few weeks ago with *Julius Caesar*. There's hardly any peace and tranquility in that play, yet it is thought-provoking nonetheless, isn't it?

That stillness out of turmoil continues with the two books I am sending you this week. I'm sure you are familiar with the tragic saga of Louis Riel. The English hated him, the French loved him. Of course, I don't mean the English and French of Europe when I say that. I mean the people from that nation that materialized north of the United States. The English and Irish and Scottish of Ontario were newly calling themselves Canadians, while the French-speaking Métis of the Red River Settlement were not. In one man, the tensions and resentments of a new nation were symbolized. It was a complicated mess whose effects are felt to this day. Would the Parti Québécois have been elected in 1976 had Louis Riel and the Red River Métis been treated more fairly by Ottawa? Or would that have led Ontarians to elect an "Ontario Party" advocating union with the United States? What is clear—and you must surely know this from your own personal experience in politics—is that once prejudice and bad faith are entrenched among a people, it's very hard to get them to get along.

Louis Riel, by the Canadian graphic artist Chester Brown, is a serious work that tells a serious story in a thoughtful and evocative manner. The drawings are compelling and the storytelling is both gripping and subtle. Louis Riel comes across as he likely was: a strange and charismatic man, religiously crazy at times but also genuinely concerned about the fate of his Métis people.

The description "strange and charismatic" could also be applied to the Japanese writer Yukio Mishima (1925–1970). If Riel was religiously crazy, then Mishima was aesthetically crazy. You might have heard about how Mishima died. He's as well known for his death as he is for his writings. The life of an author should not normally be conflated with his work, but a healthy writer who, at the age of forty-five and at the height of his fame, commits suicide by ritual disembowelment and beheading—what is popularly called *harakiri*—after taking over a military base and exhorting the army of his country to overthrow the government, cannot but attract attention for reasons other than his books. In this case, life and work are intimately linked. Mishima's end had less to do with politics and restoring Japan to a supposed former glory than with personal notions he had about death and beauty. He was obsessed by death and beauty. The characters in his novel *The Sailor Who Fell from Grace with the Sea*—Fusako, the mother; Noboru, her son; and Ryuji, the sailor—demonstrate this. They are exquisitely realized. One gets a sense of them not only in their physical being but in their inner makeup too. All are, in their different ways, beautiful. And yet their story is riven by violence and death. I won't say anything more.

I'll confess that when I first read *The Sailor Who Fell from Grace with the Sea* in my early twenties, I hated it because I loved it. It and Knut Hamsun's *Hunger* are the only masterpieces I've read with the breathless feeling that I possibly could have written them myself. Those two stories were in me, I felt, but a Japanese writer and a Norwegian writer got to them before I could.

I should explain why I am sending you two books this week. I'm off on a holiday and don't want to worry about books being lost in the mail. So these are your April books, *Louis Riel* for April 13 and *The Sailor Who Fell from Grace with the Sea* for April 27.

How curious and unrelated they seem. I doubt Mishima had ever heard of Louis Riel, and there's nothing in *Louis Riel* to make me think that Chester Brown is an admirer of Mishima. But I've always liked that about books, how they can be so different from each other and yet rest together without strife on a bookshelf. The hope of literature, the hope of stillness, is that the peace with which the most varied books can lie side by side will transform their readers, so that they too will be able to live side by side with people very different from themselves.

Yours truly,
Yann Martel

REPLY:

April 29, 2009

Dear Mr. Martel,

On behalf of the Right Honourable Stephen Harper, I would like to acknowledge receipt of your correspondence, with which you enclosed a copy of *The Sailor Who Fell from Grace with the Sea* by Yukio Mishima and a copy of *Louis Riel, A Comic-Strip Biography* by Chester Brown.

The Prime Minister wishes me to convey his thanks for sending him these books. You may be assured that your thoughtful gesture is most appreciated.

Yours truly,
S. Russell
Executive Correspondence Officer

CHESTER BROWN (b. 1960) is a Canadian cartoonist who is part of the alternative comics movement and the creator of several graphic novels and comic series. His comics are generally grim, classified in the genres of horror, surrealism and black comedy and focusing on darker subjects like mental health issues and cannibalism. His best-known work, *Louis Riel: A Comic-Strip Biography*, was five years in the making. Some of his other works include *The Playboy*, *I Never Liked You* and the comic book series *Yummy Fur* and *Underwater*. Born and raised in Montreal, Brown now lives in Toronto.

YUKIO MISHIMA (1925–1970), born Kimitake Hiraoka, was a Japanese novelist, short story writer, poet and traditional kabuki playwright. His best-known novels, *Confessions of a Mask*, *The Temple of the Golden Pavilion*, *The Sailor Who Fell from Grace with the Sea* and the *Sea of Fertility* quartet, have insured his enduring fame in Japan and around the world. Mishima committed suicide after taking over a military base with his own private army, ostensibly as a protest over Japan's drift away from its traditional values.

BOOK 55:

THE GIFT
BY LEWIS HYDE
May 11, 2009

To Stephen Harper,
Prime Minister of Canada,
A gift to be shared, like all gifts,
From a Canadian writer,
With best wishes,
Yann Martel

Dear Mr. Harper,

One of the strengths of non-fiction is its ability to focus. Whereas fiction can be as broad as the humanities, non-fiction tends to specialize, like a science. Writers of fiction commonly hear from their editors that they must "show, not tell." They must do so because fiction creates new, unfamiliar worlds that must be felt and not only described. Non-fiction, on the other hand, relies on a world already in existence, our own, with its true history and real historical figures. Of course, that history and those figures must be made to breathe with life on the page; good writing is always essential. Nonetheless, that basis in the factual world frees non-fiction writers from the cumbersome task of wholly invent- ing characters and situations and gives them far more liberty to straight-out tell. What is gained is an ability to cover a single topic deeply. What is lost is broad appeal. With non-fiction, the reader must be more actively interested in the subject covered. For example, a history of feudal Japan will likely attract fewer readers than a novel about feudal Japan. Such was the case, at least, with James Clavell's novel *Shogun* and I don't think it's unusual.

The result of this specialization is that the world of non-fiction is more fragmented. A novel is more like another novel than a work of non-fiction is like another work of non-fiction. Proof of that is in the names we give to these categories: we know what fiction is, so we call it that, and under the label we comfortably place the plays, poems, novels and short stories of the world. But what about those books that aren't fiction? Well, we're not so sure what they are, so we define them by what they are not: they are *non*-fiction. The result of this lack of convention, with great non-fiction, is a high degree of originality.

A sterling example of how original non-fiction can be is the book I am sending you this week. In *The Gift*, Lewis Hyde looks at the meaning and consequence of a gift, that is, of an object or service that is given for nothing, freely, without expectation of a concrete or immediate return. With that single notion in mind, Hyde evokes an array of peoples, places and practices and makes a coherent whole of what would be a novelistic mess. You'll see for yourself. The Puritans in America, Irish and Bengali folklore, the Trobriand Islanders off New Guinea, the Maori of New Zealand, the potlatch of the Pacific Coast First Nations, Alcoholics Anonymous, tales of Buddha, the Ford Motor Company, the fate of unexpected sums of money in an urban ghetto of Chicago, Martin Luther, John Calvin, the lives of Walt Whitman and Ezra Pound, to mention just a few references that I remember—all are woven together as Hyde lays out his thesis on the differences between the exchange of gifts and the exchange of commodities. The currencies involved in these trades are radically different. In the first, sentiments are exchanged; in the second, money. The first creates attachment; the second, detachment. The first creates a community; the second, liberty. The first builds capital that does not circulate; the second loses its value if it does not keep moving. These ideas are examined in the light of the many anthropological and sociological examples in the book.

Art is at the heart of *The Gift*. Hyde sees every aspect of art as a gift: creativity is received as a gift by the artist, art is made as a gift and then, rather awkwardly in our current economic system, art is traded as a gift. That certainly rings true with me. I have never thought of my creativity in monetary terms. I write now as I did when I started, for nothing. And yet the artist must live. How then to quantify the value of one's art? How do we correlate a poem's worth with a monetary value? I use the word again: it's awkward. If Hyde favours the spirit of gift-giving over that of commercial exchange, it's not because he's a doctrinaire idealist. He's not. But it's clear what he thinks: we've forgotten the spirit of the gift in our commodity-driven society and the cost of that has been the parching of our souls.

The Gift is a refreshment to the dried-up soul. For Lewis Hyde, the spirit of the gift goes far beyond Christmas and birthdays. It's actually a philosophy. And it's hard not to adhere to it after reading hundreds of pages on gift-making and gift-giving in all corners of the world. Perhaps we have forgotten a little how good it feels to give freely, how what is given to us must be passed on, so that the gift can live on, swimming about human communities like a fish, always alive so long as it keeps moving. Perhaps that's why the things we value the most are often those that we were given. Perhaps that is our more natural mode of exchange. At the very least, after reading this book you'll never think of the word "gift" in the same way.

One last point, made in the spirit of Hyde's book. I have now sent you fifty-seven books of all types, and there will be more to come, as long as you are Prime Minister. I imagine these books are lying on a shelf somewhere in your offices. But they won't be there forever. One day you will leave office and you'll take with you the extensive paper trail that a prime minister creates. That trail will be placed in hundreds of cardboard boxes that will end up at the National Archives of Canada, where in time they will be opened and the contents parsed by scholars. I would feel sad if that were the fate of the books I have given you. Novels and poems and plays are not meant to live in cardboard boxes. Like all gifts, they should be shared. So may I suggest that you share what I have shared with you. One by one, or all together, as you wish, give the books away, with only two conditions: first, that they not be kept permanently by each recipient but rather passed on in a timely fashion, after they've been read, and, second, that they never be sold. That would keep the gift-giving spirit of our book club alive.

Yours truly,
Yann Martel

P.S. Could you please thank S. Russell on my behalf for his or her reply for the last books I sent you, the Mishima and the Chester Brown. [See the REPLY *section of Books 53 and 54.]*

REPLY:

May 22nd, 2009

Dear Mr. Martel,

On behalf of the Right Honourable Stephen Harper, I would like to acknowledge receipt of your recent correspondence.

Thank you for writing to share your views with the Prime Minister. You may be assured that your comments have been carefully noted. For more information on the Government's initiatives, you may wish to visit the Prime Minister's website, at www.pm.gc.ca.

Yours sincerely,
L. A. Lavell
Executive Correspondence Officer

LEWIS HYDE (b. 1945) is an American poet, translator, essayist and cultural critic. He has edited a book of essays by Henry David Thoreau and translated the poems of the Nobel Prize–winning Spanish poet Vicente Aleixandre. He has also written a work of cultural criticism, *Trickster Makes This World*, and a collection of poems, *This Error Is the Sign of Love*. Formerly an instructor at Harvard University, Hyde now teaches writing at Kenyon College and is a Fellow at Harvard's Berkman Center for Internet and Society

BOOK 56

THE STRANGE CASE OF DR. JEKYLL AND MR. HYDE
BY ROBERT LOUIS STEVENSON

May 25, 2009

To Stephen Harper,
Prime Minister of Canada,
Good luck with your Mr. Hyde,
From a Canadian writer,
With best wishes,
Yann Martel

Dear Mr. Harper,

A story can sometimes capture in an image what might otherwise float around unexpressed. You must have had that experience yourself, in which a book or article or movie said cogently what you had been thinking in a vaguer way. A perfect example of a story that brings this sort of clarity is Robert Louis Stevenson's *The Strange Case of Dr. Jekyll and Mr. Hyde*. First published in 1886, it was an instant success, read by everyone who read (including Queen Victoria and Prime Minister Gladstone), and it has become an enduring classic. The moral categories of good and evil have been known since the beginning of time, and each one of us comes to know them formally as a result of instruction by our parents and our teachers, and intimately as a result of direct experience. But I suspect that most of us would claim that we long ago gave the keys to the house to good, and threw out evil. In other words, we live with good and evil by thinking of ourselves as good, not perfect, perhaps, but good enough, certainly better than our neighbours, and we use whatever rationalizations are necessary to maintain this self-image. Evil we consider as something essentially external. Other people are evil: criminals, bad cops, corrupt politicians, loitering youths, and so on. We find plenty of evil in the world, just not in ourselves.

The brilliance of Stevenson's tale is in the way he portrays the forces of good and evil: he incarnates them as two full-blooded characters in the body of one duplicitous person. Because as I'm sure you know, even if you've never read the short novel, Dr. Jekyll and Mr. Hyde are not two people but one. Each is the embodiment of one of the moral extremes battling within the same person, different not only in character but in appearance. Tall, handsome Dr. Jekyll, of impeccable reputation, is the good incarnation of this tortured person, while the shrunken, heartless Mr. Hyde, of unremitting ill repute, is the evil incarnation. But they are in dialogue. That's the genius of the tale. Living within the same soul, the two are aware of each other and in cease-less conflict. And we know which one is destined to win. If Dr. Jekyll won, if good went on being good, that would be matter for an inspiring sermon, but not for a ripping yarn. We need Mr. Hyde to win the day—but only briefly, don't worry—to feel the frisson that is horror fiction's specialty.

The novel is told in ten chapters. The first eight are effective but conventional. Strange, terrible events take place, the telling is partial and puzzling, suspense keeps us reading—it has all the trappings of a fine Gothic horror story. Then, in Chapter 9, we learn from a minor character, a fellow doctor friend of Dr. Jekyll, that the evil Mr. Hyde, a brute and a murderer, is none other than a transmogrified Dr. Jekyll. That would have been a stunning revelation to a reader who knew nothing beforehand of the story. But the reason *The Strange Case of Dr. Jekyll and Mr. Hyde* rises above the standard horror story is to be found in Chapter 10, the last and longest, told in the racked voice of Dr. Jekyll himself. In that chapter lies the greatness of the novel. To speak of good and evil as they usually are, with a smile of self-satisfaction and a censorious finger pointing outward, is tiresome. None of that here. In Chapter 10, "Henry Jekyll's Full Statement of the Case," we have a man openly acknowledging and discussing his evil side and what he seeks to do with it. His idea is to give body to his evil side so that the good side might be more purely good, untroubled by the siren call of evil. Mr. Hyde is created, then, to make Dr. Jekyll better. But oh, the temptation of evil! Dr. Jekyll looks on in fascinated horror at the outrages his alter ego commits. Slowly the fascination consumes him. While at first he alchemically switches back to Dr. Jekyll with ease, in time the efficacy of the potion that allows him to do so wears out. The dominant Dr. Jekyll begins to lose ground to Mr. Hyde until the natural being of the man *is* Mr. Hyde.

To have this battle told *from the inside*, in the very voice of the tortured double combatant, is gripping reading, one that magnifies to an appalling degree the struggles each one of us, if we are morally lucid, must go through. This is the reason for the ongoing appeal of the story. We are all Dr. Jekylls and the moral question put to each of us is the same: what will you do with the Mr. Hyde lurking in you?

By my reading of the original tale, the evil that torments Dr. Jekyll is quite clearly a sexual one, the Victorian repression of a homosexual urge. See what you think, see if you find the hints pointing to the same conclusion. But the tale, like any great story, can also be read in a way that mirrors each reader's personality. You, a politician, for example, must feel every day the inner tensions between the public good you desire to bring about and the evil that you must commit to do so. To have those opposing urges clothed in the vivid, contrasting frames of Dr. Jekyll and Mr. Hyde should help you in your struggle to become Prime Minister Jekyll.

A last observation: rarely has a story been so well served by its title. *Dr. Jekyll and Mr. Hyde*—the words roll off the tongue with such ease, the counterpoint of the titles Dr. and Mr. pleasing and the names highly unusual yet easy to remember. Curiously, the reader is never given an explanation as to how Mr. Hyde gets his name. Dr. Jekyll takes his potion in his laboratory, turns into another being, steps in front of a mirror, and "I saw for the first time the appearance of Edward Hyde." Clearly, Stevenson knew the names worked. Medicine is held to be a profession that does good, but the second syllable of the good doctor's name rhymes with "kill." As for Mr. Hyde, he is what Jekyll wants to "hide." It all works so well that anyone who has read the story remembers it fully just by recalling the title.

Yours truly,
Yann Martel

P.S. I have received yet another reply from S. Russell, your executive correspondence officer, this time for the gift of Shakespeare's Julius Caesar. *[See the REPLY section of Book 51.] That's two letters in short order, after a silence of two years. I can see why in the case of* Julius Caesar. *In the letter that accompanied the play, I spoke about my concerns over new guidelines for the Social Sciences and Humanities Research Council and the Canadian Periodical Fund. That's political stuff, the very fodder of a correspondence officer in a prime minister's office. But a response to my gift of Chester Brown's* Louis Riel *(Book 53) and Yukio Mishima's* The Sailor Who Fell from Grace with the Sea *(Book 54) came as a surprise.*

But I guess anything to do with Riel is political, still, and merits a response from you, however indirect. I wonder if I might receive a reply directly from you one day. There's quite a choice of books you can write to me about, that's for sure.

REPLY:

June 16, 2009

Dear Mr. Martel,

The Office of the Prime Minister forwarded to me a copy of your letter on May 5, 2009, regarding the Budget 2009 decision to allocate the temporary increase of Canada Graduate Scholarships (CGS) awarded by the Social Sciences and Humanities Research Council of Canada (SSHRC) to students pursuing business-related degrees. I regret the delay in replying to you.

The Government of Canada recognizes that talented, skilled and creative people are the most critical element of a successful national economy, and has committed to strengthening Canada's People Advantage in our Science and Technology (S&T) Strategy, *Mobilizing Science and Technology to Canada's Advantage*. Our government has not only maintained, but increased the level of ongoing federal support for graduate students in Canada. In Budget 2007, we expanded the CGS program to support 5,000 students annually across all areas of study. Of these recipients, 2,600 are supported by SSHRC, 1,600 through the Natural Sciences and Engineering Research Council of Canada (NSERC), and 800 through the Canadian Institutes for Health Research (CIHR).

Budget 2009 announced a further, temporary increase in the number of CGS awards that will be granted in 2009–2010 and 2010–2011 as part of *Canada's Economic Action Plan*. This increased funding will help students deepen their skills through further study at a time when they face a weakening labour market. Of the 2,500 additional scholarships made available through Budget 2009, 500 will be awarded by SSHRC to students pursuing business-related degrees.

The S&T Strategy addresses the need to foster more advanced business training in Canada as a means to improve innovation and the overall health of the economy. Our focus on business-related studies will provide additional support and encouragement to students pursuing advanced training in an area critical to Canada's future economic success.

This government recognizes the important contribution of all social sciences and humanities disciplines to a vibrant economy and society. Research in the social sciences and humanities advances knowledge and builds understanding about individual groups and societies. Knowledge and understanding informs discussion on critical social, cultural, economic, technological and wellness issues. They also provide communities, businesses and governments with the foundation for a vibrant and healthy democracy. SSHRC will continue to award Canada Graduate Scholarships across the full range of social sciences and humanities disciplines through the ongoing CGS program. Over the next three years, SSHRC will award an expected 5,700 Canada Graduate Scholarships, and 5,200 of these—more than 90 percent—will be available in all areas of the social sciences and humanities.

The additional awards will be granted in keeping with SSHRC's mandate to support excellence in research and research training in the social sciences and humanities. They will help to ensure that top graduate students in business-related fields of study contribute to enhancing Canada's prosperity.

Thank you for writing and please accept my best wishes.

Yours sincerely,
Tony Clement
Minister of Industry

ROBERT LOUIS STEVENSON (1850–1894) was a Scottish novelist, poet and travel writer. Though he suffered from ill health throughout his life, he travelled widely and lived in various locales, including the south of France and the South Seas. He lived in Samoa with his wife, Fanny, and is entombed there at Mount Vaea. His other books include *Treasure Island*, *The Black Arrow* and *Kidnapped*.

BOOK 57

HIROSHIMA MON AMOUR
A SCREENPLAY BY MARGUERITE DURAS
Translated from the French by Richard Seaver
AND A MOVIE BY ALAIN RESNAIS
June 8, 2009

To Stephen Harper,
Prime Minister of Canada,
From a Canadian writer,
With best wishes,
Yann Martel

Dear Mr. Harper,

For the first time I'm sending you an original screenplay and
with it, naturally, the movie that was made from it. *Hiroshima
Mon Amour* was written by Marguerite Duras (1914–1996), who
is often associated with the Nouveau Roman literary movement
in France, and directed by Alain Resnais (born in 1922), who is
often grouped with the French Nouvelle Vague film movement.
Nouveau roman, *nouvelle vague*—that's the adjective "new"
twice. And indeed, Duras and Resnais and their cohorts in the
1950s and '60s were doing something new in their respective
attempts to break from the conventions of the past to better
address the needs of the present. Despite dating from half a
century ago—the movie was released in 1959—the newness of
Hiroshima Mon Amour hasn't worn off.

You'll see that right away. The movie seems to have all the
traits of a staid classic. It's shot in black and white, the style of

the clothes worn by the characters would now be called vintage, the cars seen in the movie are now antiques, and so on. But right away the movie subverts expectations. The subject matter, for example. So many movies nowadays merely entertain; that is, they amuse without challenging, titillating spectators but not actually upsetting them. Nothing like that with *Hiroshima Mon Amour*. The very title makes that clear. Hiroshima will always be best known for one thing: for having been the unhappy and devastated target of the world's first atomic bomb. That title starter is followed by *Mon Amour*. My love? The-horrible-death-of-70,000-men-women-and-children-instantly-and-then-at-least-another-100,000-as-a-consequence-of-radiation-sickness *My Love*? Be forewarned: this is not a movie that goes particularly well with popcorn.

The mode of narration is another challenge. Despite the lack of any special effects, the movie is hardly an example of cinematic realism. Outwardly, it's about a French actress shooting a movie on peace in Hiroshima who meets a Japanese architect with whom she has a brief love affair. But that's like saying that *Death in Venice* is about an old fag who goes to Venice and dies. The trappings of plot in *Hiroshima*—as in *Death in Venice*—are secondary. What really determines the shape of the movie are the forces of pain, longing, memory and time. Duras's screenplay and Resnais's film are like opera: they're all about emotion. The story is therefore minimal, the characters are known only as He and She, the sequence of events is unpredictable. *Hiroshima* is a *reactive* movie, in the same sense that emotions are reactive. And so it has the features of strong emotion: it is wilful, stubborn, awkward, strangely attractive. Next to it, the usual fluff we get in cinemas today, so formulaic and clichéd, comes off as reactionary.

Hiroshima Mon Amour is sober and radical. It's a beautiful, intelligent and moving experience. I hope you rise to its challenge.

Yours truly,
Yann Martel

P.S. And still another reply. Though this one doesn't mention the book it is meant to acknowledge. If I go by the date, May 22nd, it must be a thank-you for my gift of The Gift, *by Lewis Hyde.* [See the REPLY section of Book 55.] *I get the sense that L. A. Lavell, another of your executive correspondence officers, didn't spend much time on the book. Will you ever write to me?*

MARGUERITE DURAS (1914–1996) was a French writer and film director. She was a member of the French Resistance during World War II. Her book *L'Amant* (*The Lover*) won the Prix Goncourt in 1984. Duras is buried in Montparnasse Cemetery, Paris.

ALAIN RESNAIS (b. 1922) is a French filmmaker. He began making films when he was fourteen. His documentaries include an Academy Award–winning film biography of Vincent van Gogh (*Van Gogh*, 1948), *Nuit et Brouillard* (*Night and Fog*, 1955) and *Guernica* (1950). He frequently adapts other works of art into films.

BOOKS 58 AND 59:

RUNAWAY
BY ALICE MUNRO
AND
THE DOOR
BY MARGARET ATWOOD
WITH
CAMINO
MUSIC BY OLIVER SCHROER
June 22, 2009

for *Runaway*:
To Stephen Harper,
Prime Minister of Canada,
To honour a great Canadian writer,
From another Canadian writer,
With best wishes,
Yann Martel

for *The Door*:
To Stephen Harper,
Prime Minister of Canada,
Another great Canadian writer,
From a Canadian writer,
With best wishes,
Yann Martel

for *Camino*:
To Stephen Harper,
Prime Minister of Canada,
Haunting, beautiful music,
With best wishes,
Yann Martel

Dear Mr. Harper,

Have you called Alice Munro? I remember when I won the Man Booker Prize I got a phone call from Prime Minister Chrétien. I was living in Berlin at the time, he was calling from Ottawa, so the call required a little bit of organizing. I spoke with an aide, he took my phone number and we agreed on a time the next day. At the appointed time, the phone in my office rang, I answered and it was Jean Chrétien. Though I knew it would be him, it still came as a shock. I had the Prime Minister of Canada on the line! And he wanted to talk to me! We spoke for a few minutes. He congratulated me on my win. I replied I was happy to have won a third Booker for Canada. He said he found writing a book hard work. He was referring to his memoir *Straight from the Heart*. Writing a book *is* hard work, I said, but well worth the effort. He agreed. We went on like this for a few minutes, two strangers chatting amiably. Then he said he had to go, I promptly thanked him for calling me, saying I was honoured, and I wished him a good day. He thanked me and wished me the same. I was touched that a man so busy and important should take a moment to speak to me. After all, what did he gain from it? It was a private phone call to one Canadian. At most, he might gain one vote. But that wasn't the reason. He was Prime Minister of Canada, Prime

Minister of *all* Canadians, and clearly he felt it was his duty to speak to a Canadian writer who had just received a high honour, even if he hadn't read the book for which that writer was honoured.

And now Alice Munro has been honoured with the Man Booker International Prize, given out only once every two years to a writer for their outstanding achievement in fiction. After the Albanian writer Ismail Kadare in 2005, after the Nigerian writer Chinua Achebe in 2007, our very own Alice Munro has won the 2009 Man Booker International Prize. Highly worthy of commendation, no?

In honour of Alice Munro, I'm sending you this week her 2004 collection of short stories, *Runaway*, both in print form and as an audiobook read by the actor Kymberly Dakin. There's no particular reason why I chose to send you the audiobook. I just happened to see that it was available and what with it being summer and the travelling that summer often brings on, I thought it might be pleasant for you to pop the CDs, nine in all, into your car's CD player and immerse yourself in Munro's intimate stories. In the second story of the collection, "Chance," a curious coincidence will jump out at you. The protagonist, Juliet, mentions that she and a fellow teacher have gone to see a "revival of a movie." What's the movie? *Hiroshima Mon Amour*, the very movie I sent you last week. How likely is that? (Did you enjoy it?) Alice Munro is very well known and hugely admired, so I feel a little silly talking of her work, but in case you aren't familiar with it, I will say the following. Much fiction—my own included—relies on the extraordinary, on characters unlikely to be met, and events unlikely to be shared, by the reader. Stories of this kind are like a trip abroad; we are refreshed by what is strange and exotic in them. This approach hasn't been Munro's. Her stories are about people who could be our neighbours and what happens to them might very well be familiar to us. Does this make these stories boring, uninteresting, banal? Under another writer's pen, it might. But under Munro's, it doesn't. By force of telling details and psychological candour, the lives of her characters become as interesting to us as our own lives are interesting to us. It's not that Munro makes the ordinary extraordinary. She doesn't. What she does is restore to the ordinary its vital, pulsing feel. Her stories are less about the great upheavals that can tear a life apart and more about the smaller ups and downs that define it. In a word, her stories are about texture. What I like about Alice Munro is that she makes me like my neighbours more, because after reading a collection of her stories my neighbours all seem like they could be characters in her stories, and that's an endearing quality in people, that they seem as rich as fiction.

Runaway, both print book and audiobook, counts as Book 58. I'm leaving shortly on that expedition I was talking to you about in my letter that accompanied Book 52, *Burning Ice*: I'm off to trek the mountains and forests of Peru for three weeks to see the effects of climate change on the tropical environment. I'm not sure about mailing you a book from the Amazon, so I've decided to include Book 59 in this week's package, a two-for-one deal that I've done before. And what book would go more naturally with an Alice Munro book than one by Margaret Atwood? The two names are so often paired, one would think they were conjoined twins. They are no doubt Canada's best-known writers on the international stage, along with Michael Ondaatje. And since we're speaking of the prize, Atwood won Canada its second Booker (while Ondaatje won Canada its first).

I have selected for you Margaret Atwood's latest collection of poetry, *The Door*. I haven't sent you poetry in a while and Atwood is a versatile writer, as adept with poetry as she is with fiction. What's great about a collection of poetry is how much ground it can cover in so few pages. A rediscovered dollhouse, the death of a much-loved cat, aging parents, life under Emperor Caligula, war, old photographs, and many other subjects—each poem is its own world and the collection as a whole, a galaxy. The poems in *The Door* are conversational in tone yet incisive, and they range emotionally from the sentimental to the political. I would especially recommend to you the poems "Owl and Pussycat, some years later," which is about the life of the poet, and the marvellous title poem, "The Door," which is about, well, about life, all of it, the living of it and the meaning of it, all seen through the metaphor of a swinging door and all in two pages. I would also recommend, as with all poetry, that you read each poem silently first, to get a sense of it, and then aloud, so that you get its full effect.

Sending you books by two writers from the same country makes me wonder if there is such a thing as a national literature. Is there something essentially Canadian about Munro and Atwood, essentially Russian about Tolstoy and Dostoyevsky, essentially English about Austen and Dickens, and so on. Of course, the language and setting of a work give something away. A story set in Germany and told in German is likely the work of a German writer—but is it therefore a German story? If a Canadian writer sets a story in, say, India, as Rohinton Mistry did with *A Fine Balance*, is that story any less Canadian, somehow, than a story set in rural Ontario? You have suggested that Michael Ignatieff's Canadianness was somehow suspect because he spent so many years abroad. Does that purported loss of national identity apply to stories too? I think not, neither with people nor with stories. I too spent many years abroad and never felt any less Canadian for it. And I think the same can be said of a Canadian story. Let's take as an example Josef Škvorecký. He writes in Czech mostly about Czech matters, but he's been living in Canada for over forty years. Would we deny Škvorecký his Canadianness? If we do, by what standard? If it's language, again, what claim do we have on the English and French languages? We share those with many other countries. This question of a national literature is a fascinating quagmire. If such a literature does exist, it's clearly an ever-shifting, highly permeable body of work. And it engenders another question: does the country determine the nature of a writer's work or does the writer determine the nature of the country? I think it could be argued both ways. In some cases, a writer—Kafka would be one example—clearly emanates from a determining time, place, and culture. But others—Atwood and Munro, for instance—seem more universal, as if, given different circumstances but similar personalities, they might as well have come from England or France or the United States. Who's to know? Gosh, I wonder how many times I've contradicted myself in one paragraph. No matter. I asked the question about national literature without having a readymade answer.

Lastly this week, I'm sending you a music CD by a Canadian violinist named Oliver Schroer. It's called *Camino*, as in the Camino de Santiago de Compostela, named after the town in northwestern Spain that has been an important pilgrimage destination since the Middle Ages. People have walked to Santiago from all over Europe for centuries. I did it in 2001, right after finishing my novel *Life of Pi*. I walked 1,600 kilometres in five weeks. It was a luminous experience. Schroer also explored the Camino and this CD is the result of that exploration. I offer it to you simply because the music is hauntingly beautiful. Sadly, Schroer died of leukemia just last summer, which adds poignancy to his music.

A rather busy package. May you enjoy it all.

Yours truly,
Yann Martel

ALICE MUNRO (b. 1931) is a Canadian short story writer. Her stories are generally set in southwestern Ontario and focus on the daily lives of "ordinary" people; thematically, she has been compared to Chekhov. In the 1960s, she and her first husband, Jim Munro, moved to Victoria and opened Munro's Books, which survives today. Munro published her first collection of stories, *Dance of the Happy Shades*, in 1968. It was an auspicious beginning: the book won the Governor General's Literary Award and launched a career that includes sixteen books of short stories, including *Runaway*, winner of the 2004 Scotiabank Giller Prize. She lives in Ontario.

MARGARET ATWOOD (b. 1939) is a poet, novelist, literary critic and essayist. She is also known for her political and environmental activism—and her lively Twitter feed. She is the author of thirteen novels, most recently *The Year of the Flood*, and twenty books of poetry. Her books have received the Booker Prize, the Governor General's Literary Award and the Trillium Book Award. Atwood is a Companion of the Order of Canada, and lives in Toronto with the writer Graeme Gibson.

OLIVER SCHROER (1956–2008) was a fiddler, composer, educator and producer. He recorded twelve albums and contributed to or produced over one hundred recordings. He is best known for his album *Camino*.

BOOK 60

THE TIN FLUTE
BY GABRIELLE ROY
Translated from the French by Hannah Josephson
July 20, 2009

To Stephen Harper,
Prime Minister of Canada,
From a Canadian writer,
With best wishes,
Yann Martel

Dear Mr. Harper,

This week I'm sending you the French- and English-language versions of the same novel, *Bonheur d'occasion* (in English *The Tin Flute*), by Gabrielle Roy, published in 1945. I imagine you'll want to read it in English primarily, but the novel is so rooted in its language that it would be a pity if you didn't delve from time to time into the original version. If you are at all inclined to do so, I'd suggest you have a look at sections of dialogue in French. Gabrielle Roy, like Zora Neale Hurston in *Their Eyes Were Watching God*, which I sent you a while ago, uses two levels of language. When the author is speaking as the omniscient narrator, the French is formal, grammatically and syntactically correct, timeless and universal. But when her characters are speaking, then a very particular language, place and time are evoked, the vernacular French of Saint Henri, a poor neighbourhood of Montreal, in 1940. It's a French that exists nowhere else and it would be a pity if you didn't get at least a taste of it.

The title in French literally means second-hand or used happiness. The title in English expresses the same idea, but using a tiny element of the novel: Daniel, one of the Lacasse children, is sickly and always clamours for a little tin flute. It would make him so happy, to be able to toot away on one. But he never gets one because the Lacasses are too beset by poverty. With both titles and in whatever language you read it, the message of the novel, the picture it draws, is the same: one of blighted lives, of happiness denied, of unremitting misery. Quebec has changed profoundly since 1945. A younger francophone Québécois generation might even react with disbelief that such a province as Roy portrays ever existed. The Quebec of *Bonheur d'occasion* is one deeply divided between the English and the French, a gulf that Hugh MacLennan captured with the title of his novel that came out the same year as Roy's, *Two Solitudes*. The English were the elite, generally wealthy and powerful, living in exclusive neighbourhoods like Westmount, while the French were the masses, generally poor and powerless and living in inclusive neighbourhoods like Saint Henri. In the novel, English Quebeckers are hardly seen or heard. At most, their large houses are eyed with envy and astonishment by poor Québécois who wander up the mountain into parts of the city to which they do not—and feel they never will—belong. Even the English language is barely heard, only here and there in little phrases. Otherwise, the Québécois live in total linguistic and social isolation. Their isolation extends beyond the linguistic. Though unstated in the novel, the Lacasse family are who they are and where they are in part because of their religion. They are Catholics and Catholics at that time, especially the poorer ones, had enormous families. *La revanche des berceaux*, it was called, the revenge of the cradle. The English might be richer, more powerful, but we will beat them with our numbers—that was the idea. And so the families with eleven, fifteen, nineteen children. Those numbers have ensured that the Québécois have prevailed and beaten back the forces of assimilation, but they also meant a degree of impoverishment, as large families struggled to feed so many mouths and clothe so many bodies.

The novel revolves around various members of the large Lacasse family, principally Florentine, the eldest daughter, Rose-Anna, her loving mother who always tries her best, and Azarius, her well-meaning but hapless husband. Only Florentine brings in a steady revenue from her job as a waitress. But it's not much and the family is forever moving from one slum dwelling to a worse but cheaper one. Their lives are squalid and wretched. They are clothed in tatters and malnourished. They are the unhappy slaves of an economic system that doesn't need them. All they have to keep them going is their dreams. Florentine seeks refuge in love, Azarius in lofty dreams of a better future that he's incapable of bringing about, while Florentine's little sister Yvonne hides in religion. All of them are utterly powerless and warped by their ravaging poverty. Their suffering does not make them angels; it merely confirms their humanity. Their lot is so bad that their ultimate friend turns out to be war. The opportunity to join the army and gain the pittance that an enlisted man earns is finally their only way of making a living, no matter if it means that they might be killed or have to kill.

There is one character in the novel who is absent: a priest. The trappings of religion, in the form of kitsch reproductions of sacred figures, adorn the walls of the Lacasses' living room and the family's exclamations and profanities are religious in nature, but an actual servant of the Lord never appears in the novel. That puzzles me. Blame for much of the misery in the novel, certainly the spiritual misery, can be assigned to the Catholic Church. Its message of accepting suffering in this world because of future rewards in a next world had the effect of engendering profound passivity in its followers. Furthermore, the Church's rigid moral code meant that if an unmarried woman fell pregnant her life was ruined and her child would likely be deemed an orphan, shunned by society, despite having both a father and a mother. The Church then, as now in many ways, was anti-feminist and anti-modern, obscurantist and backward-looking. It fed its followers in Quebec rancid spiritual placebos while they rotted in material misery and stagnated intellectually. I wonder why Gabrielle Roy refrained from criticizing such an institution.

The quibble is minor. *Bonheur d'occasion* is fiction, but one solidly rooted in reality. It's a masterly example of the novel as memory, as document. As a Québécois myself, I read it with a mixture of shame that conditions could have been so bad for my people just a few generations ago and consequent anger at the agents responsible for those conditions. You read this novel and right away you understand the forces behind that great leap into modernity that was La Révolution tranquille, which transformed Quebec from Canada's most backward province into its most progressive.

I will end this letter abruptly. My partner Alice's waters have just broken and our first child, a boy, Theo, is on his way. A child is the best novel, with a great plot and endless character development. I must attend to it.

Yours truly,
Yann Martel

P.S. And two more replies. Tony Clement, the Minister of Industry, sent me a complete answer to my query about SSHRC's funding [see the REPLY section of Book 51: *Julius Caesar*], *while P. Monteith in your office thanked me in a much briefer way for the next book I sent you.* [See the REPLY section of Book 52: *Burning Ice.*]

P.P.S. Please excuse the somewhat tattered condition of the French version of Bonheur d'occasion. *I read it while I was in the Peruvian Amazon recently and the humidity got to it.*

GABRIELLE ROY (1909–1983) was a Quebec writer whose first novel, *Bonheur d'occasion*, won the Prix Femina; its English-language translation, *The Tin Flute*, won the Governor General's Literary Award and the Royal Society of Canada's Lorne Pierce Medal. A quotation by Roy appears on the back of the Canadian twenty-dollar bill: "Could we ever know each other in the slightest without the arts?"

WHERE THE WILD THINGS ARE

AND

IN THE NIGHT KITCHEN

STORIES AND PICTURES BY MAURICE SENDAK

August 3, 2009

To Stephen Harper,
Prime Minister of Canada,
A reminder of childhood's wonder,
From a Canadian writer,
With best wishes,
Yann Martel

Dear Mr. Harper,

In honour of my son, Theo, who is fifteen days old (and keeping me very busy), I am sending you this week two picture books, *Where the Wild Things Are* and *In the Night Kitchen*, both by the American writer and illustrator Maurice Sendak, who was born in 1928. These are unforgettable books. You read them— or more likely they are first read to you—and they stay with you the rest of your life. I'm not exaggerating. Try it yourself: mention at random to people around you, "I was sent a book called *Where the Wild Things Are*," and you'll be amazed at the number of seasoned adults who break into a smile and exclaim, "Oh, that's a wonderful book!"

There's a lovely saying: the child is the father of the man. It applies to all aspects of an adult's personality, but I think it does so especially with the imagination. From what the child imagines in dreams and fantasies comes what the adult will hold up as ideals. Hence the importance of children's literature. The fundamental role of children's literature is to encourage children to use their imagination. Because small as children are physically, large is what they can imagine. Sadly, a relation of inverse proportion sets in for many of us: as we grow in size, our capacity to imagine seems to shrink. And so we have adults with the most leaden, literal-thinking minds, beholden to the real and the factual, adults whose imagination has so shrunk that they can't even remember (let alone imagine) what it is like to be a child, even though that was once their real and factual condition. Being children, they knew no gravity of the mind but could float and leap to any place. If the expandable imagination of a child's mind is not expanded, then it will shrink all the more, harden all the more, when that child grows up. The consequence is more dire than simply an adult with a dull, narrow mind. Such an adult is also less useful to society because he or she will be incapable of coming up with the new ideas and new solutions that society needs. A skill is a narrow focus of knowledge, a single card in a deck. Creativity is the hand that plays the cards. Hence, once again, the importance of children's literature to expand the imagination at an early age.

We read (present tense) as adults because we read (past tense) as children, and we are fully alive adults in the present because in the past we were fully alive children. Books are a key link between those two states. So I encourage you not to rush through *Where the Wild Things Are* and *In the Night Kitchen*, short though they are. Let them have their slow, deep effect. In *Where the Wild Things Are*, ask yourself what Max's state of mind is, and why that should be his state of mind, and what it might mean. Is Max's relationship with the monsters what you would expect? Look at the illustrations of *In the Night Kitchen*.

Who do the cooks with their narrow moustaches remind you of? What then might it mean when Mickey escapes the batter and floats away from the oven? In other words, I would suggest that you not just read these books (and aloud, even better), but imagine them.

Yours truly,
Yann Martel

P.S. Where the Wild Things Are *and* In the Night Kitchen *are the first two books of a trilogy. If you enjoyed them, you can try to find the third book,* Outside Over There. *It's a joyful hunt, the hunt for a book.*

MAURICE SENDAK (1928–2012) was a writer and illustrator of children's literature. He was the author of more than sixteen books and the illustrator of many, many more books. His archives are housed in the Rosenbach Museum & Library in Philadelphia, and an elementary school in North Hollywood is named after him.

BOOK 62

EVERYMAN
BY PHILIP ROTH
August 17, 2009

To Stephen Harper,
Prime Minister of Canada,
A novel about where we're all heading,
From a Canadian writer,
With best wishes,
Yann Martel

Dear Mr. Harper,

Just as a new life enters my life, I thought I'd look at how an old life ends. And so I am sending you this week the novel *Everyman*, by the American writer Philip Roth, who was born in 1933. Roth has been writing for a long time. His first book, a collection of six short stories, *Goodbye, Columbus*, was published in 1959. Roth was twenty-six years old. In the fifty years since, he has published another thirty or so books, most of them novels. And since much of his work has autobiographical elements, it's not surprising that Roth should eventually turn to the subject of aging and dying.

The child is ever expanding; as its body grows in size and strength, so does its mind and its ability to take in the surrounding world. The feeling, if you remember, is rich, wondrous and chaotic, an involvement with people, animals, objects, events, places, weather and nature that results in the most intense emotions, from soaring exhilaration to wrenching anguish, from overwhelming curiosity to stupefying boredom. Those years of emotional exploration mark us for life, directing us towards who we are and what we do in our mature years.

Then we grow old. Aging is shrinking. The body grows smaller and weaker. The lucid mind stands over its decaying body like a great tree whose soil and roots are being undercut by the bend of a river. The pains of the body accumulate. It's a never-ending battle, with full recovery an ever-receding hope. The mind starts to go too, and though forgetting names and faces is not physically painful, it brings on mental anguish. To make matters worse, old age brings on loneliness, as the relations of one's working life are left behind, as friends drift away, as family members go on with their own lives. The world has left and forgotten us, it seems. The knowledge that the inevitable conclusion of this physical, mental and social breakdown is one's complete disappearance brings on inescapable gloom and acute dread. To let go of life, after a lifetime of living—is there any greater challenge?

Everyman relates the life of a nameless man who is not ordinary or generic in his life particulars—after all, he lives in a specific city, practises during his working life a particular job, has relations to family, friends and lovers that are unique to him—but is an everyman by the fact of his aging body and approaching death. The novel is in many ways a medical story, following the trials and tribulations of Everyman's body from a biological, corporeal perspective. Ailments and medical emergencies, hospitalizations, convalescences, nurses, old people—this is the universe of *Everyman*.

It's a grim tale. The conclusion is foregone. In fact, the novel starts with Everyman's funeral. Roth pulls the reader along, so that Everyman's demise, like that of Ivan Ilych, is horrifying at the same time as it is compelling. I couldn't read the novel without comparing my own imagined old age with that of Roth's protagonist. Will my heart go like his? Or will it be my back, like that of Everyman's friend Millicent Kramer, who suffers unbearable pain as the result of her spine's decomposition? What will my social relations be like? Will I be attended to, or left lonely and isolated? So many tragedies in life can be avoided, some by care and consideration, others by pure luck. I have lived a life remarkably spared of tragedy and unhappiness. But one's death, the body that falls apart, the mind that goes, that tragedy is inescapable. It is our collective and individual future.

Having said that, there are ways of approaching death that can change its meaning, if not its pain. I'm of course speaking of a spiritual approach. If death is seen as a threshold, a step up whose peculiar form requires the leaving behind of one's body, then death becomes not an ending but a beginning, a transformation. "Religious mumbo-jumbo! Ignorant claptrap!" some will cry. But one's death and the ideas one may have about its meaning are no one else's business. It's a private affair. And just as children's heads are filled with imaginative mumbo-jumbo that is the very colour and texture of a happy childhood, so can religious mumbo-jumbo be the colour and texture of a contented letting go at the end of life. In saying this, in arguing for the practical usefulness—as well as the deep joy (and the possible truthfulness)—of a transcendent view of life and death, I am straying from the narrative of *Everyman*. The novel is resolutely, unflinchingly secular. There is no redemption or grace in Roth's novel, or none that overcomes the dread of death. The ending is grim and it comes grimly. It's a tale that yields the only moral possible from such an earthbound perspective: *carpe diem*, seize the day, enjoy today for tomorrow you die.

If this is your first Philip Roth, you'll be struck at the artless simplicity of it. You don't write so many novels that have won so many awards without learning how to tell a good story well. Even if Everyman's particulars don't match yours—his sexual obsession with very young women, for example, struck me as harking to a certain kind of dated aging male who came of age in the fifties and sixties—the psychological astuteness will nonetheless bring him close to you. You may dislike Everyman in his earlier years, feeling repelled by his arrogance, his stupidity, his selfishness, but his slow, grinding end will touch you, because in that he is like you, he is like me. *Everyman* is so finely calibrated emotionally and so perfectly crafted that it resembles the symbolic element on the cover of the edition I'm sending you: a watch.

My father, Émile, who turned sixty-eight a few days ago, sent me a poem he wrote. By coincidence, it too deals with the anguish of aging and I will end this letter with it:

> I am the oldest I have ever been.
> I may even be as old as I'll ever get.
> So I want to be left alone on the shore of this river,
> to see the tide roll in and out
> and watch which boats of the past will pass by,
> which one will stop and pick me up
> and take me back there.
> This is where I am now,
> this is who I am now.
> Leave me alone.

Yours truly,
Yann Martel

PHILIP ROTH (b. 1933) is an American novelist. He has written numerous books, including the Zuckerman novels, *Portnoy's Complaint*, the National Book Award–winning *Goodbye, Columbus*, and the Pulitzer Prize–winning *American Pastoral*. Roth's works generally focus on Jewish and American identity, and are often set in his hometown of Newark, New Jersey. In 2011 Roth was honoured with the Man Booker International Prize.

BOOK 63

FLAUBERT'S PARROT
BY JULIAN BARNES
August 31, 2009

To Stephen Harper,
Prime Minister of Canada,
A fine example of a literary novel,
From a Canadian writer,
With best wishes,
Yann Martel

Dear Mr. Harper,

An unabashedly literary novel is what I'm sending you this week. You might find the statement surprising. Haven't all the novels I've sent you been literary, you might ask? They have. But the book you now have in your hands, *Flaubert's Parrot*, by the English writer Julian Barnes (born in 1946), is more self-consciously literary than most of these other books (an exception jumps to mind: the twenty-seventh book I sent you, Virginia Woolf's *To the Lighthouse*). The attempt to lure the reader with an intriguing story and interesting characters, the writing style that seeks to be like a pane of glass, invisible so that the story appears to be seen and felt directly, as if the writer were not the intermediary, all these are less prominent in Barnes's novel. Which is not to say that there aren't stories and characters and clear writing in *Flaubert's Parrot*. There are, of course. But their proportion is different. The author is not so self-effacing here, not so wholly dedicated to pleasing the reader.

The definition of a literary novel might be this: a literary novel is a novel that makes the reader work. A non-literary or genre novel builds on conventions. So a murder mystery or a thriller or a romance novel will have characters whom the reader will quickly seize and plot developments that will create definite expectations, which the author will then play with, either shattering them (it's not the doctor who committed the murder but the little old lady you didn't think twice about) or confirming them (the boy will get the girl, don't you worry). A literary novel relies on fewer conventions. The characters are more complex and layered, not so easily reduced to stereotypes, and the plot may hold many surprises. To read such a work is a more demanding experience, a train trip in which the reader isn't coddled by comforts or told of the final destination.

The literary novel is a daring gamble for its author. The risk of spectacular failure is considerable. A novel that adheres to the conventions of a genre can feature terrible writing and characters as thin as cling film, yet still be thoroughly enjoyable. In fact, many novels that are artistically trite sell very well precisely because they're enjoyable. A bad literary novel, by contrast, has few redeeming qualities. It often commits the worst sins of a book: it is boring and it lacks credibility.

This is not the case with *Flaubert's Parrot*. The work the reader has to put in is worth the effort. Why is that? Because the reader has to think. And this leads to a second definition: a literary novel is a novel that makes the reader think. This actually follows from the first definition; if a reader is working, so to speak, it is because that reader is thinking. And therein lies the strength of literary fiction, why the risk of failure is taken on: because thinking is a good and necessary activity. Whereas in our emotional lives we favour stability, seeking and staying with the familiar, keeping in touch with our parents, for example, long after they've stopped parenting us or settling down and living with the same person for years on end, establishing a routine that may last a whole adult life, such fixity is the enemy of intellect. In our intellectual lives, we seek change and evolution, we want to learn and "move with the times." In the realm of ideas, comfort and excessive familiarity are signs of stagnation, not security. And so the constant thinking is required, because new ideas only come from thinking.

All this to say: be prepared for a slower ride with *Flaubert's Parrot*. It does not shoot forward like an express train. Regularly, I'll bet, you'll say to yourself, "That was well put," or "That's a word I haven't seen in a while." I also bet you'll regularly stop reading, as if you were getting off at a station. You'll stop because you'll feel the need to think, to decide whether you agree with this or that point in the novel, or if you've understood the point at all. But if you get back on the train, you'll find the journey worthwhile and you'll be pleased with your final destination. What is that final destination? It's not for me to say, but I was impressed with the verbal and formal play in *Flaubert's Parrot* and I felt some of its knowledge and intellect rubbed off on me.

Dear, dear, I'm losing myself in abstractions. Concretely, *Flaubert's Parrot* is about a retired widower doctor who is obsessed with the nineteenth-century French novelist Gustave Flaubert. Flaubert wrote *Madame Bovary* and was one of the great stylists of the French language (don't worry, you don't need to have read anything by Flaubert to enjoy the book). There's *a lot* about Flaubert in this novel. It's not linear in its development and it's full of opinions and observations, each of which the reader is expected to react to. This is the thinking I was referring to. It's a peevish, proudly persnickety, highly intelligent novel, very much like Flaubert himself. And it's thoroughly enjoyable, if you make the effort.

If you don't make the effort, well then, you'll just find it boring and you'll want to hurry back to your received ideas. I rather hope you settle into this curious English novel that choo-choos along so nicely.

Yours truly,
Yann Martel

JULIAN BARNES (b. 1946) is the author of eleven novels, three books of stories and two collections of essays. He has also written crime fiction using the *nom de plume* Dan Kavanagh. His works frequently address themes of British and French culture and identity. His honours include the Man Booker Prize, the Somerset Maugham Award, the Geoffrey Faber Memorial Prize and the E. M. Forster Award from the American Academy of Arts and Letters. In 2004 he was named Commandeur de l'Ordre des Arts et des Lettres. He lives in London.

BOOK 64

THE VIRGIN SECRETARY'S IMPOSSIBLE BOSS
BY CAROLE MORTIMER

September 14, 2009

To Stephen Harper,
Prime Minister of Canada,
Can 130 million people be wrong?
From a Canadian writer,
With best wishes,
Yann Martel

Dear Mr. Harper,

Since I was speaking about it in my last letter, I thought I would send you an example of genre fiction, and what genre fiction has a more recognizable brand than a Harlequin romance? A word about Harlequin. Their website informs me that they are a Canadian enterprise that publishes "over 120 titles a month in 29 languages in 107 international markets on six continents." In 2007, Harlequin sold 130 million books. Since its founding, the company has sold a staggering, an unbelievable, 5.63 *billion* books. Those italics are Harlequin's: they are clearly proud of their success, and so they should be. To have retailed nearly as many books as there are people on this planet is a unique achievement in publishing. You will get a hint of Harlequin's depth of success when you look at the title page of the novel I'm sending you this week. Publishers usually mention where they have offices. To take a random example from my bookshelf, the hardcover edition I have of the novel *Slow Man*, by the Nobel laureate J. M. Coetzee, my favourite living writer, is the British edition, and it was published by Secker & Warburg. The title page informs me where they have offices: London. That's it. The publishers of Carole Mortimer's *The Virgin Secretary's Impossible Boss*, by contrast, append a condensed atlas of cities: Toronto, New York, London, Amsterdam, Paris, Sydney, Hamburg, Stockholm, Athens, Tokyo, Milan, Madrid, Prague, Warsaw, Budapest and Auckland. And their website informs me that this list is not up to date: Harlequin also has offices in Mumbai, Rio de Janeiro and even in a place called Granges-Paccot (I looked it up: it's in Switzerland).

Now, can that many people be wrong? What's the appeal of *The Virgin Secretary's Impossible Boss?*

Well, it's not the writing. Take these three lines:

"Lucky, lucky me," he drawled dryly.
"You're impossible," Andi told him impatiently.
He shrugged unrepentantly. "So I'm told."

Oh, those adverbs. They clutter the prose like too many traffic lights on a road. But they make for easy, unthreatening prose, for prose that relieves the reader of having to think very hard. Elegance may be lost, but a clarity of sorts is gained. Faults can be found in other aspects of the writing too, as they can be found in the characterization and in the plot. And yet there are those numbers. 130 million. 5.63 *billion*.

I think the appeal of a Harlequin romance lies precisely in those traffic lights. A street with traffic lights is a safe street, a street in which the movement of vehicles is carefully regulated so that everyone can get home safe and sound. There's something to be said for that kind of security. We don't always want to be driving down adventurous roads that cross swamps, deserts and mountains.

The Virgin Secretary's Impossible Boss is the story of Linus Harrison, a handsome, muscular, driven multi-millionaire, and his beautiful, independent personal assistant, Andrea Buttonfield. There are obstacles in their way, including a snow-storm in Scotland that would chill the hardiest Yukoner—a storm that strands Linus and Andi in a pub where there's only one room with one bed available to them—but they will find perfect love. Reading the book, I was reminded of Indian cinema. The usual fare from Bollywood is equally silly, unre-alistic and escapist, yet that is exactly what the average Indian viewer wants, an escape from the harsh realities of life into a glamorous world populated by rich, beautiful people where a happy ending is guaranteed. The function of genre fiction is to relax and confirm, not to stress and challenge. Genre fiction seeks to deliver one thing: emotional satisfaction.

Is that such a bad thing? I don't think so. So read *The Virgin Secretary's Impossible Boss*, and glimpse the dream world of bil-lions of people.

Yours truly,
Yann Martel

CAROLE MORTIMER (b. 1960) is a romance novelist. She has written more than 150 books, and lives in England with her husband and six children.

BOOK 65

THE TARTAR STEPPE
BY DINO BUZZATI

Translated from the Italian by Stuart Hood

September 28, 2009

To Stephen Harper,
Prime Minister of Canada,
A novel on the perils of waiting,
From a Canadian writer,
With best wishes,
Yann Martel

Dear Mr. Harper,

It's not my habit to quote myself, but to introduce the novel *The Tartar Steppe*, by the Italian writer Dino Buzzati (1906–1972), I will:

> A beautiful, masterly novel that shimmers like a mirage, bringing into sharp focus the rise and fall of our ambitions and the pitiless erosion of time. It is the story of one Giovanni Drogo—yet how many of us will be stricken to recognize something of ourselves in him?

You'll find these words on the back cover of the edition I'm sending you. The blurb is one way in which a writer can be a citizen of the arts. When giving a blurb, a writer lends his or her éclat to a book, so that the reader is guided not only by what the writer says, but by the esteem in which that writer is held by the reader. I've been the beneficiary of a good blurb: Margaret Atwood kindly read and liked my novel *Life of Pi* and her supportive words likely attracted the attention of a good number of readers. Sometimes the blurb will be by a journalist and its weight will depend on the prestige of the newspaper in which the journalist's review appeared. This system of commendation can be very effective in helping a book meet its readers, and publishers use it all the time. When you finish your book on hockey, your publisher will dream of getting Wayne Gretzky to read it and commend it. "If the Great One liked this book, I'm sure I will too," every hockey fan will say, grabbing the book off the shelf.

For this British edition of *The Tartar Steppe*, the blurb system is in full operation. On the front cover, the *Sunday Times* ("A masterpiece") and J. M. Coetzee ("A strange and haunting novel, an eccentric classic") exhort the reader to pay attention, while on the back cover Alberto Manguel, Jorge Luis Borges and I, in a few more words, explain to a prospective reader why this book must be read.

And really, it *must* be read. *The Tartar Steppe*, published in 1940, is indeed a masterpiece, insufficiently known to the reading public. It tells the story of a young officer who is posted to a remote fort on the edges of an unnamed country. And there he waits for an invasion of barbarians that never comes. He waits for thirty years, he waits his entire life away, arriving at the fort as a young man full of prospects and leaving it old and broken. Waiting—and with it the dread of expectation—is a very twentieth-century concern. If Samuel Beckett had been writing a century earlier, he would have written *Acting for Godot*. But because it was the twentieth century that paid the price for the nineteenth's actions for God and for country—all the mess of colonialism and greedy empire-building—Beckett wrote *Waiting for Godot*. Invoking the play (which I sent you a while ago, remember?) is not inappropriate. *The Tartar Steppe* and *Waiting for Godot* were written within ten years of each other, the novel in the late 1930s, the play in the late 1940s, and they speak of the same concern. But in the ten years between the two compositions, the century shifted from the modern to the postmodern, from acting to waiting, from hoping to dreading, and that shift is reflected in the two works. *The Tartar Steppe* lies at the end of a traditional aesthetic sensibility that had run its course. *Godot* is the irreverent next step, steeped in caustic humour and bleakness and far more self-conscious.

The Tartar Steppe is a sober and luminous work. The luminosity is literal: the fort is set amidst high mountains and is bathed in pure light and thin air. But the story also achieves a philosophical brightness as it follows one man's endless waiting in a setting that is stripped of all excessive adornments—it's a military fort, after all. If you want a sense of the feel of the work, imagine a room in a modern art museum that is large and flooded with natural light and that features a single, large painting, a Rothko. You see what I mean? The novel is bleak, but beautifully bleak. I've often thought of Dino Buzzati as a cheerier, warmer Franz Kafka.

See what you think. Explore Fort Bastiani with Giovanni Drogo. Fall into the routine of a military life. Try to make the grade. Most important: keep your eyes open for the enemy!

Yours truly,
Yann Martel

P.S. I forgot to mention: The Tartar Steppe *was one of the favourite novels of François Mitterrand. What a splendid blurb that would be, from the president of France.*

DINO BUZZATI (1906–1972) was an Italian novelist, journalist, playwright, short story writer, poet and painter. He worked as a journalist in Africa in World War II, and remained at the Milanese newspaper *Corriere della Sera* for the duration of his career.

BOOK 66

WHAT IS STEPHEN HARPER READING?
BROUGHT TO YOU BY
DOZENS OF GREAT WRITERS

October 12, 2009

To Stephen Harper,
Prime Minister of Canada,
A book for book lovers,
From a Canadian writer,
With best wishes,
Yann Martel

Dear Mr. Harper,

Here is a book that I hope you've already read. There's safety in being published in book form. Who knows what might happen to the letters I sent you? I print an extra copy of each before mailing it to you, and the originals are, I hope, gathering in an archive box, but these physical traces are subject to the erosion of time or might simply be lost. As for the website that bears public witness to our book club, despite the easy access anyone has to it on a computer, it too is ephemeral. Though a website may appear on a limitless number of screens at the same moment, its underlying support is far more limited: just a virtual memory somewhere that, despite all the safeguards and backups, could be compromised and its contents destroyed. More simply, a website needs to be maintained, the subscription kept up, and so on. After you leave office, I'm not sure there will be a reason to keep www.whatisstephenharperreading.ca going.

Hence the satisfaction in seeing the letters—or at least the first fifty-five in the English Canada edition (sixty in the Quebec edition)—published as a book. Books last. They last first of all because they are cleverly constructed. I'm stating the obvious here, but a book's cover serves not only as decoration, allowing its contents to be visually represented, but as protection. If you remember the edition of Flannery O'Connor's *Everything That Rises Must Converge* that I sent you, the thirty-sixth book, it was over forty years old, and that was a run-of-the-mill paperback with the thinnest of covers. Imagine the durability of a proper hardcover book. Such books can last for hundreds and even thousands of years. But books last for another reason. Words are oral artifacts, originally travelling from the mouths of speakers into the ears of listeners, vanishing upon being heard like waves crashing upon a coastline. The amazing, civilization-making cleverness of books is that they preserve, like a refrigerator, the freshness of words so that they can burst unspoken from the minds of writers into the minds of readers through the medium of sight. But the value of a book still remains in what it says, not in what it is. Of course, some books are valued for their own sake: Gutenberg Bibles, for example, of which fewer than fifty copies exist. But most books are merely messengers, conveying a message to whoever wants to look and read. Since millions of people love to read, millions of books are produced. So *What Is Stephen Harper Reading?*, the book version, will last because it will find protection in all the homes and libraries that shelter it.

I won't say anything about the book except the following: though your name appears in it over and over, in the title, in the inscription, in the first line of each letter, the main subject is not actually you but the books I discuss. *What Is Stephen Harper Reading?* is a book about books. Eventually, there will be a complete edition. How many letters that book will contain, when it comes out, depends on you.

During a radio interview I did a few days ago in Montreal while promoting our book, the host mentioned that the Quebec journalist Chantal Hébert had sent you a book called *Fearful Symmetry: The Fall and Rise of Canada's Founding Values*, by the economist Brian Lee Crowley, and that you had written back to her, thanking her for the book and saying "... and I have read it"! Well, I don't have to ask what she has that I don't. I know the answer: I haven't sent you a single book on economic or political theory, or, for that matter, much non-fiction of any sort. Good of you to have read *Fearful Symmetry*. I'm not familiar with it. I hope you liked it. But is there any space on your reading list for a novel, a play, a poem? Last week you sang poetry to the Canadian people. No one expected "With a Little Help from My Friends" from you. And look at the effect you had. People were amazed. You made the front page of newspaper after newspaper, and often with a big photo of you at the piano. It goes to show how art can amaze, connect and unify.

Yours truly,
Yann Martel

BOOK 67

WAITING FOR THE BARBARIANS
BY J. M. COETZEE

October 26, 2009

To Stephen Harper,
Prime Minister of Canada,
A cautionary tale,
From a Canadian writer,
With best wishes,
Yann Martel

Dear Mr. Harper,

A few letters ago—number 64, to be precise, concerning Carole Mortimer's novel *The Virgin Secretary's Impossible Boss*— I mentioned in passing that J. M. Coetzee is my favourite living writer. Then in the next letter, in my discussion of blurbs, his name came up again, since a commendation of his graces Buzzati's *The Tartar Steppe*. Natural, then, to send you a novel by this superlative writer. John Maxwell Coetzee was born in South Africa in 1940 (he's now an Australian citizen). He's been showered with honours, notably two Booker Prizes and the 2003 Nobel Prize in Literature, and with good reason: he's an artist of the highest order, characterized by a style that is spare yet highly evocative and novels that are finely crafted, morally engaged and hypnotically compelling. To show him off to you, I've selected his third novel, *Waiting for the Barbarians*, published in 1980. The nameless Magistrate who is the story's protagonist lives in a frontier town on the edges of an equally nameless Empire. Some unbarbaric barbarians—they're mostly just peaceable nomads and fisherfolk who regularly barter with the townspeople—live just beyond. Relations between the barbarians and the citizens of the town are fine. Life is good and quiet. But then Colonel Joll, from the Third Bureau, arrives and informs the Magistrate that the barbarians are restless and a massive attack by them is imminent. It must be pre-empted. Two barbarians have recently been captured—a boy who is ill and his elderly uncle—for allegedly stealing cattle. They are promptly tortured—*tortured*—under Joll's supervision, and the uncle dies as a result. The boy is kept alive only so that he can guide Joll and his acolytes into the desert to capture more barbarians, who are brought back to the town where they too are tortured. Eventually Joll returns to the capital to make his report. The Magistrate comes upon a barbarian girl begging in the streets. Her ankles have been broken, her eyesight partially ruined, her father tortured and killed before her, and now she has been left behind after her fellow prisoners were released. He takes her in. But the Magistrate's descent into moral (and physical) hell has just begun, because Colonel Joll returns, with a battalion of fresh troops . . .

I leave it to you to discover what happens next. But is there not something about this set-up that sounds familiar? The frontier town, the barbarians, the waiting for their expected invasion—that's right: it's very much like the premise of *The Tartar Steppe*. No coincidence there. Coetzee drew inspiration from Buzzati's novel, hence his words of praise for the Italian novel: "A strange and haunting novel, an eccentric classic." Of course, the novels are very different. Whereas *The Tartar Steppe* is a philosophical novel bathed in sunlight, silence and solitude, *Waiting for the Barbarians* is a social work, rooted in the body and crowded with people, politics and pain. Coetzee may have started his creative journey with Buzzati, but his destination is very much his own.

Which leads us to the topic of where writers get their ideas. Like Coetzee, I too have been inspired by books. My novel *Life of Pi*, for example, was partly inspired by a review I read of the novella *Max and the Cats*, by the Brazilian writer Moacyr Scliar. And then other books, on religion, on animal behaviour in the wild and in captivity, on survival at sea, gave me further ideas and the facts from which I could weave my story. It is also true that an important source of inspiration for a writer is his or her life—but there's something grander afoot in fiction than mere autobiography, even with a writer whose life is so interesting a simple accounting of it reads like a novel. Fiction, art in general, is the forum of all possibilities, the agora where ideas of every kind assemble. And so the essential need for the thinking person to dip into art regularly, because in art life is discussed and displayed in all its manifestations, from the most conventional to the most heinous to the most idealistic. Contemplating this vast display not only of what life should be, but of what life is, plants the seed of wisdom. To shun art, then, is to shun living beyond the narrow confines of one's own experience. By contrast, to plunge into art is to live multiple lives. Art is a microscope or a telescope, either way making other realities, other worlds, other choices brighter, clearer, closer to us. Art the pregnant dream from which realities are born.

The nature of inspiration and creativity is relevant to every endeavour. The premium put on creativity varies. In the arts, in the sciences, in commerce, creativity is highly valued, while in politics, I would venture, its value is lower. A politician wants to claim to have good ideas, not necessarily original ones. Some politicians may have the luck of putting forward ideas that are both good and original—Tommy Douglas's advocacy of universal public health care is an obvious example of original public policy—but I believe the more common observation is that too much originality is a danger in politics. After all, politics, especially democratic politics, is the most social of activities. Politics is moved forward essentially by meetings and committees; that is, by people putting their heads together and hammering out policies. The political ideas of the lone, original mind will often be quixotic, simplistic, hare-brained or dangerous. I believe your own career shows the truth of what I'm saying. Throw your mind back to your early days in the Reform Party, and look at you now. What happened to the originality of the Reform Party, to all those new solutions and new approaches it came up with to solve Canada's problems? They've been ditched and forgotten, that's what. As Prime Minister, you have slowly been moving to the centre, espousing those trusted ideas that have been built over decades, that may not be original but are tried and true.

The value of a novel, then, is not that you will read it and smack your forehead and scribble down a new bill you intend to propose to the House. No. The originality of fiction addresses the individuality of its reader. How that reader then acts with others—in other words, becomes political—will involve a dilution of that originality, a regard for the conventions and sensibilities of others. And that's all right. We have to get along with others. But the cost of an artless life is that in being fed no originality, the person's sense of individuality is eroded. Which is not only sad but dangerous, since the citizen whose precious individuality is not nourished is more easily led astray by the claims of demagogues and tyrants.

But to return to J. M. Coetzee's *Waiting for the Barbarians*: it is a fine novel, moral but not in a way that is preachy. Hard to read it and not feel indignation at the wickedness of agents of the state who in the name of the law take the law in their own hands. It is the perfect cautionary tale for a politician.

Yours truly,
Yann Martel

J. M. COETZEE (b. 1940) is a South African novelist, literary critic, academic and translator who now lives in Australia. His novels have twice won the Booker Prize—for *Life & Times of Michael K* and *Disgrace*—and in 2003 he was awarded the Nobel Prize in literature. He is also an advocate for animal rights.

BOOK 68

GENERATION A
BY DOUGLAS COUPLAND

November 9, 2009

To Stephen Harper,
Prime Minister of Canada,
A time capsule,
From a Canadian writer,
With best wishes,
Yann Martel

Dear Mr. Harper,

And sometimes a book can be a time capsule, capturing the intellectual and moral state of a particular era, its joys and anxieties, its tastes and trends. I would say that Douglas Coupland specializes in writing books of this nature. Take his latest novel, *Generation A*, which I am offering you this week. From the very first pages it jumps out: the language, the preoccupations, the political and technological references, the humour—they're all so *now*. Contrast this with, say, Tolstoy's *Ivan Ilych*. In that novel, if you remember, context is nothing. The setting, the names of the characters, their class, their dress, the games they play—all these are of minor concern to the reader. One could easily imagine the exact same story being told by an American writer of the 1950s (William Faulkner, perhaps), a Japanese writer of the 1960s (Yukio Mishima) or an African writer of the 1970s (Wole Soyinka, maybe). In each case the peripheral details would be different, but the central drama would be the same. Great novels of this kind are often called timeless because they escape the strictures of time and don't seem to age. In fact, timelessness is the most conventional attribute of literary masterpieces. If it's old and great, then it must be timeless. But what's wrong with being *timely*? Must all writers strive for soaring timelessness and leave behind the earthy humus of the local, the topical, the trendy, the here and now? Is the stuff of archaeology not worth our literary consideration?

Of course it is, and Douglas Coupland's *Generation A* is scintillating proof. I must admit I read the novel enviously. Oh, to have written something so clever, funny, heartfelt and original. The story is set in the very near future and is variously narrated by Zack, Samantha, Julien, Diana and Harj, who are respectively from the United States, New Zealand, France, Canada and Sri Lanka. They are linked by the fact of each having been stung by a bee, an exceptional occurrence in a world where bees are thought to have disappeared. They are eventually brought together by a French scientist, Serge. And then—well, you will see. The narration is layered, there are passages that are very funny, others that are wise, and the language crackles with vitality throughout. It's a story about reading and storytelling, the power of reading to strengthen the individual and of storytelling to solder the group together.

Generation A is time-specific. Context is everything. And here, it's a quality. In the future, if people are curious about what it was like to live in our times, in the early twenty-first century, they will do well to read Douglas Coupland.

Yours truly,
Yann Martel

DOUGLAS COUPLAND was born on a NATO base in Germany in 1961. He is the author of the international bestseller *Jpod* and thirteen other novels including *Player One* (his novelized Massey Lecture), *The Gum Thief*, *Hey Nostradamus!*, *All Families Are Psychotic* and *Generation X*. He is also a visual artist and sculptor, furniture designer, clothing designer (for Roots) and screenwriter. His most recent book is the collection *Highly Inappropriate Tales for Young People*, illustrated by Graham Roumieu.

BOOK 69

PROPERTY
BY VALERIE MARTIN
November 23, 2009

To Stephen Harper,
Prime Minister of Canada,
A novel on corruption,
From a Canadian writer,
With best wishes,
Yann Martel

Dear Mr. Harper,

I'm afraid this is going to be a busy letter. The book first of all. The novel *Property*, by the American writer Valerie Martin, was fervently recommended to me some time ago. I finally got around to reading it last week and I'm glad I did so. It's a hypnotic read. From the very first paragraph, I was sucked into the morally corrupt life of Manon Gaudet, a woman of the American South from around the year 1810. Manon and her detestable husband own slaves, but it can also be said that slavery owns them. *Property* is about the insidious nature of injustice, how a system that is corrupt destroys not only its victims but also perverts its victimizers, blind though the victimizers may be to the injustice. So Manon owns Sarah, a beautiful slave who is her husband's mistress, but she cannot *own* Sarah and then blithely live her *own* life. I italicize those two owns, one a verb used to indicate the ownership of another human life, and the other an adjective to indicate the ownership of Manon's life, because the first precludes the second, the verb precludes the adjective. Manon cannot own Sarah and then live an unsullied moral life. Her slaves obsess and corrupt her, as they do her husband and the entire white class of the antebellum South. Antebellum and postbellum, actually; the American South is still getting over the scars of slavery. The title of the novel is very apt. Sarah the slave is Manon's property, but Manon is little more than the property of her husband because of the patriarchal society in which they live, and both are the property of the appalling system that was slavery.

The novel works because of the intelligent voice of its narrator. Manon is unremitting in her aversion to hypocrisy, her own and that of the people around her, but she never manages to improve herself. She is lucidly corrupt, her heart poisoned and her life bitter. It makes for a fascinating story, one that is contemporary, even eternal, because the nature of systems is to exercise an insidious power, for better and for worse. An educational system can improve us, for example, while an economic system can corrupt us.

I was in Ottawa promoting my book of letters to you and while there I did a reading at a studio and workshop on Elm Street called Patrick Gordon Framing. When I got there I was surprised to find that a show of paintings had been organized around the theme of our little book club. Over twenty-five artists had used the books I sent you as their inspiration. It makes for a great show. I include an invitation to the opening. The show runs until December 19. You can also find information on it at www.patrickgordonframing.ca.

One piece in particular struck me. The artist Michèle Provost took the first line of the first book I sent you (*The Death of Ivan Ilych*), the second line of the second book (*Animal Farm*), the third from the third (*The Murder of Roger Ackroyd*), the fourth from the fourth (*By Grand Central Station I Sat Down and Wept*), and so on, for the first sixty-five books, and she strung these sentences together to create a work called *A Right Honourable Summary*. This random arrangement of words or sentences to create a text with a surprising new meaning was a game invented by the French Surrealists. They called it *cadavre exquis*, exquisite corpse, the coinage coming from one of the first times they played the game. The result of a *cadavre exquis* delights by the mad juxtapositions that chance creates. Provost's *cadavre exquis* is particularly successful. She was at my reading in Ottawa and she kindly gave me two copies of a beautiful, handmade audiobook version of *A Right Honourable Summary*, one copy for you (number 1 of 12) and one for me (number 6 of 12). It comes with a booklet that has on its last pages tiny, colourful reproductions of all the book covers. To see all those covers lined up like that is not only visually arresting, it's also a great aid in identifying the origin of the lines in the audio book. Lynda Cronin reads the text in a convincing manner, weaving with her voice a story that Leo Tolstoy, George Orwell, Agatha Christie, Elizabeth Smart and all the other authors I have sent you could not have imagined. To give you a taste, here's how it starts:

During an interval in the Melvinski trial in the large building of the Law Courts the members and public prosecutor met in Ivan Egorovich Shebek's private room, where the conversation turned on the celebrated Krasovski case. With the ring of light from his lantern dancing from side to side, he lurched across the yard, kicked off his boots at the back door, drew himself a last glass of beer from the barrel in the scullery, and made his way up to bed, where Mrs. Jones was already snoring. There was nothing to be done. And, for a moment, at that gaze, I am happy to forego my future, and postpone indefinitely the miracle hanging fire. "O my teacher, behold the great army of the sons of Pandu, so expertly arranged by your intelligent disciple the son of Drupada."

At that time "everybody else" was my father and his mistress, Elsa. My Lady Baroness, who weighed three hundred and fifty pounds, consequently was a person of no small consideration; and then she did the honours of the house with a dignity that commanded universal respect.

And so on. It's a most curious and bracing new tale.

Yours truly,
Yann Martel

VALERIE MARTIN (b. 1948) is the author of nine novels, three collections of short stories and a biography of St. Francis of Assisi. She was raised in New Orleans and now lives in upstate New York. Her novel *Mary Reilly* won the Kafka Prize and was made into a film. *Property* won the 2003 Orange Prize.

BOOK 70

TROPIC OF HOCKEY
BY DAVE BIDINI
December 7, 2009

To Stephen Harper,
Prime Minister of Canada,
A book for the hockey fan in you,
From a Canadian writer,
With best wishes,
Yann Martel

Dear Mr. Harper,

Perhaps you've already read the book that accompanies this letter. I can't imagine that someone before me hasn't thought of offering it to you. You're a big hockey fan and *Tropic of Hockey: My Search for the Game in Unlikely Places* by Dave Bidini is all about hockey. But I'd say it's a cut above most hockey books because it's written by someone who (a) has the game in his blood, and (b) knows how to write. The hockey knowledge is evident. The book is replete with anecdotes, stories and events from the history of hockey, featuring a good number of players who will be familiar to you, I'm sure, but were unknown to me. And the knowledge goes deeper than that. This is no academic or journalistic account. Bidini is hockey mad. As he relates in his book, he played as a teen, but gave up when the pressure became too much. Then as an adult he started to play again in a rec league in Toronto and hockey became a central part of his life. So this book is both knowledgeable and personal.

And then the man can write. Take the following line. Bidini and his wife have just left Hong Kong by train, heading for Beijing:

> Just two hours out of town, all the glitter and sparkle of Hong Kong had given way to a country of stone and dust and the scrabblings of life, as neglected as the crumbs of an eraser that has rubbed out centuries of progress.

How's that for an image that captures the difference between the dynamism of Hong Kong and the failures of Communist China? Bidini can also be very funny, as in this description of the special talent of Kareem, the world's first Sudanese hockey player, who plays for the Al Ain Falcons of the United Arab Emirates:

> Of all the Al Ain players, Kareem had the hardest slap shot, due in part to the fact that his wind-up started from behind his head. The only problem with Kareem's shot was that he had no idea where it was going. When he wound up in the offensive zone, the Falcons ducked and covered, as if he were flinging dinner plates at them. Bear [the coach] had to remind him: "Shoot at the goalie, Kareem, at the goalie."

Tropic of Hockey is about one man's love for the game and his quest for its soul. This quest leads him to places where you wouldn't expect to see ice hockey. And different as those places are, the spirit of the game, by Bidini's reckoning, burns with the same intensity as it does in his rec league in Toronto. He finds in Harbin, northern China, in Dubai, in Miercurea Ciuc, Transylvania, the refreshing purity of a game that is not mere entertainment but a way of meeting and being, hockey as culture rather than business, "the spirituality of sports, sports as life," as he puts it at one point. Bidini contrasts this kind of hockey with what he feels is the packaged product the NHL puts out today.

Nothing beloved can be reduced to *mere* entertainment, to mere anything. So just as I have an exalted view of literature and bristle at the notion of art as mere entertainment and cannot fathom anyone having a good, thinking life that doesn't include reading, so Dave Bidini exalts, bristles and cannot fathom on the subject of hockey. Each one of us cares, defends and justifies what he or she loves. Put all those passions together, and you have a society, a culture, a nation. A last word, then, on *Tropic of Hockey*: it's the most Canadian book I've sent you.

Yours truly,
Yann Martel

As a musician, DAVE BIDINI (b. 1963) was the co-founder of the Rheostatics and is the leader of Bidiniband. He has also made a name for himself as a writer with the success of his journalism, plays and his books *The Best Game You Can Name*, *Baseballissimo*, *On a Cold Road* and *Tropic of Hockey*. Bidini wrote and hosted the Gemini Award– winning small-screen adaptation of *Tropic of Hockey*, called *Hockey Nomad*. His newest book is about Gordon Lightfoot and the Mariposa Folk Festival of 1972. He lives in Toronto with his wife and their two children.

BOOK 71:

THE FINANCIAL EXPERT
BY R. K. NARAYAN
December 21, 2009

To Stephen Harper,
Prime Minister of Canada,
If only we really were experts,
From a Canadian writer,
With best wishes for Christmas and the New Year,
Yann Martel

Dear Mr. Harper,

R. K. Narayan is the mercifully shortened *nom de plume* of
Rasipuram Krishnaswami Iyer Narayanaswami. He was Indian
and lived from 1906 to 2001. If you've never heard of Narayan,
look at the commendations on the back of the book I'm sending
you this week, the novel *The Financial Expert*, and you will see
the kinds of writers with whom Narayan is classed: Tolstoy,
Henry James, Chekhov, Turgenev, Conrad, Gogol, Jane
Austen. One commentator makes mention of the Nobel Prize,
which Narayan never obtained but would have well deserved.
I remember reading an interview with Narayan in an Indian
newspaper on my second visit to India and feeling a sense of
privilege that I was in his country while he was still alive. R. K.
Narayan was a gentle giant of English-language literature.

Like William Faulkner with his apocryphal Yoknapatawpha
County and Thomas Hardy with his semi-fictional Wessex,
Narayan invented a place, the town of Malgudi, and then spun

fictional tales about it, but all so that he might speak about real life. His characters are ordinary enough and their lives move along in ways that are neither settled nor too jarring, yet the grand march of existence, its glory and its misery, rises up from the pages of his novels. Notice the language of *The Financial Expert*. Aside from the odd word or phrase—dhoti, sacred thread, betel leaves, a lakh—the English is nearly classical, and Narayan's portrayal of India is neither folkloric nor exaggerated. He speaks not of India-the-peculiar, but of India-the-universal.

The Financial Expert tells the story of Margayya, the expert of the title, who lives on the edges of the banking world of Malgudi, helping peasants fill out forms and secure loans. His office is no more than a piece of lawn in the shade of a banyan tree and the tools of his trade are all contained in a little box. Margayya has large ambitions, though not, it seems, any way of fulfilling them. But Lakshmi, Goddess of Wealth, for whom he prays and fasts for forty days, finds grace in him and Margayya manages to do well for himself. But at a price: he becomes wealthy with money, but poor in his relations with his wife and son and others. As you can imagine, this price will have to be paid.

Margayya's fortunes are determined by turns of fate as incalculable as a win at bingo. For example, his first wave of wealth comes as a result of publishing a book. He is not its author. It is penned by one Dr. Pal, who quite unexpectedly gives him the manuscript, no strings attached. Later on, Margayya and his wife receive a letter saying that their estranged son, Balu, has died. The news proves to be false, the product of a madman who writes postcards to people he selects randomly to inform them of false calamities. I believe the arbitrariness of fate is the theme of *The Financial Expert*, and the title is therefore ironic: we are experts at nothing. We are rather at the mercy of the gods, Narayan is saying, and any sense of control that we might have is illusion. What do you think of this interpretation of the novel?

Christmas is upon us and then a new year, and so I wish you and your family health and happiness and the serenity to accept what 2010 will bring.

Yours truly,
Yann Martel

P.S. Copenhagen—what a mess. It would be interesting to read The Financial Expert, *published in 1952, long before climate change was detected, in the light of that disastrous, save-the-world conference.*

R. K. NARAYAN (1906–2001) was an Indian novelist and short story writer. Most of his stories are set in the fictional town of Malgudi in southern India. He was the author of numerous novels, short story collections, mythologies and non-fiction books.

BOOK 72:

BOOKS: A MEMOIR
BY LARRY McMURTRY

January 4, 2010

To Stephen Harper,
Prime Minister of Canada,
A life in books,
From a Canadian writer,
With best wishes,
Yann Martel

Dear Mr. Harper,

I haven't sent you much non-fiction since the start of our little book club, but how could a book called *Books* not catch my attention as I was browsing at McNally Robinson last week? (As you've perhaps heard, McNally Robinson, a fine independent book chain, has just filed for bankruptcy protection. By the sounds of it, their main Winnipeg store and the one here in Saskatoon will survive, but their venture in suburban Toronto has cost them dearly. The travails of independent bookselling are another story, although not unrelated to your latest gift.) *Books* is about a life in books. Its author is Larry McMurtry. If you think you've never heard of him, I bet you're more familiar with his work than you realize. McMurtry, a disciplined writer, ten pages a morning, every day, no exception, for years, has published many books, as you'll see if you flip to the second page of *Books*, where his works are listed in a long column. So far, McMurtry has to his credit thirty-six novels, one collection of short stories, and three collections of essays. Except for *Lonesome Dove*, which I remember hearing about when it won McMurtry the Pulitzer Prize in 1986, none of the titles were familiar to me. That is, with the exception of those that were adapted for the screen. Remember *Hud*, with Paul Newman? It was based on McMurtry's first novel, *Horseman, Pass By*. His novel *The Last Picture Show* was also turned into a successful Hollywood movie, as was *Terms of Endearment*. More recently, McMurtry co-wrote the brilliant screen adaptation of Annie Proulx's novella *Brokeback Mountain*.

So, a novelist who has done very well in Hollywood. But the book in your hands is called *Books*, not *Movies*. McMurtry, it turns out, has lived with and for and by books his whole life, writing them, reading them and selling them. He is, to use a term that comes up frequently in his memoir, a bookman. His personal library consists of approximately 28,000 volumes. His used bookstore, Booked Up, in Archer City, Texas, has over 300,000 books. He has worked in the used-book trade for over fifty years, starting as a book scout, hunting for rare books, and then moving on to open his own used bookstore, first in Georgetown, a neighbourhood of Washington, DC, and then in Texas. And throughout—the pretext for the scouting and the selling—he has read and reread thousands upon thousands of books. In one chapter, McMurtry makes mention of a "minor English literary figure" named James Lees-Milne (try saying that name ten times over), the author of several "not particularly good books on architecture, a few bad novels, several readable biographies, and twelve glorious volumes of diaries." He comments: "I have read the whole twelve volumes several times and I am sure I will keep rereading them for the rest of my life." I wonder if there's anyone else on this planet who can claim to have read the twelve-volume diaries of James Lees-Milne *several times*. And it's clear that McMurtry's judgments on Lees-Milne's other books, the not particularly good ones, the bad ones and the merely readable ones, are the result of having read every single one. Elsewhere, McMurtry, in discussing his interest in the world wars of the twentieth century, talks about reading Winston Churchill's massive history of World War II, all five million words of it. And so on, authors minor and major, works single and in multiple volumes—they've all been taken in by a mind voraciously open to the written word.

What kind of intellectual autobiography does such a mind yield? Is the reader, the average reader who's never heard of, let alone read, James Lees-Milne, reduced to feeling ignorant or half-literate? The answer is no, as you'll find out as soon as you start on *Books*. Because books, if read well, feed your humbleness, not your arrogance. Books are about life, and life is a humbling experience. Ask any old person.

Books is about McMurtry's life with books, mostly the books he's read and traded, and about the subculture—and wavering fortunes—of antiquarian book traders. The wisdom in it comes off naturally and easily. And the chapters are very short; some don't even stretch to a full page, and very few are longer than three pages. I liked that right away. All those books read, yet the man writes these itsy-bitsy chapters. The tone is equally approachable. McMurtry was born on a ranch somewhere in Texas to parents who didn't own a single book, and the feel of the man, as I sense it in this memoir, reminds me of the best of Prairie folk here in Saskatchewan, smart but modest.

A book asks you to measure yourself against it. The relationship is one of comparing and contrasting. Done lucidly, this can be an act of self-definition that leaves one a little more knowledgeable about oneself and, sometimes, a little wiser. One thing I learned from reading *Books* is that I'm not the bibliophile that Larry McMurtry is. He clearly loves not only the messages that books deliver, but their medium, that construction of ink, paper and cardboard, with its long history and technical lingo. I'm too much of the nomad, unwilling to weigh myself down, to attach myself in this way to books. McMurtry balks at e-books. I don't. McMurtry loves owning old or rare books. I don't. To me, a book is a sustained whisper and it matters not a jot whether that whisper is conveyed by an inexpensive Penguin paperback or an incunabulum. The book that is an art object is something other than literary. It belongs in a museum rather than a library. Having said that, I'd love to visit McMurtry's personal library and his used bookstore. And I love wandering about the stacks of the library at the University of Saskatchewan. Larry McMurtry and I certainly agree on this point: books, owned or borrowed, old or new, nourish and sustain the soul.

I hope you enjoy, in this new year of 2010, this celebration of book culture.

Yours truly,
Yann Martel

LARRY McMURTRY (b. 1936) is an American novelist, essayist, screenwriter and bookseller. He owns Booked Up, a store specializing in antiquarian and scholarly books, in his home town of Archer City, Texas. He is the author of more than forty books.

BOOK 73

THINGS FALL APART
BY CHINUA ACHEBE
January 18, 2010

To Stephen Harper,
Prime Minister of Canada,
A great novel from Africa,
From a Canadian writer,
With best wishes,
Yann Martel

Dear Mr. Harper,

No prorogation for me. I guess one of the differences between art and politics is that politics can stop, at least for a while, but art, the living of it, never does.

The book I have for you this week is *Things Fall Apart*, by the Nigerian writer Chinua Achebe. In case you don't know much about him: he was born in 1930 in Eastern Nigeria, among the people known then as the Ibo, now the Igbo. He was brought up speaking Ibo and English and chose to write in English. *Things Fall Apart* was his first novel, coming out in 1958. Its success was immediate, and endures. The cover of the edition I'm sending you, which dates from 1986, states that the novel has sold two million copies. Well, that fact is long out of date: it has now sold over *eight million* copies. It is the first English-language classic to come out of Africa, and is read in schools and universities around the world. As it should be. *Things Fall Apart* is an absolutely superb novel. It seems simple enough, resting on short, descriptive scenes. But the overall picture it draws is breathtakingly vast and complex, nothing short of an epic portrayal of the encounter between African and British societies in the late nineteenth century, and the ensuing wreckage of colonialism. This comment perhaps makes it sound as if *Things Fall Apart* is an overtly political novel, with the grinding of the author's axe screeching in the reader's ears. Such is not the case. Rather, *Things Fall Apart*, certainly in its first two-thirds, reads more like a work of anthropology. Achebe describes the way of life of the villagers of Umuofia, their religious beliefs and practices, their agricultural economy, their social interactions, and so on. Okonkwo is the protagonist of the story. The reader follows him through the seasons of his life, hearing about the events big and small that mark his life and make him who he is. Okonkwo is a proud man, generally fair in his dealings with his family and neighbours, a successful farmer and, when need be, a fierce warrior. He is far from perfect, just as his society is far from ideal, but both muddle along, he shaped by it and it affected by him.

And then the white man comes, in the form of missionaries. They are not intrinsically bad, these newcomers. In fact, Mr. Brown, the first missionary, is a rather sympathetic character. He is a zealous Christian, for sure, but not a blind one. He wants to convert the African heathens among whom he lives, but he is not insensitive to their feelings. He makes genuine attempts at dialogue. Alas, Mr. Smith, his successor, is not so open-minded. As for the District Commissioner, who is there to provide the colonial administrative muscle behind the religious preaching, he is even less so. Incomprehension, the white man's of the African man and the African's of the white man, wins the day—and things fall apart.

The novel is a marvel of even-handedness. It is not that the African way of life is Edenic until the arrival of the white man.

Not at all, and the novel makes that clear. Some of the religious practices of the Africans are barbaric, such as their treatment of newborn twins, who are thought to be evil and are abandoned in the forest to die of exposure. Achebe makes plain the travails of life in Umuofia. And yet the villagers manage. Life may be harsh at times, but they know who they are and where they belong. They are a people and a civilization. Not very different, really, from the people and civilization of the white man. That is the point so deftly made by the novel, that the encounter between Africans and Europeans went so poorly not because one was inferior to the other, but because they failed to understand each other and, as a direct result, to respect each other. The villagers are patriarchal, for example. Take Okonkwo and his *three* wives. An outrage. But were the Victorians any less patriarchal? The religion of the Umuofians is so much voodoo mumbo-jumbo— but is it really any different from the voodoo mumbo-jumbo of the white man? The villagers expect evil to befall the missionaries for flouting the rule of the native gods, just as the missionaries expect evil to befall the villagers if they continue to disobey the new God. And so on. The Umuofians are shown in their bigness and smallness, just as the white man is shown in his bigness and smallness. Why couldn't they properly meet and gently, slowly syncretize? It wasn't to be. Hence the heart-wrenching tragedy at the core of the novel: things didn't have to fall apart. Given better emissaries, given greater efforts to reach out, perhaps Africa wouldn't have been so wrecked and Europe so tainted.

I have rarely read a novel that so portrays a foreign reality with such an acute mix of insight, understanding and outrage. *Things Fall Apart* is a brilliant novel, Mr. Harper. I heartily recommend it to you.

I should mention that I am writing this letter in unusual circumstances. Normally I write to you in the quiet of my home office.

Not tonight. Tonight I'm sitting in the middle of the Mendel Art Gallery here in Saskatoon, on a raised platform, writing my letter in public. I'm participating in a multidisciplinary, carnival-like event called Lugo, which is bringing together dancers, musicians, actors and others in a celebration of the arts. I'm also soliciting book suggestions. I better start writing them down before the pile falls off my desk. So here goes, as they are given to me by the crowd surrounding me, suggestions of books for your consideration from Canadian readers:

Billions and Billions, by Carl Sagan

Ishmael, by Daniel Quinn

Killing Hope, by William Blum

because i am a woman, by June Jordan

The Stone Angel, by Margaret Laurence

Stella, Queen of the Snow, by Marie-Louise Gay (with this said of it by the person who made the recommendation: "It will answer many of life's pressing questions, and bring a smile to your face")

Two Solitudes, by Hugh MacLennan

The Red Tent, by Anita Diamant

Expect Resistance, by CrimethInc. Ex-Workers' Collective

Three Day Road and *Through Black Spruce*, by Joseph Boyden

The Book of Negroes, by Lawrence Hill

Long Walk to Freedom, by Nelson Mandela (I usually send you short books—which this one is not—but I highly recommend Mandela's autobiography when you have more free time. Now, come to think of it, with Parliament not sitting and all that)

The Holy Longing, by Fr. Ron Rolheiser

Staying Alive, a poetry anthology edited by Neil Astley

Your Whole Family Is Made Out of Meat, by Ryan North
(love the title)

Even Cowgirls Get the Blues, by Tom Robbins

The Secret River, by Kate Grenville

Sunshine Sketches of a Little Town, by Stephen Leacock

Money for Nothing, by P. G. Wodehouse

Che, author not given (I wonder if the person meant the
movie by Steven Soderbergh?)

The Alchemist, by Paulo Coelho

Disgrace, by J. M. Coetzee (a great recommendation—
I've already sent you a Coetzee, if you remember,
Waiting for the Barbarians)

Lion in the Streets, a play by Judith Thompson

The poetry of Emily Dickinson (which makes me think,
I haven't sent you poetry in ages)

Nervous Conditions, by Tsitsi Dangarembga (I just looked it
up on the internet—sounds really neat. Set in Rhodesia
in the 1960s and '70s, a semi-autobiographical coming-
of-age story)

Slaughterhouse-Five, by Kurt Vonnegut

Born to Be Good, by Dacher Keltner

The Golden Mean, by Annabel Lyon

The Exorcist, by William Peter Blatty

All the Names, by José Saramago

Team of Rivals, by Doris Kearns Goodwin

The Kindly Ones, by Jonathan Littell

Les Belles-Sœurs, by Michel Tremblay

One Hundred Years of Solitude, by Gabriel García Márquez

The Alphabet of Manliness, by Maddox

American Gods, by Neil Gaiman

The Tao of Pooh, by Benjamin Hoff (the person who suggested it added, "This excellent book will teach him

[that is, *you*] openness and how to value *all* people in
our community and land. Be more like Pooh, less like
Rabbit and Piglet!")

By Night in Chile, by Roberto Bolaño (more on him later,
in another letter. I'm thinking of sending you *Amulet*)

Half of a Yellow Sun, by Chimamanda Ngozi Adichie
(another Nigerian novel)

Three Cups of Tea, by Greg Mortenson

Voltaire's Bastards, by John Ralston Saul

The God of Small Things and *Listening to Grasshoppers:
Field Notes on Democracy*, by Arundhati Roy

The Master and Margarita, by Mikhail Bulgakov

Tigana, by Guy Gavriel Kay ("about the heartbreaking
lengths it is sometimes necessary to go to in order to
address the rule of tyrants")

Overqualified, by Joey Comeau

Midnight's Children, by Salman Rushdie

The Maintains, poetry by Clark Coolidge

War and Peace, by Leo Tolstoy (about as long a novel as
they get, and I've already sent you two Tolstoys, but
you should get to *W&P* before you die)

A Street Without a Name, author not given

Foxfire, by Joyce Carol Oates ("The book I re-read when
I want to remember why I write.")

*Predicting the Next Big Advertising Breakthrough Using a
Potentially Dangerous Method*, poetry by Daniel Scott
Tysdal

Death in the Afternoon, by Ernest Hemingway

The Elementary Particles, by Michel Houellebecq

Dream Boy, by Jim Grimsley

L'Avalée des avalés, by Réjean Ducharme

One Native Life, by Richard Wagamese

Yesterday, at the Hotel Clarendon, by Nicole Brossard
Ten Little Fingers and Ten Little Toes, by Mem Fox
Mid-Course Correction, by Ray C. Anderson
The End of the Story, by Lydia Davis
Story of the Eye, by Georges Bataille
Lakeland: Journeys into the Soul of Canada, by Allan Casey
The Mirror Has Two Faces, by C. S. Lewis (I find no book
    of that name by Lewis, only a 1996 American movie by
    and with Barbra Streisand, a remake of a 1958 French
    movie of the same name. I wonder what book the
    reader had in mind)
Siddhartha, by Hermann Hesse
Trainspotting, by Irvine Welsh
The Art of Japanese Bondage, author unknown (!)
The Amazing Adventures of Kavalier & Clay, by Michael
    Chabon
The Bell Jar, by Sylvia Plath
The Truth, by Terry Pratchett
A Woman in Berlin, anonymous
The Crackwalker, by Judith Thompson (which is playing
    here in Saskatoon from March 4–7 and 11–14—you
    are hereby invited)
Pinocchio, by Carlo Collodi
A Fine Balance, by Rohinton Mistry
Franny and Zooey, by J. D. Salinger

That's quite the reading list. And a reading list as it should
be: multinational and of all genres, and fresh from the minds of
the people of Saskatoon.

Yours truly,
Yann Martel

CHINUA ACHEBE (b. 1930) is a novelist, professor, poet and critic. He is professor of Africana Studies at Brown University. He is the author of five novels, four short story collections, six books of poetry and numerous other books. In 2007, Achebe was awarded the Man Booker International Prize. He lives with his wife in Providence, Rhode Island.

BOOK 74:

EUNOIA
BY CHRISTIAN BÖK
February 1, 2010

To Stephen Harper,
Prime Minister of Canada,
A book in praise of soaring over limits,
From a Canadian writer,
With best wishes,
Yann Martel

Dear Mr. Harper,

Have you ever felt limited by language? I'm sure you have. A common instance would be when you're speaking with someone and you want to convey an idea, but you've momentarily forgotten the word, it remains on the proverbial tip of your tongue, and you struggle to explain what you mean to say in a roundabout way. Another common occurrence of language limiting expression is when one is speaking in a foreign language. You, for example, have made admirable efforts to learn French, but it remains a language with which you're not fully comfortable. When you give a speech in French, I'm sure you prefer to speak from a written text vetted by a native speaker, and when you have to ad lib, I imagine you seek safety in the set phrases and expressions that you've learned; otherwise, you must struggle, trying to express your meaning in the limited knowledge you have of the language. In English, by contrast, you must feel no sense of limitations. I imagine you feel, like most native speakers of a language feel, that what you think, you express, effortlessly and without any delay or searching.

Of course, this sense of freedom, this perfect match between thought and expression, is an illusion born of comfort and familiarity. Faced with an utterly new experience, whether beatific or horrific, we often lose the capacity to speak, we are rendered speechless. And expression is more than simply a question of vocabulary. Experiences that are not emotionally overwhelming but intellectually complex can also have us struggling to speak meaningfully. In such situations, it is not necessarily words that fail us, but the preliminary understanding that leads to the choice of words. All this to say that sometimes we are tongue-tied—and we don't like it. We value expression. So, humming, hawing, non-sequituring, we struggle until we manage to put idea or experience into words.

The book I am sending you this time—the poetry collection *Eunoia*, by the Canadian writer Christian Bök (pronounced "book"), both the book and the CD (read with great gusto by the author)—is all about limitations and the soaring over-passing of them. Bök, a fervent admirer of Oulipo, the French experimental writers' collective, has taken one of their favourite techniques, the lipogram, to a very high level. A lipogram is a composition in which a letter is missing throughout. A fine example of a lipogram is Georges Perec's novel *La Disparition*, written entirely without the most-used vowel in French, the letter *e*. If you think a lipogram sounds like a gimmick, think again. In the case of the Perec novel, the letter *e* in French is pronounced the same as the word *eux*, them. *La Disparition* refers not only to the disappearance of a letter, but of *them*. Them who? Well, to start with, Perec's parents, who were Jewish and who were swallowed up by the Holocaust. *La Disparition* is a metaphor on the wiping-out of a good part of

Jewish civilization in Europe, something very much equivalent to an alphabet losing one of its key letters. No gimmickry there, I don't think.

Bök has taken the challenge even further. With *Eunoia*, he has written a series of poems that omit not just one letter, but several, and not consonants, of which there are many, but vowels, and not just one, two or three vowels per poem, but *four* vowels. That leaves just one vowel per poem. The opening lines of the collection foreshadow the treat you're in for:

> Awkward grammar appals a craftsman. A Dada bard as daft as
> Tzara damns stagnant art . . .

The hero of the vowel *A* is the Arab Hassan Abd al-Hassad, while *E* features Greek Helen, who

> Restless, she deserts her fleece bed where, detested, her wedded
> regent sleeps. When she remembers Greece, her seceded
> demesne, she feels wretched, left here, bereft, her needs never
> met.

Who would have thought that Homer's *Iliad* could be retold using just one vowel? The vowel *I* allows the author to speak about his project and defend it:

> I dismiss nitpicking criticism which flirts with philistinism.
> I bitch; I kibitz—griping whilst criticizing dimwits, sniping
> whilst indicting nitwits, dismissing simplistic thinking, in
> which philippic wit is still illicit.

In O we read that

Porno shows folks lots of sordor—zoom-shots of Björn Borg's bottom or Snoop Dogg's crotch. Johns who don condoms for blowjobs go downtown to Soho to look for pornshops known to stock lots of lowbrow schlock—off-color porn for old boors who long to drool onto color photos of cocks, boobs, dorks or dongs.

With *O*, we also get a wink at *Clockwork Orange*, the novel by Anthony Burgess I sent you a while ago:

Crowds of droogs, who don workboots to stomp on downtrod hobos, go on to rob old folks, most of whom own posh co-op condos.

Even *U*, that vowel the sight of which makes a Scrabble player's heart sink, manages to speak on its own:
Kultur spurns Ubu—thus Ubu pulls stunts.

So it goes, the wit and inventiveness dancing across the pages, the stock of single-vowel words of the English language expended to discuss a surprising range of topics, from the bawdy to the lyrical, from the pastoral to the historical.

And the purpose of it all? It may seem to you to be a mere game, with the lack of seriousness that one might associate with playing. To that, two responses: first, in playing, in toying, come discoveries, the result of chance juxtapositions; and second, language is never just about itself. This language-playing that Bök delights us with comments on the world because every word, whether invested with one vowel or five, connects eventually to a concrete reality. So speaking in mono-vowels though he is, Bök is also speaking volumes. *Eunoia*, which means "beautiful thinking" and is the shortest word in English to contain all five vowels, is a narrow but perfect work. It is a gambol through language, and it would be a sad mistake to dismiss it as merely *facetious*, which word—lo!—contains all five vowels in order. After such wordplay, the tongue is better fixed in the mouth and expression comes more easily.

Yours truly,
Yann Martel

CHRISTIAN BÖK (b. 1960) is an experimental poet. He teaches in the English department at the University of Calgary. He is the author of three books.

BOOK 75:

NADIRS
BY HERTA MÜLLER
Translated from the German by Sieglinde Lug
February 15, 2010

To Stephen Harper,
Prime Minister of Canada,
A book from far away,
From a Canadian writer,
With best wishes,
Yann Martel

Dear Mr. Harper,

It happens every few years that the announcement of the winner of the Nobel Prize in Literature is a source of surprise and consternation. The gasp is audible nearly around the world: *"Who?!"* That's exactly how I reacted in 2004, I remember. I'd never heard of Elfriede Jelinek, the Austrian writer who was the recipient that year. Of course, German-language readers surely knew of her and no doubt applauded her win. The Nobel Committee has the wisdom and discernment to cast its net wide, finding worthy winners in writers who are not well known or who write from cultures on the margin of our Anglo-American-dominated world. I discovered Elias Canetti, for example, a wonderful writer, when I had another *"Who?!"* moment way back in 1981.

Well, Stockholm has done it again. A few months ago, the winner of the 2009 Nobel Prize in Literature was announced and it was—move over, Elfriede—another "obscure" woman writer who writes in German, Herta Müller. And since the Winter Olympics are on right now in Vancouver, with hosts of foreign athletes visiting our land, I thought I would heed the Nobel Committee's high commendation and offer you something by Herta Müller. *Nadirs*, her first book, a collection of short stories, is the only one I could find at McNally Robinson. It is a curious book. Right off, it feels foreign. We don't write like that in English. It's not a matter of translation. I wouldn't know it, not speaking German and so not able to compare the original with the translation, but I doubt the book is poorly translated. It is rather the sensibility. The writing feels impersonal, nearly mechanical, it is laconic in the extreme and there is little effort at being beautiful. The stories, except for anecdotal bursts, are plotless. They're full of details, yet many of them are unreal, dreamlike, nightmarish.

It helps to know a little about Herta Müller: she's from a German-speaking region of Romania called the Banat. A minority speaker in a poor country: that would explain the sensibility, so different from mine. I'm sometimes struck by the strange inner realities that come from central and eastern Europe. There are books from parts of the world that should feel more alien to me—for example, the book I sent you a month ago: *Things Fall Apart*, from Nigeria—yet don't feel so alien to me. I felt quite comfortable slipping into the African skin of Okonkwo. And then Europe, my ancestral continent, a continent on which I lived ten years, three of whose languages I speak, whose majority religion I broadly adhere to, whose people look and dress like me, produces stories that completely puzzle me. Perhaps it's the result of that very European mix of cultural diversity, economic chaos and political misery. Whatever the case, I read *Nadirs* and I thought, "Gosh, those Germans certainly know how not to have fun."

A worthy book nonetheless. A reminder that great literature brings us to foreign shores and makes us less narrow.

Yours truly,
Yann Martel

HERTA MÜLLER (b. 1953) is a novelist, poet, short story writer, editor and essayist. She was born in Romania and now lives in Berlin.

BOOK 76

ONE DAY IN THE LIFE OF IVAN DENISOVICH
BY ALEXANDER SOLZHENITSYN
Translated from the Russian by Bela Von Block

March 1, 2010

To Stephen Harper,

Prime Minister of Canada,

A novel about terrible governance,

From a Canadian writer,

With best wishes,

Yann Martel

Dear Mr. Harper,

The coolest thing happened to me last week. There was a stiff, mid-size envelope in my mailbox. I don't get as much mail as you do, but I do get my fair share (and I don't have any staff to help me with it). So what was this, what request, what demand? I noted that it came from the United States. I opened it. Between two pieces of cardboard, a smaller envelope slipped out. On the front, top left, was the return address: The White House, Washington, DC 20500. I was intrigued. *The* White House? I opened the envelope, and there it was, on White House letterhead, a handwritten note from President Obama.

I do believe my heart skipped a beat. A week later I'm still gingerly taking the note out to marvel at it. The President of the United States wrote to me—to *me*! For sure I'm going to have the note framed. If there was a way of tattooing it on my back, I would. What amazes me is the generosity of it. As you would

THE WHITE HOUSE
WASHINGTON

Mr. Martel —

My daughter and I just finished reading Life of Pi
together. Both of us agreed we prefer the story with animals.
It is a lovely book — an elegant proof of God,
and the power of storytelling.

Thank you.

know, there is a large measure of calculation in what public
figures do. But here, what does he gain? I'm not a US citizen. In
no way can I be of help to President Obama. Clearly he did it for
personal reasons, as a reader and as a father. And in two lines,
what an insightful analysis of *Life of Pi*. Bless him, bless him.

Not all heads of government are as good. For proof, the
book I'm sending you this week, *One Day in the Life of Ivan
Denisovich*, by the Russian writer Alexander Solzhenitsyn.
Joseph Stalin made his people miserable for all of his reign as
leader of the Soviet Union from 1922 to 1953. Or to put it more
accurately, whatever good he did was obliterated by the nearly
immeasurable evil that came with it. The title of most heinous
dictator of the twentieth century of course goes to Adolf Hitler,
but Hitler burned out quickly, in twelve years, and was atypi-
cal of German leadership. Stalin, in contrast, lasted. He died
an old man, still in power, a beacon of steady and stable evil.
And while his crimes—social upheaval, economic catastrophe,
massive and systematic human rights violations, widespread
famine and poverty—were worse than those of his predecessors

or successors, Russia didn't fare well before him under the Tsars, didn't fare well after him under the Soviet leaders that followed, and isn't faring well under the authoritarian regime now in place. I am reminded of that adage "Man's inhumanity to Man," but with a variation for this case: "Russians' inhumanity to Russians." It has always puzzled me how the Russians, despite the blazing individual geniuses they have produced in the arts and sciences, have otherwise been such a calamity to themselves (and to the Europeans who had the misfortune of living in the shadow of their empire). What other country has produced a Nobel Peace Prize winner—Mikhail Gorbachev—who sought only to liberate his people from themselves? And this, in a country that has never been colonized and whose ills cannot be blamed on others.

There's a paragraph on page 104 of *One Day in the Life of Ivan Denisovich* that summarizes the attitude I'm talking about:

> He could barely stand any longer. But he kept on somehow. Shukhov [that is, Ivan Denisovich] had once had a horse like that. He had thought highly of the horse, but had driven it to death. And then they had skinned the hide off him.

He had thought highly of the horse, but had driven it to death— and with no explanation as to why. It's just what you do. And the "he" mentioned at the start is not another horse but a human being, a fellow prisoner, one whom Ivan Denisovich also thinks highly of and will just as blithely see worked to death. One feels like crying out, "Where's the humanity, the benevolence, the compassion?" Well, there's precious little of that in *One Day in the Life of Ivan Denisovich*. This short novel tells the story of an ordinary day in the life of an ordinary prisoner in the Gulag, the massive forced-labour camp system that was nearly a parallel society in Communist Russia. At most, the roughest of fraternity is fleetingly expressed during moments when fear and want have momentarily abated. At all other times, each prisoner strictly looks out for himself. It makes for appalling living, lucidly documented by Solzhenitsyn, and a searing indictment of what Stalin did to his own people.

I sent you, nearly three years ago now, *Animal Farm*, by the English writer George Orwell. It's interesting to compare that novel and *Ivan Denisovich*. Both works cover the same ground, but very differently. The first portrays the evil of Stalinism by means of allegory, the second by means of realism. Which do you prefer?

I need to inform you of a temporary change in our little book club. Up till now, it's just been you and me. But I'm leaving on a four-month trip soon, in part to promote my next novel, and I was worried that the logistics of getting a book and a letter to you every two weeks while on tour would be too much of a strain. So I've decided to invite other Canadian writers to join our literary journey. I'm glad about the decision. This is certainly a case of making a virtue of necessity. After all, why should I be alone in making reading suggestions to you? My knowledge of the book world is very limited. Why not plumb the literary depths of other writers?

So your next book and letter, to be delivered to your office in exactly two weeks, on Monday, March 15th, will come from a different Canadian writer. I won't tell you who—let it be a surprise—nor do I have any idea what the next book will be. That too will be a surprise.

Yours truly,
Yann Martel

ALEXANDER SOLZHENITSYN (1918–2008) was a novelist, dramatist and historian. His most famous books include *The Gulag Archipelago* and *One Day in the Life of Ivan Denisovich*, inspired by the eight years he served in a Gulag for writing what was deemed anti-Soviet propaganda. He was awarded the Nobel Prize in Literature in 1970. Solzhenitsyn was exiled from the Soviet Union in 1974, but returned to Russia in 1994.

BOOK 77:

KING LEARY
BY PAUL QUARRINGTON

Sent to you by Steven Galloway

March 15, 2010

To Stephen Harper,

Prime Minister of Canada,

I hope this book makes you laugh, remember and look forward,

from a Canadian writer,

with thanks,

Steven Galloway

Dear Mr. Harper,

Please don't be disappointed. I know that for some time now you've been receiving books in the mail from Yann Martel, and I suppose you've grown used to this. Even though his letters have yet to garner a personal response, I like to imagine you reading them in your robe and slippers in the morning over coffee. Is that an odd thing to imagine of one's Prime Minister? Perhaps. I apologize if so—you are, however, the leader of our country, and leaders exist as much in our imaginations as in physical being.

As you've probably figured out by now, I'm not Yann. My name is Steven, and I'm a writer from Vancouver. Yann sent you one of my books, *The Cellist of Sarajevo*. I hope you liked it. If you didn't, thanks for not letting on. Our friend Yann is out on the road promoting his new book, *Beatrice and Virgil*, and he's asked me to fill in for him. I'm happy to do so, because

I fancy myself a helpful sort of guy, and because even though a lot of writer types think Yann is tilting at windmills in sending you these books, I like to think that maybe you look at some of them, and maybe you read or have already read some of them, and that no one, anywhere, would think that receiving seventy-five free books in the mail with a letter from an internationally renowned author would be a bad thing. In a way, you're in what must be the world's most exclusive book club, albeit somewhat unwillingly. I bet Mr. Obama is jealous!

There's a band from Winnipeg called the Weakerthans that I really like. They have a song called "Night Windows," written by John K. Samson, that is about the sensation you get when you think you see someone who's died, and for a moment, before you remember that person isn't alive any more, you feel about them the way you felt when they were alive, you see them as they were when they were alive, and for that moment it's as if they never died. This sensation, which is rare and wonderful and sometimes sad, is why I love reading. It's also for this reason that I've chosen to send you Paul Quarrington's novel *King Leary*.

It's a hockey novel. One of our best ones. I read somewhere that you like hockey, and recently saw you on TV at the gold-medal game sitting next to Wayne Gretzky. That must have been a fun experience. I was at home sitting next to my aunt and a guy named Jay and it was still pretty great. Anyhow, in the novel, Percival "King" Leary was once the best player in the NHL. He won the cup in 1919, scoring the winning goal after dodging Newsy Lalonde and executing a perfect St. Louis Whirligig. Except for a glass of champagne on that occasion, he has never in his life drank alcohol. His beverage of choice is ginger ale, which he maintains makes him drunker than anything else ever could. The novel opens with him as an old man in a rest home with his pal, newspaperman Blue Hermann. He's offered a whopping sum of money to go to Toronto to make an ad for a ginger ale company. The story unfolds from there, and I don't want to ruin it for you, but our King is in poor health, and he has demons in his life that he's been trying to keep at bay but which are catching up to him. He has many moments where he sees the dead, and in his case the dead have much to say about the way in which he's lived his life. It's a funny novel, a sad novel, and the sort of novel that only a Canadian would write.

Paul Quarrington died recently of cancer. He was only fifty-six. He was a terrific guy. Sometimes, reading his work, I feel for a second like he's still alive. Most people never knew Paul, or any living or dead author for that matter, but when you read a book you often have that moment Samson describes—I bet the Germans have a name for it—with a voice in your life, or the collective lives of everyone. I suppose a cynical person would call it a sort of nostalgia, but I like to think of it as a reminder. A reminder of how things were or are or could be.

Sometimes these reminders cost billions of dollars. Take the Olympics. Though I'm not a fan of the cronyism that accompanies them, I think the stories they create, and their illustration of the bond we share as Canadians, make that money well spent. But there are other ways to do this as well, ways that don't fizzle if Crosby doesn't score in overtime (phew). Books are one of the best examples of this, and they're a whole lot less expensive. Sometimes free. I hope you like *King Leary*.

Sincerely,
Steven Galloway

PAUL QUARRINGTON (1953–2010) was the author of ten novels, including *Whale Music*, *King Leary*, *Galveston* and *The Ravine*. He was also a musician (most recently in the band Porkbelly Futures), an award-winning screenwriter and filmmaker and an acclaimed nonfiction writer.

STEVEN GALLOWAY (b. 1975) is a Canadian novelist whose work has been translated into more than twenty languages. Besides *The Cellist of Sarajevo*, he has written the novels *Finnie Walsh* and *Ascension*. Galloway teaches creative writing at Simon Fraser University and the University of British Columbia.

BOOK 78:

CENTURY
BY RAY SMITH

Sent to you by Charles Foran
March 29, 2010

To Stephen Harper,
Prime Minister of Canada,
A book still patiently awaiting its readers,
From a Canadian writer,
With thanks,
Charles Foran

Dear Mr. Harper,

Books, like people, can get overlooked. I'd like to use this slot, so generously offered by Yann, to tell you about a wonderful Canadian work of fiction that still awaits real discovery. Ray Smith's *Century* first appeared back in 1986, and didn't cause much fuss. It had a decent publisher, and Smith had already released two books that had won him a small but noisy crowd of admirers: *Lord Nelson Tavern* and the humbly titled *Cape Breton Is the Thought-Control Centre of Canada*. These were charming, off-the-wall fictions, of a cheerful piece with the prankster stuff then emerging from the coastal regions of the United States. Smith, a Cape Bretoner exiled to Montreal, had his own coastal vibe, but it wasn't stoner/surfer cool: it was late-night FM radio, chill and iconoclastic, joshing of mainstream tastes with bite but no malice.

Still, *Century* didn't launch. It took Ray Smith a long time to finish, and it wasn't as easy in its literary skin as his earlier work:

more moody and anxious, less sanguine about the triumph of light over dark. It was also set mostly in Europe, and spanned a near-century in just 165 compacted, almost pointillist pages. Things had changed in Canadian culture and literature in the interim, and Smith responded by, in a sense, going even further offshore than the island he comes from (and where he now lives again, in retirement). Whatever *Century* was, it wasn't "CanLit," as the impulse or industry was being dubbed.

I called it a "work of fiction" for a reason. The book, which has six parts linked by a single character and regular tonal over-laps, could be classified as a novel of the, yikes, postmodern variety. But, besides having no interest in any desiccated academic trope, the stories are all self-contained, as in a collection. Even Smith's one discernible theme—how art must embody the morality largely absent from a corrupted world—isn't writ in BLOCK LETTERS so everyone will get it. *Century* defies categories and shrugs off expectations. Look, says the text, of course this isn't life; of course it's just a book. Allow these elegantly arranged words to fall over you, confetti at a wedding, and then decide what the marriage is composed of.

"Matter of fact," one admirer recently observed, "the textures [of the prose] may be the meanings; Smith has too much respect for language, and too little patience with theme-speak, to insist any overarching concerns upon these smart, bright words. At moments, he may even be counting on musicality to serve as medium and message alike." Actually, I wrote that about *Century*, for a preface to a new edition published in 2009. Dan Wells, editor of Biblioasis in southern Ontario, has been both reissuing old Ray Smith books and supporting his newer ones. I won't say Biblioasis has been overlooked as well, but both these men are original, nervy literary sorts, operating from either the margins, if you insist on drawing the cultural map that way, or simply from where they need to be, as artists and publishers, in order to consider their day's—or life's—work worthwhile. I'm most happy to include my last copy of the Biblioasis *Century* with this note.

Sincerely,
Charlie Foran

RAY SMITH (b. 1941) is a novelist and short story writer. He was born in Cape Breton, Nova Scotia, and taught English in Montreal. Smith is also the author of *Cape Breton Is the Thought-Control Centre of Canada*, *Lord Nelson Tavern* and *The Man Who Loved Jane Austen*.

CHARLES FORAN (b. 1960) is the author of ten books, including the novels *Carolan's Farewell* and *House on Fire*, as well as an award-winning biography of Mordecai Richler, a biography of Maurice Richard and the award-winning non-fiction work *The Last House of Ulster*. Born and raised in Toronto, he holds degrees from the University of Toronto and University College Dublin, and has taught in China, Hong Kong and Canada. A former resident of Montreal, he currently resides with his family in Peterborough, Ontario.

BOOK 79

CHARLOTTE'S WEB
BY E. B. WHITE
Sent to you by Alice Kuipers
April 12, 2010

To Stephen Harper,
Prime Minister of Canada,
A book to remind you of the pleasures of life
and of the written word,
From a writer,
With thanks,
Alice Kuipers

Dear Mr. Harper,

Yann came up with the idea to send you a book every two weeks nearly three years ago. I remember the moment it happened. We were walking together along the river in Saskatoon. He'd just got back from his visit to Ottawa and was deeply troubled that the anniversary of the Canada Council had been so unimportant to Canada's politicians. Yann, like most writers, lives and breathes books—both those he reads and those he writes. He wanted to share that passion with you.

And so we walked along the river, the sun shining as it so often does in Saskatchewan, when Yann came up with the thought that perhaps if he sent you a book every two weeks, you might read one or two of them. He was excited and I was disparaging. I thought it would take up too many hours. Yann decided to choose short books out of respect for your time, and to include a letter with each book explaining why he chose it. He reads, or rereads, every book he sends you and carefully writes his letters to you.

Along the way, I think Yann has rediscovered the joy of reading widely. As a successful writer, he often only had time to read for research. But now I see him sitting up late at night, turning the pages, kidnapped by Pearl S. Buck or dazzled by Zora Neale Hurston. He sent you my own personal favourite—*Property*, by Valerie Martin—fairly recently. My own bookshelves have been somewhat depleted by Yann's ferocious hunt for books.

It took me a while to know what to choose to send you, as many of the books under two hundred pages that I'd already discussed with Yann have long since left the house and arrived in Ottawa. But I notice that Yann hasn't given you much children's literature, and so it seemed to me that *Charlotte's Web*, by E. B. White, would perhaps interest you. I suspect you've already read it, but it certainly bears rereading. I'd say most of E. B. White's words hold up well to being reread.

Elwyn Brooks White was born in the final year of the nineteenth century. The son of a piano manufacturer, he went to Cornell University where he took a course with Professor William S. Strunk Jr. Years later, White edited, revised and added to Strunk's *The Elements of Style*—an extraordinary book that every writer should have close to hand. It is full of bossy tips on how to write well. I'm lucky enough to have an illustrated edition. It has stood on my bookshelf for years. Writing to you now reminds me that I'd like to read it again. One of the joys of reading books is that, inevitably, they lead you to read other books. They are road maps to onward journeys. Just as *Charlotte's Web* leads me to *The Elements of Style*, so, hopefully, it will lead you to another book.

It's not entirely clear when White decided he wanted to be a writer, but it's known that he turned down a teaching job with the University of Minnesota to pursue that goal when he was in his early twenties. By 1927, he was a contributing editor at *The New Yorker*, the magazine with which he was associated until his death. His wife was an editor there. He wrote many brilliant essays (a collection of which lies next to my bed) and from there went on to write *Charlotte's Web* (among other books). All this to say that writing was his life. It permeated White's family, his work and his thoughts. Writing does that to some people. He wrote, "All that I ever hope to say in books is that I love the world. I guess you can find it in there, if you dig around."

I love that he wrote that. I love it because it speaks directly to the pleasure you will get from *Charlotte's Web*. White worried that the book would be too low-key for most kids with its simple, delightful evocation of life (and death) on a farm. Yet every carefully placed word (heeding Strunk's demand in *The Elements of Style* that we OMIT UNNECESSARY WORDS!) hums with White's pleasure at being alive.

The story is about Wilbur the pig and Fern, an eight-year-old girl, and their animal friends, Templeton the rat, a goose, a sheep and, above all, Charlotte the spider. Wilbur is a sweet, innocent pig who discovers that he is being fattened up to be killed. He doesn't want to die. As he says, "I just love it here in the barn. . . . I love everything about this place." And so Charlotte puts her mind to working out a way to save him. She uses her web to write words to the people in Wilbur's life. Words such as TERRIFIC or SOME PIG. The image of the farmhand coming to pour the slops, stopping in disbelief as he stares at the dewy web inscribed with the words SOME PIG, is etched into my mind, as the words on the web are etched into the consciousness of those who control Wilbur's destiny.

Don't be fooled. The simplicity of the language, the bucolic setting, the folksy animals, all build to Charlotte's swan song—a swan song to her friend the pig which is, at the same time, White's swan song to a way of life, written in the most elegant language. Charlotte using her strength to write those words in the web reminds me of how essential words can be. *Charlotte's Web* is a testament to the power of language, both in its tale and its telling.

This is why Yann writes to you. Like Charlotte the spider, he believes that the written word can shape lives and save lives. I hope by reading about E. B. White and, more importantly, by reading his books, you'll be reminded that as we need politicians and prime ministers, so we need books and writers.

And if reading *Charlotte's Web* does not do that for you, I'm hopeful that it will evoke a time and a place that stays with you. You'll be there with Wilbur as he tries—ridiculously—to spin a web. With Charlotte as she makes the ultimate sacrifice. With Fern as she tries to pull the axe from her father's hands. And with E. B. White as he shows us Wilbur for the first time:

There, inside, looking up at her, was the newborn pig. It was a white one. The morning light shone through its ears, turning them pink.

"He's yours," said Mr. Arable.

And so now this book is yours.
I hope you enjoy it.

Yours respectfully,
Alice Kuipers

E. B. WHITE (1899–1985) was an American author, and a frequent contributor to *The New Yorker*. He wrote *Charlotte's Web* and *Stuart Little*, and the popular writing handbook *The Elements of Style* (a.k.a. "Strunk and White").

ALICE KUIPERS (b. 1979) is the author of three novels for young adults: *Life on the Refrigerator Door*, *The Worst Thing She Ever Did* and *40 Things I Want to Tell You*. Her first picture book, *The Bookworm Book by Violet and Victor Small*, is coming out in 2013. She lives in Saskatoon.

BOOK 80

FOR THOSE WHO HUNT
THE WOUNDED DOWN
BY DAVID ADAMS RICHARDS

Sent to you by Steven Galloway

April 26, 2010

To Stephen Harper,

Prime Minister of Canada,

A great Canadian novel,

With sincere regards,

Steven Galloway

Dear Mr. Harper,

It's me again. I hope you enjoyed the last book I sent you, *King Leary*. Even if you haven't yet read it, or don't intend to read it, I still hope you enjoyed receiving it. Unexpected and free books arriving in the mail have become, now that Santa Claus's cover has been blown and the Easter Bunny unmasked, one of the few joyous gifts that come my way.

The book I have enclosed for you is another one of my favourites. I was in university when I read it for the first time, and it became one of the books that made me want to become a writer. David Adams Richards's novel *For Those Who Hunt the Wounded Down* has one of the best titles of any Canadian novel, or any novel, period.

I'm sending you this novel for several reasons. For starters, it's a wonderful book. Few writers capture working-class life as well as Richards, and few are as able to make seemingly ordinary lives feel extraordinary. Richards has written thirteen novels, most of them set in New Brunswick. He was recently made a Member of the Order of Canada, and has won about every possible prize for his writing.

I think that one thing Canada is good at is being able to productively discuss ideas where there is disagreement. Tomorrow, I'll be getting up before the sun and flying from Vancouver to New Brunswick where I'll be taking part in Moncton's Frye Festival. All across Canada, literary festivals are organized by people making little or no money. They are attended by readers of all political stripes, who happily part with some of their hard-earned money to spend an afternoon or evening talking about and thinking about books and the ideas contained within them. Even when they don't like the book. And the best festivals, the ones where people are the most energetic, are in places like Moose Jaw, Campbell River and Sechelt. These festivals are often supported in part by the federal government. For this I am thankful. It makes us a better country.

Going to festivals is not about meeting the authors, though some people like that. But often meeting an author is a terribly disappointing event. Often the person's not what you expect, isn't as clever as their books, says something not so brilliant. And sometimes it's the festival-goer's fault. A few years ago, I was in my publisher's office in Toronto for some reason or another, and I was told that David Adams Richards was in the building if I would like to meet him. Well, of course I would. We met as he was coming out of the lunch room, and he had a cup of coffee in his hand. I shook his free hand with too much gusto, which made him spill his coffee all over his shoe. It was completely my fault, and I felt like an idiot. Since then I have scrupulously avoided running into him again in the hope that he didn't catch my name and that by the next time we meet I will have aged enough that he won't recognize me.

Why do I mention this in a letter to the elected leader of my country? In a roundabout way, I'm trying to show you that writers aren't elitists. We often sound like we are, and occasionally we even act like we are—when you spend most of your time in a room by yourself, misunderstandings are bound to occur. But on a base level, we're ordinary people who happen to be good at writing down stories. And I think our stories are a big part of this country. Go to Moncton or anywhere else and you'll find a lot of people who think so too.

With sincere regards,
Steven Galloway

DAVID ADAMS RICHARDS (b. 1950) is a Canadian novelist, poet, non-fiction writer and screenwriter. His novels include the Miramichi Trilogy and *Mercy Among the Children*, which was a co-winner of the Giller Prize (with Michael Ondaatje's *Anil's Ghost*) in 2001. His book about fishing on the Miramichi, *Lines on the Water*, won the Governor General's Literary Award for Non-Fiction. His newest novel is *The Lost Highway*.

BOOK 81:

DIARY OF A MADMAN
BY LU XUN

Translated from the Chinese by William A. Lyell
Sent to you by Charles Foran
May 10, 2010

To Stephen Harper,
Prime Minister of Canada,
China's Tolstoy, China's Hugo,
from a Canadian writer,
with thanks,
Charles Foran

Dear Mr. Harper,

I read a newspaper article about a poll conducted by the largest online media company in China. The poll produced a list of the country's ten most significant cultural icons of the twentieth century, as chosen by the Chinese themselves. A full five of them were writers and three more were singers/actors. One, curiously, was a rocket scientist, while the final cultural icon was an obscure soldier who became the focus of a propaganda campaign.

The names on the list were familiar to me from fifteen years of reading and writing about China, and five years of living in Beijing and Hong Kong. Three of the choices, author Louis Cha and singers/actors Leslie Cheung and Faye Wong, were alive until shortly before the poll was conducted. Others, such as author Lu Xun and opera singer Mei Lanfang, continue to exert influence many decades after their deaths. I noticed strong patterns to the selections and remarked on how difficult, and extraordinary, these lives had been. I decided as well that, while far from definitive, the list was sound, and a window onto the values and sentiments of the Chinese people.

I also had a thought: imagine replacing these names with equivalents from the West. For Faye Wong, substitute Madonna; for Leslie Cheung, Elvis Presley with a twist. Mei Lanfang has been called China's Paul Robeson, and scientist Qian Xuesan's impact was akin to that of Robert Oppenheimer. Further back, Lao She's novel *Rickshaw* asserted the same kind of moral force as John Steinbeck's *The Grapes of Wrath*, while Qian Zhongshu's *Fortress Besieged* could be likened to a Shanghai version of F. Scott Fitzgerald's *The Great Gatsby*. Louis Cha's populist *wuxia* novels are the match of Zane Grey's westerns and John Ford's films. As for Lu Xun, the oldest and most revered of the ten, he has no exact parallel. To appreciate his significance, it is necessary to look to Tolstoy's importance to nineteenth-century Russia or Victor Hugo's to the Europe of his age.

The exercise left me wondering to what extent most of us really know China. Can someone claim to know the United States, say, if they've never seen a western or heard of *The Grapes of Wrath*? If they are oblivious to how Elvis Presley and Madonna altered the pop landscape? Our understanding of China remains stubbornly imprisoned by the most obvious markers: its rapacious economy and repressive political system, a population of staggering size and expectations. Yet a country is foremost a culture and a culture is the sum of the values and efforts, dreams and yearnings, of the people who dwell in it. To understand a nation, you must be intimate with its dreams and with its dreamers.

As it happens, Lu Xun has been a touchstone for me since I first started thinking about China. To the extent that this towering figure is known in the West, it is for his short stories, which literally birthed modern Chinese literature in the 1920s, and which remain vivid, unsettling examinations of a crumbling society and an enduring psyche. I hope you enjoy this sampling of Lu's most essential work.

Best wishes,
Charlie Foran

REPLY:

May 20, 2010

Dear Mr. Foran,

On behalf of the Right Honourable Stephen Harper, I would like to acknowledge receipt of your recent letters, with which you enclosed a copy of *Century*, by Ray Smith, and one of *Diary of a Madman*, by Lu Xun.

The Prime Minister wishes me to convey his thanks for sending him these publications. You may be assured that your thoughtful gesture is most appreciated.

Yours sincerely,
S. Russell
Executive Correspondence Officer

Lu Xun (1881–1936) was a Chinese essayist, short story writer, poet, teacher, editor and translator. His works were approved by the Communist Party, though he was never a member. He is considered one of the major Chinese writers of the twentieth century.

BOOK 82:

THE GREY ISLANDS
BY JOHN STEFFLER
Sent to you by Don McKay

May 24, 2010

Dear Prime Minister Harper:

As everyone on the planet probably knows by now, Yann Martel is busy touring with his new book, and has asked other writers to take over in his absence. Today it is my pleasant duty to present you, and readers of his website, with a classic of Canadian writing, John Steffler's *The Grey Islands*.

When I say "classic," I am placing it among other master-pieces of environmental writing like Thoreau's *Walden*, Aldo Leopold's *Sand County Almanac* and Gary Snyder's *The Practice of the Wild*; it is a book that engages wilderness in an intense way that alters our way of perceiving it. Unlike those texts, *The Grey Islands* is, technically, fiction, but it is based on John Steffler's actual experience alone on the uninhabited Grey Islands off the coast of Newfoundland's Great Northern Peninsula. It contains some of the most vivid, and varied, writing anywhere, including prose narrative, lyric poetry (which frequently registers aspects of the place in acute close-up), tall tale, ghost story, essay, dream sequences, maps, census charts and songs. What emerges is an unforgettable evocation of this remote windswept island and a record of one man's difficult passage into wilderness. But along with this, there's an increasing focus on the former residents of the island and the fishermen who still visit it, the narrative opening itself to include their voices in the many-threaded weave.

I'd be hard pressed to say whether I love this book more for its central story (the progress of the protagonist from town planner to pilgrim) or for its wonderful nooks and crannies. There is such economy in the language, and such a sure musical sense in Steffler's ear, that each of the passages—whether in the voice of a Newfoundland fisherman or the narrator-as-poet— hums with its own energy. When I first read it, back in the eighties, I found it hard to believe he was really pulling it off, making a book so various, with such diverse parts, yet working as an organic whole. It still seems unlikely, as unlikely as Confederation, another structure whose mysterious strength— as Canadians discover over and over—lies in its diversity.

I realize that this gift may be redundant—John Steffler having been the Parliamentary Poet Laureate a few years ago. (If you already have a copy, perhaps you wouldn't mind passing this one along to another parliamentarian.) *The Grey Islands* should be as inescapable for Canadians as *Walden* is for those south of the border, an iconic book that sets dramatically before us, in a way that is richly complex, at once meditative and entertaining, the difficult and essential encounter with wilderness.

As a bonus, I'm also including the talking-book version, published by Janet Russell of Rattling Books, the intrepid Newfoundland publisher of such distinguished books as Mary Dalton's *Merrybegot* and Michael Crummey's *Hard Light*—two more books that should be included in any Canadian's reading repertoire. On the CD, narrated by John Steffler himself, you will also hear Frank Holden speaking the part of Carm Denny, a deceased resident of the island, thought to be mad. It's a passage not to be missed, and includes the greatest bath scene anywhere. Eat your heart out, Hollywood. My thought is that, given what I'm sure is a very tight schedule, you might squeeze the CD in now, and reserve the book for a time of greater leisure.

Strong writing enables us to live imaginatively as well as practically; it enlarges the scope of life. When it engages the theme of wilderness, it can also enhance our understanding of ourselves as citizens of the world, as well as of a country. Of course such understanding will embrace not only our hardihood and courage, but our disgraceful blindness to the value of wilderness in and for itself. While that blindness was certainly part of the colonial experience, it remains a lamentable feature of some current attitudes, attitudes often registered in government policy. In the end, reading books like *The Grey Islands* can help make us better, more thoughtful, inhabitants of the planet.

I hope you will find this a stimulating addition to what must by now be a pretty fascinating, and eclectic, library.

Yours sincerely,
Don McKay

JOHN STEFFLER (b. 1947) grew up in Ontario and now lives in Newfoundland. After working a variety of jobs, including carpenter, deckhand and shoemaker, he became an English professor. His books of poetry include *That Night We Were Ravenous* and *The Grey Islands*. His novel, *The Afterlife of George Cartwright*, was a finalist for the Governor General's Literary Award and won the Thomas Head Raddall Atlantic Fiction Award. Steffler was Canada's Parliamentary Poet Laureate from 2006 to 2008.

DON MCKAY (b. 1942) is a Canadian poet, professor and editor. His books of poetry, which frequently address ecology, include the Governor General's Literary Award–winning *Night Field* and *Another*

Gravity, and the Griffin Prize–winning *Strike/Slip*. McKay is a co-founder of Brick Books, a Member of the Order of Canada and a birdwatcher.

BOOK 83

CALIGULA
BY ALBERT CAMUS

Translated from the French by Justin O'Brien

Sent to you by René-Daniel Dubois

June 7, 2010

To Stephen Harper,

Prime Minister of Canada,

Caligula, an extraordinary play

About pain

The quest for Power

And human scale,

With respect,

René-Daniel Dubois, O.C.

Dear Mr. Harper,

It is with strong feelings that I send you today *Caligula*, by Albert Camus.

You will note that I am enclosing two versions: one, the original, in French, of course, but also an English version, in a skilful translation by Stuart Gilbert.

I think—mistakenly, perhaps, and please correct me if I am wrong—that if you are not yet familiar with this author, the opportunity of comparing form and content from one language to another can only prove to be enlightening.

There are many reasons for my having chosen this work.

Here are two of them.

The year 2010 marks the fiftieth anniversary of the death

of Albert Camus, one of the most important writers of the twentieth century.

I usually refrain from categorizing authors as being either "major" or "minor": I have always thought that literature is a treasure in which each contribution is essential, and the older I grow the clearer this becomes to me. There is a style or none, a voice or none. If there is a voice, there is literature. If not, it isn't literature.

However, Camus—among very few others—is clearly an exception. He not only talked, he dove in, canvassing the woven link between the soul of humanity and its rebellion. From this immersion, he brought back exceptional works, notably *The Rebel*, a deeply moving and passionate essay on the genesis and history of this rebellion, and *Caligula*, of course, the play which is the transposition of this *Rebel*. Not just a simple sketch, nor a dialogued representation, but more: an incarnation.

If, for example, one compared *The Rebel* with the plans of a mechanical device as drawn by engineers, *Caligula* would constitute the locomotive itself, charging ahead, never veering from its course, crushing everything in its path.

The second reason behind my choice relates to the fact that while the character of Emperor Caligula may have seemed to Camus to be an excellent illustration of the myth seething through the events of his time—just before World War II—it is certainly plausible to claim that in our time this myth acts overtly and has become . . . omnipresent. It has even succeeded, in the Western public sphere, at least, in repressing anything that might tend to contradict it. Revenge against life and its corollary, the cult of pure blind power, are to be seen everywhere today. Signs of their reign assault our eyes wherever we look.

Albert Camus has left us an extraordinarily inspiring body of work that can undoubtedly help us to better define who we are, what drives us, and to better understand our fellow man as well as our era.

At the heart of this work is *Caligula*.

Albert Camus achieved with Caligula what Sigmund Freud, in his own times, did through Oedipus: from an ancient story, he brought forward an essential myth for all people of all eras. And he gave it a name.

The storyline? Very simple.

Caligula, the emperor of Rome, beloved by all, has just lost Drusilla, his sister who was also his lover. He becomes a monster. Why? Because this loss makes him see that, simply put, "Men die; and they are not happy."

Drusilla's death has awakened in him a yearning for the impossible. In his quest, he will be ruthless.

My wish for you, Mr. Prime Minister, is that reading this appalling yet magnificent play will provide you with as luminous a source of inspiration as it did for me.

Respectfully,
René-Daniel Dubois, O.C.

ALBERT CAMUS (1913–1960) was an author, journalist, essayist, playwright and one of the essential philosophers of the twentieth century, primarily for his work on the theory of the Absurd. He was born in French Algeria, and participated in the French Resistance during World War II. He received the Nobel Prize in Literature in 1957.

RENÉ-DANIEL DUBOIS (b. 1955) is a Quebec playwright, actor and director. His plays include the Governor General's Literary Award–winning *Ne blâmez jamais les bédouins* and *Being at Home with Claude*, which was made into a film.

BOOK 84

NIKOLSKI
BY NICOLAS DICKNER
Translated from the French by Lazer Lederhendler
Sent to you by Émile Martel
June 21, 2010

To Stephen Harper,
The splendid translation of a most
entertaining Québécois novel,
From a Canadian poet and translator,
Émile Martel

Dear Mr. Harper,

In a democracy, it is a cherished privilege of the citizen to address directly the leader of his or her country. We all know in our hearts that it is the duty of the leader to respond to these efforts. Matters of interest or concern may need to be addressed this way, and adequate responses often ensure an element of serenity to the citizen who has initiated the dialogue, as well as provide the leader with clues about the soul and the mind of his or her fellow citizens.

When Yann asked me to join in on the What Is Stephen Harper Reading? book club, I was positively elated because it gave me a role, as a poet and as a translator, in this campaign, which, you will have learned, has been noted and admired in many a country and matches a cherished belief I have in international cultural relations, a foreign policy your government absurdly dropped, which was not only a great loss to Canadian artists and creators, but also a blow to Canada's image abroad.

The novel I'm sending you today was published in French in Montreal in 2007 and received the Governor General's Literary Award for translation to English in 2009; so you have two books here resulting from the special and exceptional talents of two artists: a novelist and a translator.

The book, *Nikolski*, by Nicolas Dickner, was very well received both in Quebec and in France; it won many prizes, and has been beautifully translated by Lazer Lederhendler.

The profession of translator is a discreet and humble one. We translators are seldom noticed and hardly anybody ever believes that we did our work right. There is always a nuance, always the shadow of an emotion that we missed, or there is a smell or a taste that we have exaggerated or understated. Whatever we do, we know that another translator in a few years will do differently, may even do better, just as a reader or a writer who understands both languages is likely to say that the original is much, much better than the translation. Of course it's better! Most of the time.

But the translator can sometimes take some sort of a revenge. There is an anecdote I like to tell: Shakespeare wrote *Hamlet* near the end of the sixteenth century. About one hundred years later, Voltaire was born in France. Two pillars of European and world culture. Naturally, Voltaire knew of Shakespeare and read his works. One day he wanted to share with his readers, in French, the most famous line uttered by Hamlet:

To be or not to be, that is the question.

How would these ten words be translated in a way that respected not only the desperate intensity of the original English, but adopted the common form of French verse in use at the time, the twelve-syllable rhyming "alexandrins"? This way:

Demeure, il faut choisir, et passer à l'instant
de la vie à la mort, et de l'être au néant.

An interesting exercise would be to take Voltaire's two verses
without knowing Shakespeare's original verse and translate
them back to English. Translation can be a magical cave revealing beauties even the author did not know about . . .

Returning to *Nikolski*, whichever version you read first, the
French original or the English translation, your attention will
be drawn to the cover illustration: three fish, the same three fish,
actually, but swimming in different directions, horizontally in
one and vertically in the other. I believe there is a slightly different message there, although I'm not sure what that message
is. What do you think?

The novel is a splendid construction of twisted and adventurous lives where various characters hover around each other
in a dance of chance and luck, mostly around the Marché Jean-
Talon in Montreal, but also in other places in Canada—among
them the Prairies and the north shore of the Saint Lawrence—
and in distant Caribbean countries. Piracy is important in this
book, and navigation. And a fishmonger, and . . . and . . . You'll
love that crowd once you get to know Noah and Joyce and the
narrator who sells used books on rue Saint-Laurent.

The French version has a dedication from Nicolas Dickner
to our granddaughter Catherine, encouraging her to "return
to the novel." She'd told us that she hadn't read a novel in a
while. But she already had a copy of the book. So allow me to
encourage you, too, to return to the novel, fulfilling the wish
of Nicolas Dickner.

With my best wishes,
Émile Martel

Born in Rivière-du-Loup in 1972, NICOLAS DICKNER grew up in Quebec and studied visual arts and literature in university. Afterwards, he travelled extensively in Europe and Latin America before settling in Montreal. His first novel, *Nikolski*, won three awards in Quebec, one in France, and was the winner of Canada Reads 2010. He currently writes a weekly column for *Voir*, and his most recent book is *Apocalypse for Beginners*.

ÉMILE MARTEL (b. 1941) is a writer and translator. He worked as a diplomat from 1967 to 1999, serving twelve years at the Canadian Embassy in Paris, four of them as the minister for cultural affairs. He has published seventeen books of poetry and fiction, thirty Spanish and thirteen English translations, most of them in cooperation with Nicole Perron-Martel. He was awarded the Governor General's Literary Award for *Pour orchestre et poète seul* in 1995. He is the President of the Centre québécois du PEN international.

BOOK 85

HOW I LIVE NOW
BY MEG ROSOFF

Sent to you by Alice Kuipers
July 5, 2010

To Stephen Harper,
A book to colour your imagination,
Sent by a writer,
Alice Kuipers

Dear Mr. Harper,

Books sometimes come to you at serendipitous times. For me, the reading of *How I Live Now* by Meg Rosoff coincided with a time in my life when I was spending several weeks in rural England. The novel is wonderful. It starts with fifteen-year-old Daisy arriving in the UK to stay with her cousins on a farm. Their mother leaves, and then a war begins. Rosoff never tells the causes of the war. Daisy is not interested. She's too busy falling in love with her cousin, the compelling and startling Edmond. Soon the events of the war separate them and Daisy is transformed.

In the UK this Easter a strange thing happened. The skies closed because of the giant ash cloud from the Icelandic volcano. Planes were prevented from flying. I was in Devon in a cottage on Dartmoor. After a couple of days with no flights, I began to notice how eerily quiet the skies were. I lolled in the flower-filled garden, the moors spread before me, the book dangling from my hand as I stared into the empty blue above. The extraordinary story of Daisy and her cousins roaming around a rural landscape blighted by rationing and violence had seeped from the pages, staining my imagination. The creepy silence of the skies echoed the cessation of flights in the novel. I couldn't laze around the garden without feeling the cousins hurtling around behind me on their way to their barn. I couldn't get up and walk over the moors without seeing Daisy frantically searching for Edmond.

Meg Rosoff published *How I Live Now* in 2004 and gave up her career in advertising shortly after that. It was her first book but since then she has published many more (a thrilling discovery for me as I now have all the rest to read). She regularly updates her blog at www.megrosoff.co.uk. She wrote of her most recent novel:

> For the best part of two years, the book has been constantly in my space, whining, stonewalling, refusing to play ball. I've been hating it, loving it, neglecting it; threatening, cajoling, pleading, throwing it out with the bath water, retrieving it; practicing tough love, bribery and suggesting it go play in traffic. Once I even told it I wasn't its real mother.

She seems to feel that her book is somehow alive. I wonder if she felt the same way when writing *How I Live Now*. I'm going to hazard a guess that she did. Writers feel that way about their characters and their stories. And when a writer is as talented as Rosoff, the reader feels life pulsing from the pages of her books.

Rosoff's writing is brave and moving. She writes of a teen-ager who is sent to England because she is destroying herself—both emotionally and, we discover, physically. It's almost too late for Daisy, yet during her time in this country at war, she discovers that she is so much more than she gave herself credit for. It's a classic story of trial and redemption, and it's a love story. It's a story of survival and of longing. This novel is *alive*. It leaves the page and tints your imagination like water coloured with a drop of blue dye.

This year as the sky lay empty of planes, as the moors before me filled with Daisy and her story, life spilled from Rosoff's pages and *I* felt more alive.

I hope that this novel comes at a serendipitous time for you too (although maybe without the drama of an entire country shutting down its airspace!). May it stain your imagination blue.

Yours respectfully,
Alice Kuipers

REPLY:

September 3, 2010

Dear Ms. Kuipers,

On behalf of the Right Honourable Stephen Harper, I would like to acknowledge receipt of your correspondence, with which you enclosed a copy of the book entitled *How I Live Now*.

Thank you for sending this book to the Prime Minister. Your thoughtful gesture is most appreciated.

Yours sincerely,
T. Lewkowicz
Executive Correspondence Officer

MEG ROSOFF (b. 1956) is an American writer. After working in publishing and advertising in New York City in the 1980s, she moved to London, where she still lives. She has written books for children, young adults and adults.

BOOK 86

STUNG WITH LOVE:
POEMS AND FRAGMENTS
BY SAPPHO

Translated from the Greek by Aaron Poochigian
July 19, 2010

To Stephen Harper,

Prime Minister of Canada,

Poetry that has crossed the desert of time,

From a Canadian writer,

With best wishes,

Yann Martel

Dear Mr. Harper,

I'm back and you're still there. So let's resume this lopsided duet where I read, think, write and mail, and you say and do nothing. Your silence doesn't particularly bother me. It's future generations who will damn you or, more likely, mock you. Me? I feel like a cowboy in a western who is about to cross a fearsome desert. To comfort myself, I talk out loud. Does my horse answer me? No, it doesn't. Would I therefore want to do without it? No, because without it I would lose what defines me as a cowboy—and I would have to cross that desert on foot. You are my democratic horse through which I exist as a democratic cowboy. Better to ride on your sullen back than to be trampled down by a dictator. As for these troubled times, the desert that faces us? I have faith that we'll get through it, somehow. I'll be guided by the books I read and the people I meet. And you, our leader? I don't know. Do blind horses get across deserts? Are they not swallowed up by the sands?

Before I go on, I should ask: have you enjoyed the books that some fine fellow Canadian writers have sent you while I was on tour for my latest novel? I am grateful to Steven Galloway, Charlie Foran, Alice Kuipers, Don McKay, René-Daniel Dubois and Émile Martel for contributing to your burgeoning library. Those are interesting titles they sent you.

Poor Greece. It has certainly received a beating these last few months. The mismanagement of its finances has cost the country—and a number of European banks—very dearly. I'm not entirely sympathetic to their woes. By the sounds of it, the blame for the problems of the Greeks can largely be laid upon the shoulders of the Greeks—and then they were preyed upon by greedy banks, who saw profit in making easy loans to them. A real mess, an insolvency that will tar and mar the country for years to come.

Yet a country can't be reduced to its pockets, whether deep or full of holes. Poor Greece, rich Greece, mismanaged Greece, recovering Greece—next to that monolith of a proper noun those adjectives are mere twigs. Greece is Greece is Greece, and there is much to that. For starters, the language and its alphabet, lovely and arresting. I count the Greek language as one of the most pleasing vocal instruments our species has come up with. Italian, spoken next door, perhaps has a more lissome, mellifluous form, but Greek has the staccato intensity of *content*. Western philosophy, and therefore Western civilization—since before we *do* we must *think*—started with the Greeks, specifically with the Greeks living in Ionia, in Asia Minor, now Turkey. They became known as the pre-Socratics since they were not quite weighty enough to be given their own name but rather became defined by the illustrious philosopher whom they preceded. Nevertheless, those pre-Socks—Thales, Anaximander, Anaximenes, elsewhere the formidable Parmenides of Elea, besides others—are important because they were the first to try to understand the world by relying not on myth but on reason. They *observed* the world, something that hadn't been done before in the West. That inspired intellectual approach, which brought Greece a blaze of renown, was such a singular achievement that when the Italians did the same some two thousand years later, inspired in part by the rediscovery of some forgotten Greek philosophers named Plato and Aristotle, it was called the *renaissance*, after the initial *naissance* brought about by the ancient Greeks.

Well, at the same time that the Greeks were thinking, some of them were also feeling. So Sappho. I haven't sent you poetry in a long while. Sappho was a woman who lived on the island of Lesbos roughly between the years 630 and 570 BCE. She is held to be the first woman poet in literary history. Those who came before her have been lost to time. Sappho's poetry itself—some 9,000 lines in total, it is estimated—has barely survived the predation of time and exists only in fragments. In the late nineteenth century in the Egyptian town of Oxyrhynchus, an ancient garbage dump containing vast quantities of papyrus was discovered. Much of it had been used by the ancient Egyptians as stuffing to fill the empty spaces in coffins and mummies. In one mummified crocodile's stomach, a fragment of poetry by Sappho was found. (That must have been one happy croc, to be digesting a morsel of Sappho's poetry for centuries.)

Though Sappho wrote on a variety of subjects, she is best known for her love poetry. It is simple and moving. Take this fragment:

Sweet mother, I can't take shuttle in hand.
There is a boy, and lust
Has crushed my spirit—just
As gentle Aphrodite planned.

Weaving was a female activity. A virginal girl who properly
married would continue weaving as the head of her household.
But if she was led astray . . . It's interesting to note the feminine
empowerment in this fragment. The girl is aware of the options
that are available to her. It is for her to choose whether to take
hold of the shuttle again and focus on her weaving, or turn to
the boy. Another fragment gives us a clue about her choice:

Since I have cast my lot, please, golden-crowned
Aphrodite, let me win this round!

Here's another heartfelt cry from twenty-six centuries ago:

That impossible predator,
Eros the Limb-Loosener,
Bitter-sweetly and afresh
Savages my flesh.

Like a gale smiting an oak
On mountainous terrain,
Eros, with a stroke,
Shattered my brain.

But a strange longing to pass on
Seizes me, and I need to see
Lotuses on the dewy banks of Acheron.

Acheron was one of the rivers of the Underworld, and the lotuses on its edge were associated with forgetfulness. The poet is so lovesick that she wants to die and eat the flowers of amnesia.

Some of the poems are surprisingly explicit:

> Time and again we plucked lush flowers, wed
> Spray after spray in strands and fastened them
> Around your soft neck; you perfumed your head
>
> Of glossy curls with myrrh—lavish infusions
> In queenly quantities—then on a bed
> Prepared with fleecy sheets and yielding cushions,
>
> Sated your craving . . .

It's the "yielding cushions" that really makes this hot stuff. Sappho laments the ravages of old age:

> As you are dear to me, go claim a younger
> Bed as your due.
> I can't stand being the old one any longer,
> Living with you.

She also widens her gaze to topics that might be called political, and what she has to say is pertinent to this day:

> Wealth without real worthiness
> Is no good for the neighbourhood;
> But their proper mixture is
> The summit of beatitude.

I'll quote one last fragment, a prescient one:

> I declare
> That later on,
> Even in an age unlike our own,
> Someone will remember who we are.

Indeed. Sappho lived among people who were mostly illiterate. Amazing that poetry performed aloud and preserved initially only in the memories of her listeners should survive to this day. They are fragments, true, and who is to say what treasures were obliterated by time (or continue to lie dormant in a mummified animal lying under Egyptian sands). But what survives still speaks—and what more can one ask of a poem? The passion of Sappho's poetry has something volcanic to it: the print may be thin and black, but just beneath it runs molten magma.

So when you have Greece on your mind, as I'm sure you have recently, I hope you manage to take the long view. Economics is a short-term concern. What endures is art. Ask any crocodile how to survive a desert and it will tell you: better to have a poem in your stomach than a number in your head.

Yours truly,
Yann Martel

SAPPHO (CA. 630–570 BC) was a lyric poet in Ancient Greece, born on the island of Lesbos. Her poetry, which frequently focused on themes of love and companionship, survives mostly in fragments (potsherds and papyri).

BOOK 87

SWEET HOME CHICAGO
BY ASHTON GREY

August 2, 2010

To Yann Martel
Ashton Grey

To Stephen Harper,
Prime Minister of Canada,
A genie escaping a bottle,
From a Canadian writer,
With best wishes,
Yann Martel

Dear Mr. Harper,

A few weeks ago I was at the Saskatchewan Festival of Words. It's a friendly celebration of literature held in the pleasant Prairie town of Moose Jaw. I'm sure you've been (to the town, I mean). One of the days I was there, as I was leaving the public library where the festival takes place, a man on a park bench hailed me. He was holding a baby in his arms and was sitting next to another man. I might've just waved and walked on, but there was that baby. I have a baby. So I approached the two men. It turned out that the other man was the dad, and the genial man who had called out my name was his friend. The three of us chatted for a few minutes. I was about to go when the man holding the baby asked me if I would buy his book. I had noticed the thin volumes spread out in a half-circle on the ground in front of him. "Special Festival price, seven dollars," he said. I gave him ten, he signed my copy, and I walked away with *Sweet Home Chicago*, by Ashton Grey. I saw Mr. Grey again the next day, on Main Street this time, near the Mae Wilson Theatre, still hawking his opus. Someone told me that Mr. Grey, who looked to be in his thirties, couldn't afford the bus from Winnipeg to Moose Jaw, so he'd hitchhiked to come sell his book at the Festival of Words. Such dedication, I thought. And he had the good karma earned from holding a baby the previous day.

I decided to read his book and now I pass it on to you. *Sweet Home Chicago* is forty-nine pages long. I remember Mr. Grey saying on the park bench that he didn't like calling it a novella. I didn't ask what he had against the term, but out of respect for his wishes, let's call it a long short story. If you look on the copyright page, you'll see that it was "first printed" in 2009 and then printed again by Bindle Stick Publications of Hamilton, Ontario, in 2010. The number 3 appears below that information. My guess is that *Sweet Home Chicago* is onto its third printing. Now, whether Bindle Stick Publications is Mr. Grey's own self-publishing operation and he lives in Hamilton, Ontario (and how he got from Hamilton to Winnipeg), or whether Mr. Grey lives in Winnipeg and does business with Bindle Stick Publications, a tiny vanity press in Hamilton, Ontario—to all these questions, your guess is as good as mine.

Sweet Home Chicago is a long short story with many flaws. There are lots of spelling mistakes. On the very first page you'll read the sentence "He reached over the bar and ceased Ronald's coat trying to jerk him awake." Ronald's coat was more likely "seized." The dialogue is consistently wrongly punctuated:

"I guess you should call the police." He said with a voice that expressed his sorrow that nothing else could be done.

That should be a comma after "police" and the personal pronoun that follows should start with a small letter, since the statement is all one sentence. On a broader level, some of the exposition is awkward, many details are unnecessary, and it's not entirely clear to me what the story is about thematically. And yet it has narrative drive, the characters have their charm, there are funny parts, and underlying it all is an uncynical tenderness. It's a booze-fuelled story, so to seek out the flaws is to soberly miss the point. Best to read *Sweet Home Chicago* with the unfocused, good-humoured indulgence of the slightly drunk. The story relates the consequences to the unnamed protagonist of being in a bar next to a man who has the misfortune of keeling over and dying right then and there. Our hero finds himself in an alcohol-soused pickle.

This story is no *Under the Volcano*. (Do you know the novel? Malcolm Lowry? It's Canadian. The over-consumption of alcohol achieves there its greatest literary expression.) But that is another book. The attraction for me in sending you *Sweet Home Chicago* lies not with the quality of the work but with the intent of the author. It's Ashton Grey's strong desire to *tell his story* that struck me, a desire so strong that he self-published it and now self-promotes it, even hitchhiking from Winnipeg to Moose Jaw to share it, and all this without any serious chance of critical or commercial success. But that's what stories do to a person and, collectively, to a people. Stories are like genies: just as a genie wants to escape its bottle, so a story wants to escape the man, woman or child in which it finds itself. A shared story is a living story. Stories are passed down through families and through history. They endure while the storytellers die. Now that Ashton Grey has committed his story to the page, it will live on. That is a good thing. We need stories, all kinds of stories, because without stories, our imagination dies, and without imagination, there is no real appreciation of life. You have the luck of owning one of the few copies of *Sweet Home Chicago*. I hope you realize what a rare privilege that is.

Yours truly,
Yann Martel

ASHTON GREY (1983–2011) was a Canadian writer, author of the novella *Sweet Home Chicago* and contributor to *Bound for Glory* magazine.

BOOK 88

AUTOBIOGRAPHY OF RED
BY ANNE CARSON
August 16, 2010

To Stephen Harper,
Prime Minister of Canada,
Poetry to make you think and feel,
From a Canadian writer,
With best wishes,
Yann Martel

Dear Mr. Harper,

"Art is heart." My uncle Vince, a photographer, said that once. What he meant is that expression that is not rooted in emotion, or that does not evoke emotion, is not art. Art can, of course, make one think. Art that aims to last should do that at least in part, since emotions tend to froth up mightily but then fade, while a thought can calmly stay in the mind for a lifetime. A thought can be fully revived simply by the act of thinking, while an emotion remembered is far more tepid than an emotion felt. A story that is all emotion, a romance, say, may move, but it will be quickly forgotten as it will leave nothing for the mind to mull over. Nonetheless, despite the perishability of emotion and the cool immortality of thought, it is emotion that marks us most. Nothing goes deeper than emotion, and after that, at a shallower level, we think. Thinking that is significant may trigger an emotion. Remember Archimedes shouting "Eureka!" (great emotion) after his discovery that a submerged object will displace its equivalent volume of water (great thought). Which do we remember most? I think it's that cry and that image of the exultant man running down the streets of Syracuse naked after jumping out of his bath.

Anne Carson's *Autobiography of Red*, then. Anne Carson is a Canadian academic. She holds a Ph.D. from the University of Toronto and is a classics scholar who has taught at UC Berkeley, at Princeton, at McGill, among other universities. Which is very impressive—but not, I would argue, an ideal background for a poet. Universities do wonders for dead poets, teaching them and therefore keeping them alive, but they're deadly for living poets. It's pretty well impossible to make a living as a poet, so many poets have sought shelter in universities, earning degrees from them and then teaching there. I don't know why that is so. Why wouldn't poets seek shelter in plumbing or farming? Whoever determined that poets should have soft, uncallused hands? The damage universities have done to poetry stems from the kind of thinking that thrives in these institutions, and which is indeed necessary if they are to produce quality scholarship: thinking that is rigorous, codi-fied, impersonal. Such hyper-thinking tends to kill the spon-taneity, the liveliness of the poetic instinct. Walt Whitman is taught in universities, but Walt Whitman would never have survived university.

Academic cleverness is on display in *Red*. The first five sec-tions—*Red Meat: What Difference Did Stesichoros Make?*; *Red Meat: Fragments of Stesichoros*; and then three appendices—and the last section, *Interview*, are interesting but in a puzzling, cool, clever, archly droll way. You have to know who Stesichoros is. I'd never heard of him. Then you have to care. I didn't really. Compared to some of the other poetry I've sent you—

Ted Hughes's *Birthday Letters* or *Gilgamesh*, for example—these sections are not memorable. Thank God they're short.

But then there's the meat of the book, the *Autobiography of Red* in question, which is by far the longest section. It's great. It's a novel in verse that tells the sad story of Geryon, a red monster, and his unhappy relationship with Herakles (or Hercules, as you might know him better). Geryon loves Herakles, and Herakles loves Geryon too, but in a fickle way, in a way that doesn't accommodate Geryon's love. So Geryon loves and suffers, while Herakles loves and cavorts about with Ancash, his Peruvian lover who loves and suffers as much at the hands of Herakles as Geryon does. The names are classical, but the setting is contemporary as are the language and the imagery. And the emotions are there. Take these lines, of Geryon and Herakles lying next to each other:

> Not touching
> but joined in astonishment as two cuts lie parallel in the
>   same flesh.

And the story ends with an astonishing image that will stay with you. I won't ruin it by quoting it out of context. You must earn the image by reading your way to it. Then it will have its emotional impact on you. And you will perhaps be left thinking.

Yours truly,
Yann Martel

ANNE CARSON (b. 1950) is a Canadian poet and professor of Classics, whose writing style crosses genre and form, combining poetry, translation, essay, fiction and criticism. Much of her work takes its cue from classical Greek literature. Carson has published fifteen books and garnered a list of accolades that includes the Griffin Poetry Prize and a Guggenheim Fellowship.

MR. PALOMAR
BY ITALO CALVINO
Translated from the Italian by William Weaver
(AND
THREE LIVES
BY GERTRUDE STEIN)
August 30, 2010

for *Mr. Palomar*
To Stephen Harper,
Prime Minister of Canada,
A book of observant stillness,
From a Canadian writer,
With best wishes,
Yann Martel

for *Three Lives*
To Stephen Harper,
Prime Minister of Canada,
Pretty much one of the worst books I've ever read,
From a Canadian writer,
With best wishes,
Yann Martel

Dear Mr. Harper,

Perhaps you noticed that the last book I sent you, the poet Anne Carson's *Autobiography of Red*, starts with a quotation from Gertrude Stein. That got me thinking. Every literate person has

heard of Gertrude Stein. Paris fixture for forty years; friend of
Ernest Hemingway and Sherwood Anderson, of Pablo Picasso
and Henri Matisse; coiner, it is said, of the term "the lost generation" to designate those American writers who were born out
of the disillusionment that followed the First World War; sayer
of "A rose is a rose is a rose" to debunk literary pomp and pretence; and so on—Gertrude Stein is a name that has endured. I
have in mind the image of a smart, genial, open-minded woman
who liked to be at the centre of things. All artists need patrons
and supporters, and what a nice thing it must have been to have
Gertrude Stein play that role, to be admitted into her salon in
Paris in rooms full of stunning modern art, and to be offered
drink and food and conversation, if one were a young and poor
expatriate writer or painter. If Paris was a moveable feast, as
Hemingway put it, I imagine Gertrude Stein as the hostess of
that feast.

But who has *read* Gertrude Stein? Her *Autobiography of Alice
B. Toklas*, which is purportedly about her lifelong companion
but is in fact about both of them and their lively lives in Paris,
is Stein's best-known work. Though as biography it's fanciful, with the facts largely filtered by a cheerfully opinionated
subject, it's still not a work of fiction. What of Stein's true
fiction? I had never read anything by her, and couldn't even
think of a title. So there, my choice was made.

I found *Three Lives*, a collection of three long stories first
published in 1909 and more recently reprinted by Penguin
Classics. The introduction by an American academic whetted
my appetite. In it I discovered that the style of each of the
stories was highly influenced by a different modern painter. So
"The Good Anna" was marked by Paul Cézanne, "Melanctha"
by Picasso and "The Gentle Lena" by Matisse. How odd and
intriguing, I thought. In what way could brush strokes affect

the writing of words? How could the play of paint on a two-dimensional surface influence the composition of a story on a page? I settled in for a thrilling Modernist ride. I have often thought that no one has pushed and pulled the English language quite so much as the interwar writers of the last century. Hemingway, William Faulkner, James Joyce, Virginia Woolf, John Dos Passos, e. e. cummings, to mention only a smattering off the top of my head—they made English say new things in new ways. I thought I would witness such experimentation with *Three Lives*.

Well, I was disappointed, angrily disappointed. It's all very well to have ideas and theories, and experiments do need to be made, in art as well as in science, and one should make allowances for risk-takers—but my God, what a boring book! I worked my way through "The Good Anna" and started "Melanctha," but forty pages in my reading ground to a stupefied halt, and I gave up. Of what I read, I have this to say: there is no concern for realism in either setting or psychology; there is no eye for detail or ear for dialogue; nearly everything is told, not shown; the characters are only fitfully plausible; there is only the odd heartbeat of a plot; the language is plain and unappealing; and the repetition—which was announced as Stein's great gambit—is as interesting as watching paint dry, which is the only link I can make between *Three Lives* and what Cézanne, Picasso and Matisse did. Most surprising to me, coming from someone I thought would be a fountain of bon mots, was the utter wit-lessness of Gertrude Stein's writing. Oh yes: the racism, that too came as a surprise. I noted a few squeaks by the author of the introduction to explain it away, but I took little heed of this warning. After all, there's that line in Hemingway's *The Sun Also Rises*, of the character Robert Cohn, how he had "a mean Jewish streak." That second adjective wouldn't pass muster nowadays. But it's just one line among many, one line in a magnificent body of work that only there jars with its prejudice. It's a smudge upon the timeless art made by a man who is of his time, formed and limited by its biases. And more to the point, *The Sun Also Rises* is not *The Protocols of the Elders of Zion*. The comment on Robert Cohn is a line in passing, a throwaway line in no way central to the novel. Gertrude Stein's *Three Lives* is something else. See how this paragraph sits with you:

> Rose Johnson was careless and was lazy, but she had been brought up by white folks and she needed decent comfort. Her white training had only made for habits, not for nature. Rose had the simple, promiscuous unmorality of the black people.

As for our heroine:

> Melanctha Herbert was a graceful, pale yellow, intelligent, attractive negress. She had not been raised like Rose by white folks, but then she had been half made with real white blood.

Rose Johnson is a proud one:

> "No, I ain't no common nigger," said Rose Johnson, "for I was raised by white folks, and Melanctha she is so bright and learned so much in school, she ain't no common nigger either, though she ain't got no husband to be married to like I am to Sam Johnson."

They're a fine pair, Sam and Rose:

> The child though it was healthy after it was born, did not live long. Rose Johnson was careless and negligent and selfish, and

when Melanctha had to leave for a few days, the baby died.
Rose Johnson had liked the baby well enough and perhaps she
just forgot it for awhile, anyway the child was dead and Rose
and Sam her husband were very sorry but then these things
came so often in the negro world in Bridgepoint, that they
neither of them thought about it very long.

I like the "*perhaps* she just forgot it" and then the huffy, what-
you-making-so-much-trouble-about "anyway" that follows.
As for the death of a baby not being thought about for "very
long," I'd think that'd be inaccurate even of a mother gnu who's
just lost a baby gnu to a lion on an African plain, let alone of
two human beings. And this tripe appears in the first two pages
alone. After that, it gets no better, it goes on and on in the same
register, because "Melanctha" is all about black folks as they
exist in Gertrude Stein's mind.

You perhaps see now why I stopped reading. Whatever
theory of literary composition Gertrude Stein might have
wanted to bring to light is buried by a thick layer of toxic racist
sludge. I'm willing to forgive the odd slip of an artist if the aim
of the work is high. But when the slip is central, when the slip
is all you see and get, then the high aim is lost. Gertrude Stein's
book is all the more galling if you consider that she was both
lesbian and Jewish, and therefore, you'd think, slightly more
sensitive to prejudice. But no, not Gertrude Stein. Stupid, stupid
woman. I see now why she has survived among readers only in
her incarnation as hostess to young greats.

Why then am I sending you her book when I so loathed
it? Because maybe I missed the point. Every reader has his or
her limitations. Clearly I'm not up to this Penguin Classic. You
might have a different opinion. Perhaps you will get something
out of *Three Lives*.

But in that order of books, of writers who try something new, there's much better than Gertrude Stein. Take Italo Calvino, for example, an Italian writer who lived between the years 1923 and 1985. I've chosen *Mr. Palomar* for you. Here you have a book that is plotless but fascinating, that is experimental yet rewarding, that is different without becoming tiresome, that is rooted but not restricted, that is beautiful though not in a classical way. *Mr. Palomar* is a book that charms and stimulates in equal measure. It makes you see both language and the world in a slightly different way.

It's a hard book to describe. I suppose one could say that it's a collection of short stories. But that's not quite right. It is indeed divided into sections that can be read in any order, like a standard collection of short fiction. But they're not stories, not really. They would be better described as fictional meditation pieces. In each one, the discreet, attentive, concerned Mr. Palomar has an encounter or an experience upon which he dwells. His name is the same as that of the famous observatory in California. That gives you some idea of the scale of Mr. Palomar's musings. And yet his scale is also very small, so that sometimes his telescopic viewing becomes microscopic. There's a pleasing harmony to that, as the very, very small, the molecular, has much the same layout as the very, very large, the cosmic, and both, to the mind, are quite dizzying in their vastness. But I'm not being concrete enough. In "The naked bosom," Mr. Palomar is walking along a beach and he sees, up ahead, a woman lying on the sand, topless. How is he to deal with this, what should he do with his gaze, where should it go? The piece, three and a half pages long, describes the choices that come to Mr. Palomar's mind and their ramifications. In "From the terrace," Mr. Palomar looks out upon Rome and contemplates the significance, from a bird's perspective, of that vast panorama of variegated roofs. In "The albino gorilla," Mr. Palomar wonders about the meaning of a gorilla holding onto an old tire. In "The order squamata," the variety of reptiles, and how they live in time, is mused about. In "Serpents and skulls," the meaning, or lack thereof, of pre-Columbian Mexican architectural motifs is discussed. And so on. The settings are varied (Rome, Paris, Barcelona, Japan, Mexico), sometimes the very large is looked at (night skies, planets, oceans), sometimes the very small (a gecko, a Japanese sand garden), throughout the language is apt and intensely evocative, and always there is a concern for the meaning of things, how *this* is related to *that*. Italo Calvino is like a spider and with his words he links the most incongruous elements so that finally everything is linked by the thin thread of a web, and order and harmony are thereby established in the universe. *Mr. Palomar* is both whimsical and philosophical, an odd mix. It's a book that assures the reader that his or her gaze upon the world is not only important, but essential, because only in watching, in observing closely, can things be seen.

Which point was entirely lost on Gertrude Stein, but we won't go there again. Enjoy *Mr. Palomar*. It brought upon me a sort of Zen peacefulness, that stillness which I mentioned so long ago to you.

Yours truly,
Yann Martel

ITALO CALVINO (1923–1985) was an Italian journalist, short story writer, editor, lecturer and novelist whose books include *Invisible Cities* and *If on a winter's night a traveler*. He left the Italian Communist party after the Soviet Union invaded Hungary in 1956.

GERTRUDE STEIN (1874–1946) was an American writer, patron and art collector. Her most famous book is *The Autobiography of Alice B. Toklas*, published in 1932. Stein is credited with coining the phrase the "lost generation." She is buried in Père Lachaise Cemetery.

BOOK 90:

SELECTED POEMS
BY AL PURDY
September 13, 2010

To Stephen Harper,
Prime Minister of Canada,
Fire in your hands,
From a Canadian writer,
Yann Martel

Dear Mr. Harper,

I met Al Purdy once. Or rather, he was pointed out to me at a small party at a literary festival in Eden Mills, Ontario. Purdy was sitting, I was standing; Purdy was elderly and revered, I was young and upcoming. I made nothing of the occasion because I had never read his poetry. He was just a name. I regret that now, not having gone over to shake his hand and chat with him. The writer as a man is like any other man until you've read him. It's only once you've read him that the writer makes a greater impression. Had I read Purdy before that party, I would have approached him with a measure of trepidation. But I gather he was exceedingly generous with writers, especially younger ones. I'm sure we would have had a good conversation.

Now I have read Al Purdy and I can see why he was revered. He's an intensely Canadian poet, which I don't mean as a limiting qualifier. Every poet comes from somewhere, but some feel more universal than others, their specific cultural origin leaving only a discreet mark upon the poetry. Not so with Al Purdy.

He's all about Canada. You see that right away in the places that inspired his poetry. The first poem in the collection I'm sending you is called "The Road to Newfoundland." Other poems mention Vancouver and BC. Still others, the Canadian Arctic. And at the centre of this poetic geography, holding it together like the fixed point of a compass (I mean here the mathematical instrument consisting of two pointed legs, one of which keeps still while the other holds a marking implement—pencil or pen—and pivots around it, describing arcs or circles; not the other compass, which uses a magnetic needle to indicate geographical direction, although it would serve the metaphor just as well), is Roblin Lake, near the hamlet of Ameliasburg, Prince Edward County, Ontario. Several poems evoke the lake, and one senses that the A-frame house Purdy built there was the capital city of his poetry (more on that A-frame a little later). Other geographies are mentioned too—Cuba, for example—yet even with these poems the sensibility is entirely Canadian. What this Canadianness means is that a reader from Canada reading Purdy's poetry will likely *recognize* our country in it, while a reader from abroad will likely *learn* about our country. But to repeat myself using different words: there's nothing local-yokel about Purdy's work. You see that in the historical, literary and political references sprinkled throughout. Al Purdy clearly was a man who read widely and thought freely.

The language is colloquial, the tone conversational. There is therefore a deceptive simplicity to Purdy's poetry. Just a guy talking on the page, with funny line breaks. But then an image hits you, and you (or, to be more accurate, I) go *Wow!* Take the first poem, the one I mentioned above. It starts:

My foot has pushed a fire ahead of me
for a thousand miles

> my arms' response to hills and stones
> has stated parallel green curves
> deep in my unknown country
> the clatter of gravel on fenders registers
> on a ghostly player piano
> inside my head with harsh fraying music
> I'm lost to reality
> but turn the steering wheel a quarter
> inch to avoid a bug on the road . . .

My foot has pushed a fire ahead of me/for a thousand miles—have you ever thought of a car in those terms? I'll certainly never forget it. And then that modern image, of a man driving an internal combustion engine, is linked to an older one, when precious fire was carried from camp to camp in a moss-lined basket. You get an inkling here of how Purdy effortlessly spans history and geography with that startling compactness that is poetry's forte. There are too many poems to discuss in detail, but if you want a taste, if you're in a rush, I'd suggest you have a look at "The Cariboo Horses," "Late Rising at Roblin Lake," "One Rural Winter," "Interruption," "Married Man's Song," "Fidel Castro in Revolutionary Square," "Hombre," "Trees at the Arctic Circle," "Lament for the Dorsets," "House Guest," "At Roblin Lake," "Poem," "Wilderness Gothic" and "Roblin's Mills (2)." That should give you an idea. But you shouldn't be in a rush. That's not the way to read poetry. No point either in reading one poem after another, page after page, like a novel. That would be like eating twenty good meals in a row. Best to read only a few poems at a time, like opening a window for a moment in the autumn to breathe in the invigorating air before closing it again. And poems thrive on increased familiarity. Repeated reading will make you comfortable with the cadence and help you unpack the imagery. I've chosen to send you *Selected Poems*, published in 1972 by McClelland & Stewart. It has a good and vigorous introduction by George Woodcock.

I will mention one other poem, "Hombre," in which Purdy remembers meeting Che Guevara in Havana, actually *meeting* him, and shaking his hand—astounding. The mythical Che. Since when do poets and politicians meet and shake hands? Have you ever met and shaken hands with a poet? Well, I guess that's the prerogative of *revolutionary* politicians, ones who are willing to go off into the jungles of Bolivia to die for a dream. Purdy met Guevara in Cuba in 1964, when the charismatic Argentine doctor was the minister of industries. Was the poet in awe of the revolutionary? No. Purdy was a man of the people, for sure, but also a democrat and one senses in the poem, as one does in the other poems inspired by his visit to Cuba, a suspicion that Castro's and Guevara's dreams for the people might not take into account what the people actually wanted. Again, Purdy shows himself to be profoundly Canadian, preoccupied with the small details of common decency rather than the grand visions of truculent idealism.

This meeting between a poet and a politician brings me back to the A-frame house on Roblin Lake, where so much of Purdy's poetry was written and where so many literarily inclined visitors came to visit. This A-frame is both a cornerstone and a crossroads of Canadian poetry. Purdy died in 2000 at the age of eighty-one and a campaign has been launched to purchase his property, create an endowment and establish a writer-in-residence program in the A-frame. It's a great idea. Literary culture, of course, is kept alive by the publishing and reading of books, but the places that inspired books are also important. After all, if the spirit of a place inspired a writer, it will likely inspire others. I myself now want to visit Ameliasburg.

And cultural memory lasts a long time. Businesses come and go, but a great poet's house—that's the stuff of plaques and museums, which the Al Purdy A-frame Trust is trying to avoid. It wants to keep Al Purdy's generosity alive. Where one poet lived and worked, others will too. That is their mission. *The Al Purdy A-Frame Anthology* was published by Harbour Publishing (they're the guardians of Purdy's legacy: they've put out a more recent *Selected Poems*, covering the years 1962 to 1996, in addition to the complete *Beyond Remembering: The Collected Poems of Al Purdy*). All proceeds of the sale of *The A-frame Anthology* go to the Trust. I meant to send you my copy, but it's too lovely. It's an evocative mix of reminiscences, poetry and photographs. I knew no more about Al Purdy than I suppose you do, yet the anthology made me feel the creative energy of the place and the fun Al and his gang had there. The A-frame Trust hasn't reached its fundraising goal yet. If you're interested in helping, please visit their website www.alpurdy.ca. You can make a donation and you can also order a copy of the anthology.

If you're lucky, one day you might end up on the shores of Roblin Lake, shaking hands with a poet.

Yours truly,
Yann Martel

AL PURDY (1918–2000) was a writer, editor and poet who lived for much of his life in an A-frame home he and his wife built in Ameliasburgh, Ontario. He is Canada's unofficial poet laureate and wrote more than thirty books of poetry, including *In Search of Owen Roblin* and *Rooms for Rent in the Outer Planets*, which was a finalist for Canada Reads in 2006.

BOOK 91:

THE NIBELUNGENLIED

Translated from the medieval German by Cyril Edwards

September 27, 2010

To Stephen Harper,
Prime Minister of Canada,
From a Canadian writer,
With best wishes,
Yann Martel

Dear Mr. Harper,

I was in Germany last week to promote my latest novel and I thought that while there I'd find something German for you. My first thought was Thomas Mann's *Death in Venice*, a virtuoso piece of short fiction. But as I was browsing through the foreign-language section of a bookstore in Frankfurt, my eyes fell upon the book I'm sending you this week, *The Nibelungenlied*. It's the medieval illustration on the cover that drew my attention, and then I was further drawn by the imprimatur just below the title: Oxford World's Classics. This was a world classic I'd never heard of—what better reason to read it? The title is somewhat unattractive, but I assure you: this is a great book.

The Nibelungenlied arose from the oral tradition and was finally written down—whether with accuracy or great liberties is not known—by an anonymous poet roughly in the year 1200, and it is, in the words of the introduction by the translator Cyril Edwards, "the greatest medieval German heroic poem or lay, a revenge saga on an epic scale, which has justly been compared with Homer." The introduction, by the way, is useful but not essential. You can plunge directly into the epic. Despite the chasm of time between then and now, and the ensuing profound changes in thinking and mores, there is an emotional appeal to the work that makes it timeless. Our world isn't inhabited by knights and damsels any longer, but love, devotion, heroism, envy, treachery, lust for revenge—these are emotions and actions we still feel today, and they continue to feature in novels and movies of all genres, from literary fiction to romances and thrillers.

The language of the work, both of the minstrel narrator and of the various characters, is gracious and courtly, full of ornate flattery. Every knight is a hero of blinding good looks, dressed in the finest garments the world has ever seen, mightier than Samson or Arnold Schwarzenegger, and richer than Croesus or Bill Gates. And the same goes for the ladies. But the action betrays the words. Treachery is done after the nicest exchanges. Queens follow up social niceties by calling each other wenches and whores, and a knight who has sworn eternal loyalty to another then proceeds to stab him in the back. It makes for glorious reading.

I doubt *The Nibelungenlied* describes with anthropological accuracy the actual ways of central Europe's nobility a thousand years ago. It is a work of literature, not of history. But there's something to be gained thereby for the modern reader. If true ways are not described, *ideal* ways certainly are. The treachery of Prunhilt, of Gunther and, especially, of Hagen—you will see how profoundly perfidious they are—stands in strong contrast to the good and honourable behaviour of those they betray, Sivrit and Kriemhilt. The characteristics of this good and honourable behaviour offer a fascinating look at the mindset of the time.

For example, you might notice the surprising cosmopolitanism. The characters in *The Nibelungenlied* come from a variety of places: Burgundy, the Netherlands, Iceland, Hungary, Austria, Denmark. (One place never mentioned by name is Germany, which didn't exist yet as a nation; Bavaria comes up in passing, but only as a dangerous nest of brigands.) Yet all these characters mix and match without any linguistic or cultural friction. And the good relations go beyond language. The Hungarian characters, with King Etzel at their head, are Huns and therefore pagans. Nonetheless, they get along very well with the Christian characters. Better than that: Etzel, King of the Huns (historically, Attila the Hun) *marries* Kriemhilt, devout Christian lady and widow of slain Sivrit.

What struck me even more in the relations between the various nobles is the material generosity of their exchanges. I had in mind that these kings and queens, these lords and ladies would keep tight control of their goods and chattels. Being at the top of the feudal pyramid, they would be the recipients of much of the commodities produced by their vassals. And don't wealthy people tend to cling to their wealth? Don't the rich *hoard*, giving to charity only as much as will not diminish their abundance, as in the parable of the poor widow in the Bible? Well, not in *The Nibelungenlied*. Take this line, describing what Kriemhilt does when she arrives at the court of her new husband, King Etzel:

> The queen then distributed gold and garments, silver and precious stones. All that she had brought across the Rhine with her to the Huns had to be given away in its entirety.

In its entirety? And this is just one instance of giving. Such abundant giving happens again and again in *The Nibelungenlied*.

People are constantly giving, giving, giving, and not just to allies, which might have an element of self-interest. No, the giving also extends to guests who are strangers. This constant gifting reminds me of a book I sent you earlier. Do you remember *The Gift*, by Lewis Hyde? It too spoke of societies based not on the hoarding of wealth but on its flow; that is, societies where wealth is perceived to increase if it is kept in motion and to decrease if it lies stagnant. I did not expect to find such a dynamic in thirteenth-century central Europe. Of course, such incessant giving was probably not the norm. I imagine that many a lord sat on his bags of gold, glowering at every passing stranger. Nevertheless, it is interesting that this is the ideal portrayed in *The Nibelungenlied*, one of wealth shared over and over. The ideal noble is noble because he or she gives without restraint.

Another surprise was the degree to which characters—kings, lords, knights, husbands and wives—consult and seek advice from each other. It undermines the authoritarian image I had of those distant times. Oh, and the women are strong. Prunhilt literally: when her new husband gets too frisky she trusses him up and hangs him by a nail for the night. But also morally— Kriemhilt for example.

And lastly, the entirely secular tint of the work. Christianity is mentioned here and there, and Jesus is invoked on occasion, but overwhelmingly the world portrayed is secular, with the pleasures and torments very much earthbound. Again, my image of a medieval Europe in a Christian deep freeze was altered.

There's a curious narrative device that occurs often: the paragraph that ends with a comment in brackets by the author. These comments often announce some future event in the story, usually tragic. The device may remove an element of suspense in the story, but a highly effective sense of foreboding is created in its stead. Since the story was initially spoken, not read, I do wonder how these brackets were signalled. These are some of the intellectual perks of *The Nibelungenlied*. Mostly, though, the ride is just to be enjoyed.

There's a sad postscript that needs to be mentioned. *The Nibelungenlied* vanished from notice in the sixteenth century. It was rediscovered some two hundred years later and became one of the canonical elements of German nationalism in the nineteenth century, used by Wagner in his *Ring of the Nibelung* cycle of operas. And then, alas, the Nazis exploited Sivrit's fate, or Siegfried's, as the name had become, as a literary warning of what might befall the Aryans if they did not resist the treachery of "lesser races." In such ways do politicians sometimes pervert literature.

Yours truly,
Yann Martel

CYRIL EDWARDS (b. 1947) is a (largely) retired lecturer in medieval German literature and philology at the University of Oxford. His books include *The Beginnings of German Literature*, translations of Wolfram von Eschenbach's *Parzival and Titurel* and Hartmann von Aue's *Iwein, or the Knight with the Lion*, and *The Little Book of Soups & Stews*. Forthcoming: *The Allotment/The Black and the Green*, a novella and selected poems.

BOOK 92:

CHESS
BY STEFAN ZWEIG

Translated from the German by Anthea Bell

October 11, 2010

To Stephen Harper,
Prime Minister of Canada,
Your move,
From a Canadian writer,
With best wishes,
Yann Martel

Dear Mr. Harper,

Do you play chess? I'm sure you have. It has a rare allure among games. Stefan Zweig puts it nicely:

> ancient yet eternally new; mechanical in structure, yet made effective only by the imagination; limited to a geometrically fixed space, yet with unlimited combinations; constantly developing, yet sterile; thought that leads nowhere; mathematics calculating nothing; art without works of art; architecture without substance—but nonetheless shown to be more durable in its entity and existence than all books and works of art; the only game that belongs to all nations and all eras, although no one knows what god brought it down to earth to vanquish boredom, sharpen the senses and stretch the mind. Where does it begin and where does it end?

(It occurs to me that Zweig's musing could also apply to sex, except for the invocation of sterility, but that's neither here nor there.) Chess *is* a game of stumping complexity. With the exception of go, I can't think of another game that offers so many possible plays. And there's another appeal to chess: the complete absence of luck. Chess is an entirely logical game in which there is no "luck of the draw." You win or you lose entirely based on the mental powers you bring to the chequered board. And so the aura of genius that surrounds the great chess players of history. But if genius it is, it's a peculiar one, deep perhaps but also very narrow, confined to the movements of pieces on a board. Bobby Fischer once said, "Chess is life." Well, not really. Life very much has an element of luck to it, the luck of where and to whom we are born, the luck of our genetic inheritance, the luck of our circumstances, and so on. Nor is life logical. In fact, according to a good number of thinkers and writers, it's not even certain that life makes sense. But chess has simple rules that yield a vastly complex game, just as life, one might argue, has simple rules that yield a vastly complex experience. And we meet opposition in life, just as there is opposition in chess, black against white. So the parallel is rough, but it pleases, this simplification of life in which only force of personality matters and fate is entirely in one's own hands. One looks at the chessboard and imagines a battle scene—or perhaps Question Period.

Stefan Zweig's *Chess* (also known at *The Royal Game* or *Chess Story*) was published posthumously after the author's suicide in 1942 in Brazil, to which he had fled with his wife to escape the Nazis. Zweig is the quintessentially continental European writer of the interwar period, a man caught between bloodbaths who tried to make sense of a world gone mad. He did this by applying himself to the "real" world in a series of biographies and by "escaping" that world in works such as *Chess*. But escape is never possible. The reality of Zweig's life seeped into his fiction. You will see this in *Chess*. The story takes place over the course of a few days on a passenger steamer travelling from New York to Buenos Aires. Aboard is the world chess champion Mirko Czentovic. Some chess amateurs lure him into a game, him against all of them. Czentovic easily defeats them. They play again. The amateurs look like they're once again going to lose. But then a voice from the crowd makes a surprising suggestion for the next move. They follow his advice, as they do for the following moves, each given urgently by this stranger. To their amazement, the game ends in a draw. The stranger reluctantly agrees to play a game one-on-one the next day with the world champion. But who is this stranger? Where—how—did he acquire his prowess at chess? *Chess* has that unity of time, action and place that Aristotle said was a key characteristic of the good story, and it is a good story indeed. It sucks you in. You climb aboard the ship in your mind and you hurry, like the chess players, to the smoking room where the games are being played. But despite the appealing fictional setting, so removed from the violent unfolding of history, the world and its troubles can't be so easily forgotten. Stefan Zweig's experience with the Nazis infuses the middle section of his novella. Chess is portrayed as a necessary escapism, an obsession that allows his character to hold on to sanity.

Because that is another appeal that chess holds: a game that is entirely logical, where wild emotions have no play, where rigorous sanity wins the day and defeat comes only from an inner lapse of reason—such a game, in a world gone mad, is a relief.

Perhaps there are days on Parliament Hill when you feel like retreating to your office and playing chess, Mr. Harper. After all, you're still stuck with a minority government, and then there's the uproar over proroguing Parliament, the fight over the Afghan detainee documents, the billion-dollar summits, the furor over the elimination of the mandatory census, the fruitless effort to kill the gun registry, the fury of the veterans' ombudsman, and other controversies—these must wear you down. You like to be in control. You have notions about how things should be, but constantly you don't get your way. Constantly, the unpredictable happens. Wouldn't it be nice if politics were a chess game and you could just sit down and bully your way to a checkmate?

Alas, thankfully, the political system in Canada is not so arranged. Instead, you're playing a life game in which you've lost a fair number of pawns. How will the game end, I wonder?

Yours truly,
Yann Martel

STEFAN ZWEIG (1881–1942) was a novelist, playwright, journalist and biographer. He left Austria in the 1930s, fleeing the Nazis, moving to England and then the United States before dying in Brazil. In addition to *Chess*, his books include *Amok* and *Letter from an Unknown Woman*, which has been adapted for the stage and screen.

BOOK 93

SELECTED POEMS
BY YEVGENY YEVTUSHENKO

Translated from the Russian by Robin Milner-Gulland and Peter Levi

October 25, 2010

To Stephen Harper,
Prime Minister of Canada,
Have you made a mistake?
From a Canadian writer,
With best wishes,
Yann Martel

Dear Mr. Harper,

Politics is the art of compromise, the saying goes. When a newspaper prints a photograph of two politicians shaking hands and smiling broadly, whether in Washington, the Middle East or elsewhere, it's likely that a compromise is being celebrated, a breakthrough in which opposing parties have reached an agreement by making concessions. The fruitful compromise is the great enabler of social peace, whether between competing groups or lone persons relating to each other. Those who stand too firmly, who are unwilling to negotiate in any way with others, are soon at the heart of incessant social friction and lose any peace they might wish to have. Compromising helps not only to establish social harmony, but also to build relationships, since a compromise is normally the result of open dialogue and increasing familiarity with one's adversary. Such relationships, in addition to making compromise possible, may also dilute the differences that provoked the antagonism in the first place. In politics, the fruitful compromise often makes the difficulties go away. Take Northern Ireland, for example. The Troubles, as they came to be called, started in the late 1960s, and for three decades Protestant unionists and Catholic nationalists were at each other's throats, killing men, women and children, some actively involved in the hostilities, others mere bystanders. The hatred could not have been more intense. Yet eventually, by dint of slow, unremitting effort, the warring parties signed a truce, the Good Friday Agreement of 1998, and now peace generally prevails in Northern Ireland. A compromise ended the Troubles and, over time, as peace becomes part of the social fabric, the root causes of the Troubles will, one hopes, disappear. The compromise of the Good Friday Agreement has made, and continues to make, the difficulties go away. That is good politics.

Now, compromise is not your way. You went into politics early on, without any entrepreneurial or significant work experience to teach you the value of yielding. There was the National Citizens Coalition, of which you were president for a few years, but being an advocacy group, it's hardly the place to learn the motto "Let's talk." You stand by your principles and ideology, and you wait—expect—the country to come round to your views. To be honest, I doubt that's going to happen. You've been in office for over four years now, at a time when the opposition has been fragmented and, in the case of the Liberals, discredited, and still you've managed only two minority governments in a row, and polls don't show your fortunes improving significantly.

Let me introduce you then to Yevgeny Yevtushenko. Yevtushenko is a Russian poet who was born in 1933. He was twenty years old, and coming of age as a poet, when Stalin died in 1953. Yevtushenko profited from the let-up in repression in

Soviet life that followed under Nikita Khrushchev and quickly became the poetic voice for a post-Stalin generation that yearned for greater freedom (it's at this time that Alexander Solzhenitsyn's *One Day in the Life of Ivan Denisovich*, which I sent you a while ago, was also published). Yevtushenko wrote poems that no poet living under Stalin would have dared to write, not if that poet wanted to stay alive. An example is *Babi Yar*, which is included in the collection of poems I'm sending you this week. Babi Yar is a ravine on the northern edge of Kiev, in Ukraine. An estimated 100,000 innocent people of all ages were murdered there by the Nazis. The victims were Roma and POWs but overwhelmingly they were Jewish. Yevtushenko, who is not Jewish, wrote the poem to protest the proposed building of a sports stadium by the Soviet authorities on the site of the massacre. The poem mourns the Jewish deaths, but also excoriates the Russian people for their Jew-hatred. It's a moving poem, and also, in taking on explicitly the victimhood of the Jews as the poet's own, affirming his common humanity with them, a brave poem coming from a citizen of a land so notoriously inimical to Jews.

Yevtushenko gained great fame and honour in both East and West in the 1950s and '60s. He travelled extensively to the West. If you look him up on Wikipedia, you will see a 1972 picture of him chatting with President Richard Nixon (which reminds me that President Obama wrote to me—who knew American presidents had such a history of paying attention to writers?). "Here," the Soviet Union seemed to saying, "is proof that we are not a repressive society. We too can produce great poetry that is critical of us, and here is our poster boy."

How does his poetry measure up? Well, in this slim volume, it fares quite well. Except for *Babi Yar*, politics intrudes very little into it. Or no more than politics might in a collection of

American or Canadian poetry. Much of it is quite bucolic, reminding me that Russia, the largest country in the world even without its former Soviet satellite states, is, ipso facto, mostly rural. Many of the poems exude a common sense and an approachable humanity that brings to mind Robert Frost.

But did he compromise himself? The Soviet Union was from start to finish a repressive state where every freedom was, if not outright curtailed, then under constant surveillance. In such a state, was it possible to be a free poet? Yevtushenko was criticized by many, including the great Russian-American poet and critic Joseph Brodsky (have you heard of him?), as a duplicitous fake, as a poet who had around his neck a collar that was tied to a leash held by the Kremlin and that he barked and growled only when and so much as it suited them.

Clearly, some writers paid a greater price for their writings, being forced either into exile, like Solzhenitsyn or Brodsky, or, worse, into jail in the Soviet Union. Was it perhaps the case that Yevtushenko hoped his country would change and open itself to greater civil liberties? Maybe he simply loved his country, including its communist ideals. Maybe the idea of permanent exile, of living forever in a country whose language, ways and food would be foreign, chilled his soul. In other words, did Yevtushenko simply believe in his country in a way that Solzhenitsyn and Brodsky did not?

I have no position on the matter. I don't know enough about Yevtushenko or Soviet history, and so cannot judge. His poetry is a pleasure to read, but the political man behind the poems remains elusive. What is certain is that Yevtushenko has been accused of compromising himself in his dealings with the Soviet state. His standing has paid a price. Compromise, you see, does not have in the arts the worth that it has in politics. The compromised artist is likely to be seen as a failure, but the compromising politician a success. If politics is the art of compromise, then art is the politics of uncompromise. Artists need and fiercely defend their freedom. It is precisely from that freedom, from that individuality, that art springs. To compromise, to conform, to give in, is to kill the creative impulse. True art is uncompromising. The great artist lets rip, saying "This is where I stand, this is my vision—take it or leave it!" In the arts, there is no parliament to which the artist is accountable, no Question Period to which he or she must submit. Art is the place for those who do not accept compromise.

Hence my question to you, Mr. Harper. Have you not chosen the wrong profession? Could it be the case that you are a frustrated artist?

Yours truly,
Yann Martel

YEVGENY YEVTUSHENKO (b. 1933) is prolific in many roles—poet, essayist, novelist, film director, screenwriter and actor. He is the best-known poet of the post-Stalin generation, and appeared on the cover of *TIME* magazine in 1962. He now teaches Russian and European poetry and film at the University of Tulsa and the City University of New York. His honours include the American Liberties Medallion and the Ovid Prize.

BOOK 94:

THE ABSOLUTELY TRUE DIARY
OF A PART-TIME INDIAN
BY SHERMAN ALEXIE

November 8, 2010

To Stephen Harper,

Prime Minister of Canada,

From a Canadian writer,

With best wishes,

Yann Martel

Dear Mr. Harper,

Three years ago (yes, that long ago) I sent you the novel *Oranges Are Not the Only Fruit*, by the English writer Jeanette Winterson. If you remember—and hopefully enjoyed—it was the story of a girl, Jeanette, who is caught between two worlds, the world of evangelical Christianity and the world of her nascent lesbian sexuality. She must choose the world to which she wants to belong. It is one or the other. She cannot be both Christian *and* lesbian, not at that time, not where she lived.

The novel I'm sending you this week, *The Absolutely True Diary of a Part-Time Indian*, by the American writer Sherman Alexie, plays out a somewhat similar conflict. Junior, the protagonist, a teenage Spokane Indian, lives on a reservation in Washington State. It's a lousy place. Most of the adults are poor, miserable alcoholics, and most of the kids are poor, miserable and on their way to becoming alcoholics. Junior decides one day to switch schools. He'll leave the school on the rez and go to the high school in Reardan, the small farming community just down the road. But there's a hitch: Reardan is an all-white school. The only other Indian there is the school mascot. And many on the rez see Junior as a traitor to his people for leaving. But Junior feels that if he stays, a part of him will die. He goes ahead and starts attending Reardan High School.

True Diary is a very funny book in a sad sort of way. The prose, simple and effective, is aimed at teens. The story will speak to any reader, teen or adult. It asks difficult questions. How do you get on with life when your life really sucks? What keeps you going when the going gets tough? Alexie's answer is that earthly salvation depends on one's spirit, on the ability to find inner resources to endure and overcome adversity. But there is a cost to every battle, even the ones that are won. So Junior does well at Reardan High, but he's also now living in a white world and leaving behind the Indian self he knew. Unlike Jeanette's dilemma in *Oranges*, which demands an exclusive choice, Junior's dilemma is less radical. It's not a question of one identity or another, but of two identities uncomfortably merging, white and Indian, hence the title: a *Part-Time* Indian. In saving one part of himself from dying on the rez, will another part of Junior die in the white world?

It would be nice to think that one day Junior will stop being tormented by these perceived existential opposites, that his Indian self will be enriched by becoming a little bit white (whatever that might mean) and his white world will profit by becoming a little bit Indian (whatever that might mean), until there is no longer any friction between the two worlds. It's good, after all, to be something only part-time. Part-time Indian, part-time white, part-time writer, part-time father, part-time this, part-time that—isn't that just another way of saying that Junior has grown into a normal, twenty-first-century hybrid human being, a rich world unto himself, varied and complex but still whole?

Yours truly,
Yann Martel

SHERMAN ALEXIE (b. 1966) is a novelist, filmmaker, poet and comedian. He adapted the screenplay for the award-winning film *Smoke Signals* from a story in his first collection, *The Lone Ranger and Tonto Fist Fight in Heaven*. Alexie is also renowned for his writings on basketball. He lives in Seattle with his wife and two sons.

BOOK 95

CAKES AND ALE
BY W. SOMERSET MAUGHAM

November 22, 2010

To Stephen Harper,
Prime Minister of Canada,
To have chatted with Thomas Hardy,
To be like Rosie,
From a Canadian writer,
With best wishes,
Yann Martel

Dear Mr. Harper,

The cover is dreadful, but the book is good. *Cakes and Ale* is the first Somerset Maugham I'm sending you. Maugham, an English writer who lived between 1874 and 1965, was a prolific author of novels, plays, short stories and travel writing. His masterpiece is *Of Human Bondage*. Oh, what the lovesick soul submits itself to! But Philip Carey's misery at the hands of Mildred will be for another time, when you have more time to read: *Of Human Bondage* is a long book, close to seven hundred pages. So *Cakes and Ale* instead, at a neat 190 pages.

Maugham would not generally be placed at the forefront of English literature, I don't think. He was too old-fashioned in his technique, too lacking in newness and experimentation. He was writing novels at the same time as his Modernist contemporaries like Hemingway, Faulkner, Joyce and Woolf were rewriting the novel. But who cares, it's not a competition. So long as the reading is enjoyable, let's keep on reading. Maugham relied on those mainstays of the good story—character, plot, emotion—and did very well with them.

Cakes and Ale features members of my own profession. I thought you might find that amusing, seeing how scribblers operate. The main characters—Edward Driffield, Alroy Kear, William Ashenden—are all writers. The first is portrayed as at the forefront of late-Victorian literature, the second as having more ambition than talent, while the last is our modest but slightly cantankerous narrator. It is said that Maugham based Edward Driffield on Thomas Hardy. Maugham mentions in his author's preface meeting the elderly Hardy once at a dinner party and chatting alone with him for three-quarters of an hour (imagine that: chatting with Thomas Hardy!), but explicitly denies the link between Hardy and Driffield. He has this surprising assessment of Hardy: "I read *Tess of the D'Urbervilles* when I was eighteen with such enthusiasm that I determined to marry a milkmaid, but I had never been so much taken with Hardy's other books as were most of my contemporaries, and I did not think his English very good." So says Maugham, but then his character William Ashenden gives the same lukewarm assessment of the fictitious great writer Edward Driffield. To give a character an aura of fame is difficult, and Maugham succeeds admirably with Driffield, but if it helps you to think of Driffield as Hardy, go for it. There's no problem with adding fiction to fiction. It will only increase your reading pleasure.

What links these three characters, certainly the first and the third directly, is the voluptuous, carefree, beautiful Rosie Driffield. She is Edward Driffield's first wife, William Ashenden's former lover and Alroy Kear's problem. Kear, you see, has been charged by Driffield's *second* wife to write the great man's biography, and the shamelessly promiscuous

Rosie is both awkward to deal with and impossible to avoid in his biography.

What is shocking to see in the novel is how considerations of class so regiment the lives of the characters. There are people one can know and visit and be at ease with, and entire classes of others that one should deal with on a stiff, strictly professional basis. Rosie stands out as the only character who lives the life she wants, unencumbered by such notions of propriety. And that means living her emotions, no matter where they lead her.

See if you like this first sample of Maugham. His short stories are wonderful too.

Yours truly,
Yann Martel

W. SOMERSET MAUGHAM (1874–1965) was an English novelist, short story writer, travel writer and playwright. He always wanted to be a writer and, with the success of his book *Liza of Lambeth*, he walked away from his position as a medical doctor. His novels include *Of Human Bondage*, *The Painted Veil* and *The Razor's Edge*, all of which have been adapted for the screen.

BOOK 96

SIX CHARACTERS IN SEARCH OF AN AUTHOR
BY LUIGI PIRANDELLO

Translated from the Italian by John Linstrum

December 6, 2010

To Stephen Harper,
Prime Minister of Canada,
From a Canadian writer,
With best wishes,
Yann Martel

Dear Mr. Harper,

One of the great monuments of twentieth-century European theatre is *Six Characters in Search of an Author*, by Luigi Pirandello. A few biographical details, quickly: Italian; 1867 to 1936; short stories, novels, plays; Nobel Prize for Literature in 1934.

Six Characters was first performed in 1921. Like many daring works, it divided before conquering the public. It made Pirandello famous around the world. It was a play like none before. It starts with a bare stage, a space not pretending to be a living room or a garden or anywhere else, but only that: a bare stage. Eventually some actors wander on, soon joined by a director, a prompter, a prop man and the various other members of a theatre company. They are about to rehearse a play. Now, the device of a play within a play is not so revolutionary. Shakespeare used it in *Hamlet*, for example. But that is a finished play within a finished play. Here, at the start of *Six*

Characters, the inner mechanics of that artifice called theatre are displayed with complete nudity, so to speak; the actors appear as themselves, standing around, chatting, smoking, reading a newspaper, and the normally hidden director and others are out in full view. It all has the appearance of real, ordinary life. Then—and this is where the Pirandellian revolution starts—the doorkeeper apologetically interrupts the director to inform him that some people are here to see him. The director is annoyed. A rehearsal is never to be interrupted! But these people, they're insisting, says the doorkeeper. In fact, they've already made their way to the stage, six of them, a man, a woman, a young woman, a young man and two children. The director asks impatiently: Who are you, what do you want?

The Father replies: "We have come in search of an author." They—that is, the Father, the Mother, the Stepdaughter, the Son, the Boy and the Child—are characters abandoned by an author. They've come to this stage hoping that the director will become the author who will allow them to fulfill their purpose. The director and the actors react with disbelief and consternation. After all, the Father and his family are not ghosts; they are flesh and blood. Yet they insist that they are characters. Do they apologize for their strange status? Not at all, because, "you know well that life is full of infinite absurdities, which, strangely enough, do not even need to appear plausible, since they are true."

The words "real" and "true" come up often in the play. They are at the heart of what the play is about. The fanciful premise of characters appearing in real life is never abandoned during *Six Characters*. On the contrary, it is insisted upon throughout. What Pirandello aims to do is blur the distinction between the real and the true, the concrete and the imaginary. Because what is real may not contain any truth beyond a base material factuality and what is true may not need the stamp of reality to be any more true. Such insistence is not twee literary fancy. Much of life is illusion. Who you were yesterday, Mr. Harper, when you were a Young Turk of the Reform Party, has vanished. It was real, but then it vanished. Who's to say that who you are today won't once again disappear into a haze as you move into who you will be tomorrow? Billions of people on Earth have similarly disappeared, their reality dissipated into nothingness, first in subtle ways as they mutated from one incarnation to the next as they grew up and then grew old, and then wholly and concretely as they were swallowed up by the oblivion of death. Compare that to the literary character. A character is always who he or she is, never changing, permanent, immortal. Every audience that has seen *Hamlet* has, eventually, died, but Hamlet remains, alive and unchanging in the pages of the play. As the Father says at one point, a character "is always 'somebody.' But a man . . . may very well be 'nobody.'"

More twee fancy, you might huff. But think of it this way, then: art is the essence of life. Art is life minus the humdrum, the ordinary, the mundane. In a novel, a character never wastes the reader's time with trips to the supermarket or with the brushing and flossing of teeth, and in a play the viewer is spared the Hellos and the How-are-yous and the other banalities that pepper our daily speech. These are left out because the novel and the play are there to relate only the essential. That being so, they do indeed have a truth greater than that of much dull and inane reality. If you continue to insist that novels and plays nonetheless lack reality, shouldn't that be said with pity rather than arrogance? Don't we want life to be more like art? Many, *many* people would like that, I suspect. And some people actually pull it off. Isn't that a common expression, to say of someone who makes a vivid impression upon us, that he or she is a "real character." That's right out of Pirandello!

Pirandello's point, as I see it, is to question the content and appearance of reality. Reality is less real than it might appear. And truth can be hard to see, let alone accept. Another way of putting it would be to say that life is more a product of the imagination than we realize. So we too, at times, are characters searching for an author, for direction, for meaning, while at other times we are actors, consciously—or perhaps unconsciously—playing our role.

I hope you get to see *Six Characters in Search of an Author* on stage one day. I saw a modern version a couple years ago in London. It was bracing stuff.

I'm sorry the translation I'm sending you is not very good. It's nearly sixty years old and in dated British English. One character even exclaims, "By Jove!" It makes me cringe, but it's the only one I could find on short notice. And the book is falling apart, too. But that's only the passing reality of an otherwise truthful work of art.

Yours truly,
Yann Martel

LUIGI PIRANDELLO (1867–1936) was an Italian novelist, poet, short story writer and playwright. He was awarded the Nobel Prize in Literature in 1934.

LE GÉANT DE LA GAFFE
BY ANDRÉ FRANQUIN

LE LOTUS BLEU
BY HERGÉ

PAUL À QUÉBEC
BY MICHEL RABAGLIATI

December 20, 2010

To Stephen Harper,
Prime Minister of Canada,
Three French lessons,
Three Christmas gifts,
From a Canadian writer,
Merry Christmas,
Yann Martel

Dear Mr. Harper,

The comic book is a well-established Franco-Belgian tradition. I grew up on it, having spent four years as a child in France. I adored Asterix and Obelix, Tintin, Lucky Luke, Spirou and Fantasio, Philemon and many others. When I returned to Canada at the age of twelve, I found the comic books that were most widely available here—Marvel Comics—to be compelling, but grim and humourless—and foreign, since Marvel Comics are American.

You've made commendable efforts to master the French language, as I mentioned in an earlier letter, so I thought I'd send you three comic books in French, *Le Géant de la gaffe*, by André Franquin and *Le Lotus bleu*, by Hergé, both from Belgium, and *Paul à Québec*, by Michel Rabagliati, who is from Quebec.

Le Géant de la gaffe features Gaston Lagaffe, an office boy who is nominally in charge of reader correspondence at the magazine where he works, *Spirou*. In fact, he does nothing but tend to his own interests, which vary from the artistic to the technological and never, ever involve letters from readers. He is prone to gaffes, which has the same meaning in French as in English. But Gaston's gaffes are in a class of their own. He is the terror of his fellow office workers and, indeed, of his entire neighbourhood. Curiously, despite his many catastrophic misadventures, he's never fired.

Each page in the album stands on its own, telling its own gag, so there is no continuous story. But the same characters appear throughout. The genius in the *Gaston Lagaffe* series is primarily visual. Take page eight, in which Gaston offers Prunelle, his boss, a ride in his ancient car. He's just installed a newfangled device, seat belts (we're in 1977). Prunelle is a little worried, but Gaston reassures him: he installed them himself. Alas, Gaston has accidentally attached Prunelle's seat belt to the motor's drive shaft, so as he drives off the seat belt starts to wind itself around the shaft, pulling Prunelle down through his seat into the frame of the car. Have a look at the middle illustration, three rows down, in which Prunelle has been completely sucked into his seat. See his raised foot, his clenched fist, hear the loud *CRRRAC* sound. It's unspeakably funny. Even better: page twenty-nine, in which Gaston has given Lebrac, a colleague, a taste of his chili-pepper sauce to see if it's spicy enough. Behold the effect on Lebrac. The drawings are extraordinarily expressive.

By comparison, Tintin is quite witless. The jokes, when there are any, aren't particularly funny. And the drawing style is more workmanlike. But the genius with Tintin lies elsewhere, in its narrative breadth. The long Tintin series—the first one, *Tintin au Congo*, came out in 1930, and the last one, the twenty-second, *Tintin et les Picaros*, in 1976—is dramatic in intent and has endeared itself to millions of readers around the world because of the adventures told within. *Le Lotus bleu*, the Tintin I am offering you this week, is an early one, from 1934 (in its original black-and-white edition), but even there the adventure sweeps you along. And some of the illustrations are nonetheless startling. Have a look at the large ones on pages six and twenty-six, for example.

And we should place Hergé in his historical context. He practically invented the illustrative language of comic strips. The way the stories are told frame by frame so that the narrative is clear and fluid, with close-ups and wide shots; the details to convey emotion, for example stars circling the head for pain or beads of water for anxiety or wonderment; the ambition to tell entire stories that are memorable and gripping—all this started with Georges Rémi (he inverted his initials to create his pen name). I don't want to venture too far, not being a historian of the subject, but I do believe that Tintin is the grandfather of the Franco-Belgian narrative comic strip. He is the giant upon whose shoulders subsequent artists stood, including Franquin and, on our side of the Atlantic, Michel Rabagliati, the author of *Paul à Québec*.

Paul à Québec is the sixth in a series. It tells a sad story, of the illness and dying of Paul's father-in-law. It's very moving. I doubt you'll be able to finish the story with your eyes still dry. *Paul à Québec* speaks with a confidence that shows how the comic book has come of age, capable of telling stories as serious as any told using solely written language, with illustrative details that are as powerful as the well-chosen metaphors of an accomplished novelist. *Paul* is entirely rooted in the language and culture of Quebec. I read it with a degree of nostalgia, recognizing many of the elements (the strange restaurant in the opening scene, for example, that stands between Montreal and Quebec). This is where I come from, I thought. These are my people, these are my stories.

I wish you and your family a merry Christmas.

Yours truly,
Yann Martel

ANDRÉ FRANQUIN (1924–1997) was a Belgian comics artist who contributed to *Spirou et Fantasio* (as part of the "School of Marcinelle" in the 1950s and '60s) and *Tintin*, and created his own strips *Gaston* and *Isabelle*.

HERGÉ (1907–1983), the *nom de plume* of Georges Remi, was a Belgian comics writer and artist. He is best known for creating the Tintin comic books. He continued to write the Tintin series during World War II. He is the recipient of the Order of the Crown.

MICHEL RABAGLIATI (b. 1961) is a Canadian cartoonist and author of the Paul series of books (*Paul in the Country*, *Paul Moves Out*, et al.). Though he read and created comics as a child, he worked as a graphic designer and illustrator for many years before drawing comics again.

BOOK 98

SIR GAWAIN AND THE GREEN KNIGHT
EDITED AND TRANSLATED BY JAMES WINNY

January 3, 2011

To Stephen Harper,
Prime Minister of Canada,
From a Canadian writer,
With best wishes for 2011,
Yann Martel

Dear Mr. Harper,

Why not start the new year, which we hope will be good, with something old and most certainly good? A few weeks ago I happened to bump into Doug Thorpe, the genial head of the English Department at the University of Saskatchewan. He's very knowledgeable about Sir Walter Scott, so I asked him if he didn't have a short Scott to propose for our reading purposes. He shook his head. "There are no short works by Sir Walter Scott. He was terribly long-winded. Every tome he wrote has at least six hundred pages." So much for Sir Walter Scott and our busy-busy-busy-short-book club. Did he have anything else to propose, off the top of his head, I asked. He thought for a second. "Have you sent him *Sir Gawain and the Green Knight?*" I hadn't. Doug invited me into his office and fished around his bookshelves for a few moments. "Here you go," he said, handing me a copy of the book in question.

Indeed, here you go. I was doubly touched by the gift in that a name on the front cover jumped out at me: James Winny, the editor and translator. James Winny taught at Trent University, in Peterborough, Ontario, where I did an undergraduate degree in philosophy. He was my tutorial leader in a first-year introductory English course I took. I'm sure Professor Winny entirely forgot me the moment our course ended, but I still remember him clearly. Once a week, eight or so of us students would troop into his office, where he would lead us into discussion on a work of literature. He was a patrician figure in his sixties, with a resonant voice and an elegant English accent, and he was friendly in a phlegmatic way. Times have changed. Now, in a university system in Canada more geared to producing economically useful workers than critically thinking citizens, it's unimaginable that eight first-year students would have hour-long weekly meetings with a full professor, but so it was at the time, in the early 1980s at Trent University. Those tutorials marked me. Once Professor Winny read aloud T. S. Eliot's *Four Quartets*. He mastered a range of English accents and he brought the poems to life for us, did he ever. I remember another discussion we had about Joseph Conrad's *The Secret Agent*, which he deemed—with an authority that nonetheless felt like a suggestion—a perfect novel. With each meeting, he made us see more in a work than our immature minds had first seized. It was a thrill to be led on such an intellectual ride.

I remember James Winny clearly, but I hadn't thought of him in ages, and here, twenty-five years later, his name and his work were suddenly before me. It's been a pleasure to be in the orbit of his mind again. I wish I had been in a class in which he discussed *Sir Gawain and the Green Knight*.

Sir Gawain was composed by an anonymous poet in the late fourteenth century "in a regional dialect characteristic of northwestern England," as Winny's introduction informs us. The advantage of the Broadview edition I'm sending you is that it's a bilingual one, with the original text printed on the even pages, on the left, and the translated text on odd pages, on the right. To me, the Middle English dialect is nearly opaque, and I have no patience for this kind of linguistic game. To every language I don't speak I'm ready to grant all the beauty and subtlety the human mind can come up with, and a cultural content greater than any museum could fit in its galleries, but the first thing *I* notice is the barrier of incomprehension. I might as well be talking to a clarinet—except a clarinet is meant to be beautiful, while a language is meant to communicate, with beauty a bonus. I find that my eyes, looking at the Middle English text on the left, jump about, seeking words or phrases it can understand, and they quickly grow weary of the exercise, whereas the pages on the right, in modern English, shatter and grip with their clarity. I don't so much see the words as the images they convey. But see for yourself. Perhaps you'll find enjoyment in deciphering the Middle English.

What surprised me in Winny's translation into modern English of *Sir Gawain* was how close the story was brought to me. Over and over as I read the poem, one thing came through: personality, be it that of Sir Gawain, or the Green Knight, or Lord and Lady Bertilak. Compare that to another work of old European literature I sent you recently, the German *Nibelungenlied*. I never imagined Sivrit or Kriemhilt, Prunhilt or Hagen as real people. They were rather literary symbols embedded in a vivid story. Sir Gawain is also such a symbol—for the codes of chivalry and courtly love, which can be seen as medieval ideals that tried to reconcile the loving kindness of Christ with the brutal social realities of the time— but he's a symbol whose human form seems palpably real. Take these lines:

> And when the knight saw his blood spatter the snow
> He leapt forward with both feet more than a spear's length,
> Snatched up his helmet and crammed it on his head,
> Jerked his shoulders to bring his splendid shield down,
> Drew out a gleaming sword and fiercely he speaks—
> Never since that man was born of his mother
> Had he ever in the world felt half so relieved—
> "Hold your attack, sir, don't try it again!"

It's the leaping forward, the rush to get his equipment in place, the plain statement of his relief and then the fearful warning—I can't imagine Sivrit of the *Nibelungenlied* displaying such all-too-human emotions.

Or take the stanzas in Part Three in which Sir Gawain, resting in his bed, is repeatedly tempted by Lady Bertilak. The eroticism of those pages reached up and tempted *me*. I don't know how Sir Gawain resisted those very human feelings.

What's fascinating to read is the conscious working-out in Gawain's mind of what his code requires of him. We see a man trying to uphold his ideals, and lamenting his failure when he doesn't manage it. It's not only interesting; it's moving. Each one of us, you and me, must struggle every day to live up to our ideals.

Sir Gawain is a work of remarkable intimacy. That is achieved not only by the small number of characters, but also by the interiority of the drama. Despite being spread over much of the British isle, a wide geographic scale for the time, the story essentially unfolds in the close company of Sir Gawain. The reader is Sancho Panza to his Don Quixote.

The descriptions of the seasons, winter in particular, are lovely. The hunting scenes are breathtaking. And all is carried to the reader by a poetic language that is clear, vigorous and true, that truth whereby language sorts and makes sense of reality.

Such language comes from great writers, and our anonymous poet from northwestern England was surely that, a great writer.

I've told you nothing of the plot. Sir Gawain is at Camelot with Arthur and the other Knights of the Round Table. It is Christmas, many games are being played, and a good time is being had by all (in this story, there is much having of a good time, the comfort of it, the fun of it). Then into the hall enters a knight who is a stranger to everyone. He is a giant, but he makes a striking impression for another reason: both he and his horse are entirely green, bright emerald green. He rides in, dismounts and tells the revelers he wants to play a Christmas game: he will receive an unprotected blow from anyone in exchange for returning a blow a year and a day later. He taunts the court until Gawain steps forward. Gawain takes hold of an axe. The Green Knight stands unflinching. Gawain slices his head off. Far from falling over dead, the Green Knight leans over and reaches for his head and lifts it in the air. The head speaks: *See you in a year and a day, Sir Gawain*. The Green Knight then climbs onto his horse, head still in hand, and rides off.

A year goes by quickly when its end is dreaded. In the fall, Sir Gawain sets out to find the Green Knight and fulfill his part of the terrible bargain . . .

Sir Gawain and the Green Knight can be read as a Christian allegory—though one that treads lightly, aware of the weakness of the flesh—or it can be read simply as a good story. Either way, I hope it helps you prepare for the challenges, temptations and rewards of 2011.

Happy New Year.

Yours truly,
Yann Martel

JAMES WINNY taught English at Trent University, Cambridge and Leicester University, England. He translated and edited works by Geoffrey Chaucer as well as *Sir Gawain and the Green Knight*, and wrote introductory texts to literature by John Donne and Shakespeare.

BOOK 99:

A HISTORY OF READING
BY ALBERTO MANGUEL

January 17, 2011

To Stephen Harper,
Prime Minister of Canada,
A history of reading, a history of being,
From a Canadian writer (and reader),
With best wishes,
Yann Martel

Dear Mr. Harper,

I have only now and then sent you non-fiction, but Alberto Manguel's *A History of Reading* is so perfectly suited for our sort-of dialogue that I've chosen it for this week. It's an engagingly erudite and cosmopolitan work that effortlessly whizzes through history and over borders, as if planet Earth were a book and Manguel had carefully read it through, noting every reference historical, literary, religious, philosophical, physiological, archaeological, sociological, biographical, commercial, geographic, technical, personal and anecdotal that had to do with reading. As it turns out, reading is everything. Not because everyone is a reader of books. That is not the case. Rather, because the world, and everything in it, is indeed a book of sorts. Manguel quotes Walt Whitman from *Leaves of Grass*:

> In every object, mountain, tree, and star—in every birth
> and life,

As part of each—evolv'd from each—meaning, behind
the ostent,
A mystic cipher waits infolded.

(Good stuff, Whitman. He's a thrilling poet, one whose poetry quickens the reader's sense for life.) The world, like a book, demands elucidation. So a paleontologist reads a fossil the way a reader reads a detective novel, wondering *What happened here?* So a lover reads the face of his or her beloved the way a reader reads a romance, finding comfort and security there. So a politician reads a poll the way a believer reads scripture, asking *What is my fate?* And just as it's a pity when a reader finds it not worth his or her time to finish one book, and then another, and then another, and so on, until that reader becomes, ipso facto, a non-reader, so it's a pity when a man, woman or child turns from the world, feeling it not worth the read. In both books and world there is mystery, a "cipher . . . infolded," and what a joy it is to bathe, to swim, nearly to drown in that mystery. Among the many fine qualities of Manguel's book is this one, that by dint of the abundance of curious and interesting facts, it jubilantly makes the case that we are a curious and interesting species.

Unlike a novel, which is like a long thread that must remain taut if it is good and so requires on the part of the reader an attention that is regular, if not constant, *A History of Reading* is composed of many short, colourful threads and benefits from stint reading. Manguel's style is leisurely and elegant and it links with no apparent strain its many elements. Despite its breadth, *A History of Reading* remains a personal work, not only because Manguel's charming, urbane *I* voice regularly slips in to share an experience or anecdote from his long and satisfying life as a reader, but because it really *is* a personal work. Note the article in the title; it's A *History*, not The *History of Reading*. With this choice, Manguel is merely reflecting one of the delightful powers of a reader: to select and interpret as he or she wishes. Manguel's history of reading might be very different from yours or mine. His is rich, varied, joyful. What would yours be like?

I do believe that my next package to you, book and letter, will be my last.

Yours truly,
Yann Martel

Internationally acclaimed as an anthologist, translator, essayist, novelist and editor, ALBERTO MANGUEL (b. 1948) is the best-selling author of several award-winning books, including *A Dictionary of Imaginary Places* and *A History of Reading*. He was born in Buenos Aires (where he served as a reader for the writer and librarian Jorge Luis Borges), moved to Canada in 1982 and now lives in France, where he was named an Officier de l'Ordre des Arts et des Lettres in 2004.

BOOK 100

SCORCHED
BY WAJDI MOUAWAD

Translated from the French by Linda Gaboriau

January 31, 2011

To Stephen Harper,
Prime Minister of Canada,
A voice that rises up against erasing,
From a Canadian writer,
With best wishes,
Yann Martel

Dear Mr. Harper,

This letter, I'm quite sure, will be my last one to you. I said, over and over, that I would persist with our exclusive book club as long as you were in power. But selecting a book for you; reading or rereading it; thinking about it; writing the letter that goes with it; having the letter translated by my parents and discussing that translation with them; scanning the cover of the book; uploading the English and French letters onto their respective websites; and finally mailing book and letter so that they reach you on time every second Monday—all this takes time and effort, and while it's been a great pleasure for me (I don't know about you), I've been doing it for close to four years now and I want to move on. I have the luck of living with two pregnancies at the moment: the first is my partner Alice's, who is carrying our second child, a girl due at the end of May, and the second is mine, a new novel gestating in my head. I'm having a small writing studio built in my backyard so I can have a space to take care of my novel not far from where Alice and I will take care of our new baby. I'm very excited about the new novel. It will be called *The High Mountains of Portugal* and it shimmers in my mind like snow-capped mountains catching the sun. I already have lots of notes written, I've been gathering material I intend to read for research, and the story in my head is bursting with promise. I can't wait to get started on it. I'm of course equally excited about the new addition to our family. Both babies will require lots of joyful work.

And it so happens that this is the hundredth letter I've written to you. One hundred. One, zero, zero. The same as $1 + 1 + 1 +$ $1 + 1 + 1 + 1 + 1 + 1 + 1 + 1 + 1 + 1 + 1 + 1 + 1 + 1 + 1 + 1 + 1 + 1$ $+ 1 + 1 + 1 + 1 + 1 + 1 + 1 + 1 + 1 + 1 + 1 + 1 + 1 + 1 + 1 +$ $1 + 1 + 1 + 1 + 1 + 1 + 1 + 1 + 1 + 1 + 1 + 1 + 1 + 1 + 1 +$ $1 + 1 + 1 + 1 + 1 + 1 + 1 + 1 + 1 + 1 + 1 + 1 + 1 + 1 + 1 + 1$ $+ 1 + 1 + 1 + 1 + 1 + 1 + 1 + 1 + 1 + 1 + 1 + 1 + 1 + 1 + 1 +$ $1 + 1 + 1 + 1 + 1 + 1 + 1 + 1 + 1 + 1 + 1 + 1 + 1 + 1 + 1.$ That's a lot of letters and books. And come to think of it, it's the same number of chapters as in my novel *Life of Pi*. One hundred is a nice round number and a good number to end on. (The number of times you personally have written back to me is also a nice round number, by the way: 0. That's zero, naught, nada, zilch.)

It's true, too, that I'm tired of using books as political bullets and grenades. Books are too precious and wonderful to be used for long in such a fashion.

Now what would be your send-off book? The question pre-occupied me. We started on a strong note—with *The Death of Ivan Ilych*, by Leo Tolstoy, if you remember, which I sent you on April 16, 2007—and I wanted to end on a strong note. The answer came naturally when I received an invitation from the artistic director for French theatre at the National Arts Centre, in

Ottawa, a one-minute walk from where you work. I was invited to participate in an evening event called *Mais que lit Stephen Harper?*, in which books and reading would be celebrated. I eagerly accepted and I hope that you will come, too. Take this as a personal invitation. The event is at the NAC's nine-hundred-seat Theatre Hall at 7:30 p.m. on Friday, February 25. It's sold out, but I'm sure two tickets can be found for you and Mrs. Harper, if you want.

The invitation, I mean *my* invitation, came from Wajdi Mouawad. There, I knew what book to send you, I had our hundredth book. Wajdi Mouawad is not only the artistic director for French theatre at the NAC, he's also a brilliant playwright. I liked the idea of ending our book club with a play of his for a number of reasons. Firstly, because I haven't sent you enough drama (or poetry). Secondly, because what better way to signal to you that art is partial and unfinished because its meaning is forever changing and evolving, that art demands a constant and renewed involvement on the part of the reader, listener, viewer, that art is the work and joy of a lifetime for maker and receiver, what better way to signal that than by sending you a play script, a play on the page, which is partial and unfinished because it's unstaged? By doing so, I end our book club not with a full stop, but with suspension points. Thirdly, a play by Mouawad is an excellent choice for our final book together because he's a multilingual Québécois of Lebanese origin, and thus a typical hybrid Canadian, and I wanted to end with a Canadian writer. Fourthly, I'm sending you *Incendies—Scorched*, in Linda Gaboriau's lively English translation—because, as I'm sure you already know, the Quebec filmmaker Denis Villeneuve's cinematic adaptation of the play has just received the nod of an Oscar nomination for best foreign-language film. Yet another Canadian work of art receiving international acclaim. Fifthly, and lastly, I'm sending you a Mouawad play because, as I said, he's brilliant. The man has got fire in his guts and bile on his tongue. He's an Angry Young Man (do you know the movement? British, postwar, vocally dissatisfied with the status quo—I once saw their emblematic play, John Osborne's *Look Back in Anger*, and years ago, while living in Mexico City, I had the privilege of meeting and hearing a reading by another of their lions, Arnold Wesker).

Scorched is appropriately titled. Part of the action of the play takes place in a war-torn country which, though unnamed, is obviously Lebanon, a hot place where one is likely to be scorched by the sun. But more to the point, the play scorches the soul. It tells the story of a twin brother and sister, Simon and Janine, and their mother, Nawal, who falls into complete silence for a reason her children will discover only after her death. The play turns on a revelation that is truly disturbing. I read it and felt dazed. And this is after merely *reading* it. The effect upon hearing it from a stage, revealed by an actor, brought to life, would be something close to shell shock, I'd think. And the emotional impact lingers in the mind, too. I don't think I've ever read a story that more potently symbolizes the horror and insanity of war. In a few pages the power of art is revealed: just a few people talking on a stage, pretending to be someone else somewhere else, quite obviously a *device*—and yet, at the end of it, you walk away feeling as if you'd lived through a war that's ripped your life apart.

I'd love to see the play staged, and I can't wait to see the movie.

Now that we're closing down our literary duet, there are so many books I regret not sending you. Ralph Waldo Emerson, *Tristram Shandy*, Martin Buber's *I-Thou*, Dante's *Divine Comedy*, Knut Hamsun's *Hunger*, more of J. M. Coetzee, the list goes on.

Oh well, they will wait for you on a shelf in a bookstore or library somewhere. Books are patient. They have time. They'll still be there long after you and I are gone.

What I've been trying to do in this long epistolary dead end with you, beyond the plying of irony, is to make the following point: that the books available in bookstores and libraries throughout Canada, that the exhibits to be seen in this nation's galleries and museums, that the movies coming out of this country, that the plays and dance pieces seen on its stages, that the music heard in its concert venues, be they bars or orchestra halls, that the clothes that come from our designers, the cuisine from our best restaurants, and so on and so forth with every creative act of Canadians, that all these cultural manifestations are not mere entertainment, something to pass the time and relax the mind after the "serious" business of the day is over with, the earning of money—no, no, no. In fact, these manifestations are the various elements that add up to the sum total of Canadian civilization. Take these away and nothing worthwhile remains of Canadian civilization. Corporations come and go, leaving hardly any trace, while art endures.

Yet it is corporations and their voracious demands that regulate our lives nowadays, far more than theatres, bookstores and museums. Why is that? Why is it that people work so crazily hard these days, at the expense of family, health and happiness? Have we not perhaps forgotten that work is a means to an end, that we work so that we may live, and not the other way round? We've become slaves to our work and have forgotten that it's in moments of leisure and stillness, when we're free from working with a hoe or at a keyboard, that we can contemplate life and become fully ourselves. We work, work, work, but what mark do we leave, what point do we make? People who are too beholden to work become like erasers: as they move forward, they leave in their wake no trace of themselves. And so that has been the point of my fruitless book-gifting to you: to raise my voice against Canada becoming a nation of erasers.

Yours truly,
Yann Martel

WAJDI MOUAWAD (b. 1968) is a Lebanese-Canadian actor, playwright and director. His play *Littoral* won the Governor General's Literary Award for Drama, and *Incendies* was adapted into an Academy Award–nominated film. He is a Chevalier de l'Ordre des Arts et des Lettres and an Officer of the Order of Canada

IN SEARCH OF LOST TIME
BY MARCEL PROUST

Translated from the French by C. K. Scott Moncrieff and Terence
Kilmartin, revised by D. J. Enright, in a six-volume box set
February 28, 2011

To Stephen Harper,
Prime Minister of Canada,
We must find the time,
From a Canadian writer,
With best wishes,
Yann Martel

Dear Mr. Harper,

I wanted to offer you one last book. All the books I sent you
earlier were comparatively short, usually under two hundred
pages. But this one is far, far longer. I've chosen to send you a
six-volume box set of Marcel Proust's complete *In Search of
Lost Time* not to thump you with a 4,347-page club of irony,
but because it's a work I've been meaning to read for years. It's
surprising that I've never read *À la recherche du temps perdu*.
After all, French is my mother tongue and I lived in France
for ten years, the first four in the very arrondissement where
Proust was born, the sixteenth. And I've read other very long
novels, *The Brothers Karamazov*, by Dostoyevsky, and *War and
Peace*, by Leo Tolstoy, for example. So why did I never take
on Proust's masterpiece? I suppose for the same reason that
many books are left unread, a mixture of fear and slothfulness,

fear that I wouldn't understand the work and unwillingness to spend so much intellectual energy reading all those pages. But as you and I both know, fear and slothfulness lead nowhere. Great achievements only come through courage and hard work. In sending you Proust's monument, then, I'm reminding myself that I, too, must read it. I'm committed to reading it from start to finish before I die, and I hope you join me in making that same commitment.

Proust's ten-page description of the eating of a madeleine is famous. It is, apparently, a bravura piece of writing, moving, profound, life-changing. The experience of reading *In Search of Lost Time* as a whole is said to be life-changing. I don't need my life to change, I don't think, but I do want to discover what people mean when they say that of Proust's masterwork of nostalgia. I want to understand how ten pages can be devoted to the eating of a small cake and how my life could possibly be different afterwards. I invite you to join me, on your own time, in reading this mammoth novel. I do believe it will bring stillness to our souls.

And now our little book club truly comes to an end. The project has been, in many ways, as much a gift to me as it has been to you. Because of it, I have read or reread over one hundred books. I will miss the challenge of finding you a new short book every second week. But in foregoing that activity, I hope to find the lost time I need to read Marcel Proust. I hope you find the time, too.

Yours truly,
Yann Martel

MARCEL PROUST (1871–1922) was a French novelist, critic and essayist. He is buried in Père Lachaise Cemetery in Paris.

The award-winning author of *The Facts Behind the Helsinki Roccamatios*, *Self*, *Life of Pi*, *Beatrice & Virgil*, and *101 Letters to a Prime Minister*, YANN MARTEL was born in Spain in 1963. He studied philosophy at Trent University, worked at odd jobs—tree planter, dishwasher, security guard—and travelled widely before turning to writing. *Life of Pi* won the 2002 Man Booker, among other prizes, and was an international bestseller.

Yann Martel lives in Saskatoon with the writer Alice Kuipers and their children.